RIDE A WHITE SWAN

IN MEMORIAM

Mark 'Marc' Feld Bolan, 30 September 1947–16 September 1977
June Ellen Child Feld Bolan, 23 August 1943–31 August 1994
Michael Norman 'Mick(e)y' Finn, 3 June 1947–11 January 2003
Steve Currie, 20 May 1947–28 April 1981
Stephen Ross 'Steve Peregrin(e) Took' Porter,
28 July 1949–27 October 1980
Keith John Moon, 23 August 1946–7 September 1978
John Alec Entwistle, 9 October 1944–27 June 2002
Henry Kenneth Alfred 'Ken' Russell,
3 July 1927–27 November 2011
John Robert Parker Ravenscroft, 'John Peel' OBE,
30 August 1939–25 October 2004
Roger Scott, 23 October 1943–31 October 1989

equitare in cygno albo

RIDE A WHITE SWAN

The Lives and Death of
MARC BOLAN

LESLEY-ANN JONES

HODDER &
STOUGHTON

First published in Great Britain in 2012 by Hodder & Stoughton
An Hachette UK company

1

Copyright © Lesley-Ann Jones 2012

A CIP catalogue record for this title is available from the British Library

'One Another's Light' © Brian Patten from Collected Love Poems (Harper Perennial)
Reproduced by kind permission of the author.

Endpaper photographs courtesy of: Jeff Dexter, Harry and Sandra Feld,
Steve Harley/Comeuppance, Lesley-Ann Jones, Caron Willans.

Hardback ISBN 978 1 444 75877 1
Trade Paperback ISBN 978 1 444 75878 8
eBook ISBN 978 1 444 75880 1

Printed and bound by CPI Group (UK) Ltd, Croydon, CR0 4YY

Hodder & Stoughton policy is to use papers that are natural,
renewable and recyclable products and made from wood grown in sustainable
forests. The logging and manufacturing processes are expected to conform
to the environmental regulations of the country of origin.

Hodder & Stoughton Ltd
338 Euston Road
London NW1 3BH

www.hodder.co.uk

For Mia, Henry & Bridie

To Ed

'Lou Reed told me, "I heard T. Rex on the radio this morning. It sounded like today's music, really powerful. You can't beat a good song. He had a great voice." Made my day.'
Tony Visconti

'I like peasant people. We're . . . from all corners of the globe, a gang of peasants who want to be in musical entertainment. This is the whole idea. It's like in medieval days. A few people just got together and made some music to make themselves happy, and then to make other people happy off it. That's really all it is for me.'
Paul McCartney

'He was a good friend. A good musician. He had a great style. And, you know, he's another artist we miss.'
Ringo Starr

'Bowie and I got married, then we split up around 1973 . . . no, really, we were never enemies. The press made all that up. They did it with Bowie and Bolan, but those guys were good friends . . .'
Alice Cooper

'Marc's music has left a strong legacy. It is gratifying to see that he is "the one" from that period, after being so critically derided at the time. So many bands and musicians have nodded towards his sound. His infectious songs are still on the radio, on adverts and in films. He was the winner in the end. Maybe he had to die young for that to happen; but it would be great if he could look down from somewhere and know that he is still a star – and always will be.'
Marc Almond, Soft Cell

'The only people for me are the mad ones, the ones who are mad to live, mad to talk, mad to be saved, desirous of everything at the same time, the ones who never yawn or say a commonplace thing, but burn, burn, burn, like fabulous yellow Roman candles exploding like spiders across the stars …'
Jack Kerouac, 1922–69

ONE ANOTHER'S LIGHT

I do not know what brought me here
Away from where I've hardly ever
been and now
Am never likely to go again.

Faces are lost, and places passed
At which I could have stopped,
And stopping, been glad enough.

Some faces left a mark,
And I on them might have wrought
Some kind of charm or spell
To make their fortunes work,

But it's hard to guess
How one person on another
Works an influence.

We pass, and lit briefly
By one another's light
Hope the way we go is right.

Brian Patten

Contents

Fade-in . . .

Santa Monica Pier, August 1989. A few of us are hanging, minding our own business, wondering what the night will bring. The Who are in town, which is why we are here: for *Tommy*, with special guests Elton John, Steve Winwood, Phil Collins and Billy Idol, at the Universal Amphitheatre LA. The extravaganza is a 25th anniversary nod to when late, lamented Moonie joined the band, but they don't wreak havoc the way Keith once did. Who could? Anyway, those days are gone. The Who are more than twenty years into their career now (as it turns out, not even halfway through). Daltrey and Townshend are being millionaire rock stars somewhere. Not that they'd hang out with the likes of us anyway. But Entwistle does. Preferring the pack over the in-crowd on away nights out, he pitches up with a bottle of brandy and skips a light fandango . . . or something. We shiver in the mists falling in off the ocean. The moon is out.

Most of the rides are now closed, but the Ferris wheel's still open, electric fireworks sparking a granite sky. A motley crowd is assembling, there's quite a scene going on. Fishermen gather with rods poking out of holdalls, and set themselves up along the railings. An ancient trio starts palming a set of rust-rimmed drums. 'Hello darkness, my old friend . . .' the Simon & Garfunkel song from 1964 about the assassination of JFK. The drummers smile, chuffed that we recognise it. One tips his hat, like a hobo in a cartoon. He offers candy, shrugs when we refuse it, strikes up another familiar pop tune as he shoves the lollipop in his cheek. A hunchback shuffles by with a bubble machine, frothing the air with dreams.

'La, la, la, la-la la-laaa . . .'

'Hear that?' says John.

'Hear what?' I murmur.

'They're playing T. Rex.'

'Who is?'

'The steel drummers.'

'. . . an' I love the way she twitch, a-ha haaaa . . .'

'Can't be. How would they know it?'

'Everybody knows it.'

'Must be twenty years since that was a hit.'

'Eighteen.'

'How do you know?'

'March '71', John declares. 'We were at Record Plant when it came out.[1] Didn't do much here. Back home, 'Hot Love' was huge, remember? Something like six weeks at Number One. We were out that year . . . Lifehouse. '*Who's Next.*'

'What happened?'

'Glam happened. Rock'n'roll got very us'n'them.'

'Did you ever meet Marc Bolan?' I ask him, as we wander off in search of more drink.

'*Meet* him,' laughs John, 'we went on tour with him!'

'Never knew that.'

''67, I think it was. Before your time. Kit and Simon [Lambert and Napier-Bell] brought a bunch called John's Children out to support us in Germany. Mad, they were. Puppets on pills. Didn't last long. Out-Who'd The Who, the bastards. Keith was not thrilled. Kicked ten weeks of shit out of their gear one night and nearly wrung their flamin' necks, not that it stopped them.'

'Doing what?'

'Can't remember.'

'Really?'

'Blood.'

'Actually?'

'Gore. Chains. Chairs. Feathers. Pillow fights gone mental. Crowd went nuts for it.'

'How bitter a thing to look into happiness through another man's eyes.'

'Fuck off, Orlando.'

'What was he like?'

'Orlando?'

'*Bolan!*'

John smiles.

'Nicest little bloke you ever did meet.'

Lights are winking across the water over in Malibu. Colony-ites bunk down when night drops in. The Pacific laps, only yards from their windows, licking silently into rock pools and tiny coves. This place is the capital of Californian cool, where a 12,000 square-foot pad on the most desirable beach in the world is the least you could want. Where the sand is only public below the tide-line. Where celebrities hang together, coming and going as they please, jogging, barbecuing, riding ponies in Topanga Canyon, tripping down to Gladstone's for a little seafood or to Santa Monica for a burger, and never having to worry about being watched. In a place where everyone is someone, it is easy to be no one at all. Could a guy like Marc Bolan really have settled here, and for this kind of life?

'Malibu was a new rock'n'roll status thing back then,' remembers Jeff Dexter, Marc's oldest, closest friend. 'It was what they all aspired to. It showed the world they'd made it. Our Kid had several good pals here along the beach.'

'When I was expecting with Rolan, Marc and I would come down to Santa Monica Pier and look out towards Malibu,' Gloria Jones tells me. 'In many ways, it seemed like another world. That was our dream, to live here together. We were both very comfortable with the idea of growing old. We knew what kind of a life we wanted. We had it all planned. Marc was so excited about it. Our idea was to relocate from London, buy a great house, have more children and bring them up beside the ocean. We were definitely going to get married and live here, we spoke about it often,' says Marc's partner and the mother of his only child.

'We were just going to make a nice family and grow old together. It's what he wanted at that point in his life. Marc had been lost for a while, but he'd found himself again. This was absolutely where he wanted to be. It's been thirty-five years since he died, which I find so hard to believe. But even now I close my eyes at night and it's still Marc, holding me. I smell him. I can still hear him – talking, singing, laughing, just being himself. He's around me. He has never gone away. We were as one, right from the beginning, me and Marc. It was unlike anything, what we had. In some ways, we still have it.'

In the early hours of 16 September 1977, as they were making their way home from Morton's nightclub in Mayfair, Gloria lost control of the purple Mini she was driving across Barnes Common. The car collided with a steel-reinforced concrete post, and wound up in a tree. Marc, not yet thirty, died instantly. Gloria's injuries were so terrible that she learned of Marc's death only on the day after his funeral.[2] She was unable to fly home to her family in America, as she recalls it, for almost four months.

The past doesn't die, it's never over. Gloria knows. She gets on with her life. What choice? The memories linger. Now and then she'll turn a corner and find herself back there. Her injuries may have healed, but not her heart. If she could turn back time, would she do things differently?

'Where do you start?'

I knew nothing about Marc Bolan the one time I met him. I was tagging along with my junior school classmate Lisa and her mother Hyacinth (who later became the well-known celebrity-and-sports photographer Hy Money) to a Sunday afternoon gathering in the back of a local pub. The Three Tuns hosted the Beckenham Arts Lab, of which David Bowie was a founder and regular member. Hy, a beautiful, exotic Indian painter, was part of their cool creative circle. She had often sketched and photo-graphed me – gawky, freckled, bespectacled me, why would she? But that was Hy, she embraced us all. I'd banged a tambourine during the odd soirée at her home, the lamentable extent of my musical ability.

My childhood was not so easy; I spent much of it inside books. *Black Beauty, Anne of Green Gables, Little Women* and *Malory Towers* were my favourites. I was still a *Bunty* and Girl's World girl. A Brownie. I did ballet and tap, I liked football. The 'hippie movement' and the 'underground music scene' (whatever they were) might as well have been happening on the moon. In some ways they were, I think.

Hy had said that she wanted to treat us to 'something special'. I had never seen a sitar, let alone heard one played live. The sound of that instrument is so familiar to me now that I could not say I remember accurately how or indeed whether it affected me that day. I do remember how taken I was by the young man playing it. I had no idea at the time that he was the brilliant Lithuanian-born musician and artist Vytas Serelis, nor that his companion was the singer-songwriter Marc Bolan of 'cult underground duo' Tyrannosaurus Rex.

Marc did not join in with the music that day. He stood quietly to one side with David, watching Vytas play. He made no impression on me, so could not have gone out of his way to draw attention to himself. I didn't realise, when it happened, that the curly-haired boy in the Three Tuns that day was the same guy who exploded as if out of nowhere in 1970 with 'Ride a White Swan'.

Lisa Money and I went on to different secondary schools. I had a new best friend at Bromley Grammar, Natasha Holloway. 'Face of '68' teen idol Peter Frampton graced our bedroom walls momentarily. His father Owen was Head of Art at Bromley Tech. We returned a couple of times to the Arts Lab with Hy, who was now getting into photography. The Frampton posters were relegated to the drawer under the bed, and replaced with amateur pictures of David Bowie.

Bolan and Tyrannosaurus Rex were by now gaining momentum and seeping into mainstream consciousness, thanks largely to the enthusiasm of the late DJ John Peel – whose self-styled remit was to champion the cause of acts he liked the sound of, as yet unsigned. I was still a little too young to be aware of all this. I don't think I started listening to music radio until 1970, Radio London and Radio Caroline having passed me by. My parents might have dipped in and out of the Light Programme, and they later followed *The Archers* on BBC Radio 4. But ours was not the kind of household to tune in to Tony Blackburn's new Radio 1 Breakfast Show, which kicked off in 1967 with 'Flowers In The Rain' by The Move. This was probably because we were not driven to school, so there was none of the car-listening we do on the school run now.

We got the bus in those days, and transistor radios were banned by the conductors. We were, at least, allowed them in the playground during break. I didn't get my first Sony Walkman until I went to college, by which time most of my radio-listening was done on Friday and Saturday evenings while getting ready to go out, or when I returned home after a hard night's partying. Album culture was all-consuming. We carted our precious poly-thene-protected vinyl everywhere. Having since read and absorbed plenty about that period in broadcasting history, I sometimes feel as though I experienced it all first-hand. I know that I didn't, though.

David Bowie was always a big deal to us – mostly because he was a local hero, the kind that means the most. He was one of us. Not that we fancied him. He was a side-order rather than a dish. I remember having a thing about his eyes. The right pupil was so massive that it almost obliterated the iris. One eye was lumi-nously blue, the other dull and grey. He had a penchant for odd outfits – a washed-out pink t-shirt over a blouse with a wallpaper pattern, say. One half of his hair might be ruffled, the other side swept straight back. His teeth were awful. He would sit there surrounded by gerbil-cheeked girls and moody guys. Most of them had guitars. Giggling behind Hy, clicking away with her camera, Natasha and I made a pact to find out where he lived. This turned out to be a sprawling flat in Haddon Hall on Southend Road, a huge Gothic mansion with turrets and stained glass. Unbeknown to our mothers, we used to get the 227 bus there after school. The autograph we were on the hunt for took several attempts as David was never at home when we called round. From time to time his American girlfriend Angela, later briefly his wife, would stand chatting to us on the doorstep. She must have been sick of pests like us, but at least she was nice about it. She was bleached-looking and beautiful, despite an odd nose, and huge hands. She gave us signed photos, knowing full well what we really wanted. We kept on trying, and one day he was there.

He could not have been more friendly. We could not have been more thrilled to be drinking tea with the object of our affections, particularly as we were there behind our parents' backs. Tash and I sat gushing ludicrously about astrology, re-incarnation, karma, Tibet – all the mystic stuff we'd read that he was into. We thought we sounded intelligent. I don't think he noticed. He asked if we believed in UFOs, and what we thought of Marc Bolan.

'I like him,' I said. 'Have you met him?'

'He's a friend of mine,' said David. 'We're doing some stuff together. Hey you never know, one day we might be in a band.'

He told us about his many failed auditions for *Hair*, the risqué stage musical of the day. Tash asked about *Space Oddity*. David said he was 'out of his gourd' and 'totally flipped' over it.

That he was still struggling to find his way, there being no suggestion at that point that he would become one of the most iconic rock stars in history, with a string of alter egos, images and recordings unlike anything we'd seen or heard before, was way over our heads. He would achieve massive success as an actor, with movies like Nicolas Roeg's *The Man Who Fell To Earth* and stage roles such as *The Elephant Man* on Broadway. Against the odds, in July 1973, we'd attend his legendary gig at Hammersmith Odeon, the night he retired Ziggy Stardust and the Spiders from Mars. But I'm getting ahead of myself.

Someone else of enduring significance was living at Haddon Hall with David when we first started going there. We might even have passed him on the path, not realising who he was.

8

Tony Visconti, a beautiful and charismatic young American musician, had arrived from New York in the Summer of Love to hone his skills as a record producer. He was determined, he said, to discover the next Beatles. What he found, instead, was Tyrannosaurus Rex. As the Sixties waned, Tony was still unaware that his protégé's popularity would, in his imminent electric incarnation, eclipse Beatlemania and fulfil his wildest wish. For a moment, at least.

Young fans had no idea at the time of the influence of Brooklyn's answer to George Martin over two of the greatest rock acts to emerge as glam. Producers were not yet celebrities, they were still back-room boys. They had moved on, but not much, from traditional white-lab-coated 'Artistes & Recording Manager' status, when they did everything from dictating instrumental arrangements to telling their charges what to wear. While we'd vaguely heard of the 'Fifth Beatle', as some people called George Martin (while others applied that term to their manager, Brian Epstein), Visconti, at the turn of the Seventies, was nothing like a household name. By the time I was old enough to understand how records were actually made, he was kind of a legend.

So Tony Visconti was producing Marc Bolan while David Bowie was still struggling. Bowie even supported Tyrannosaurus Rex on those early tours – as a mime artist. Their young friendship took on a competitive dimension, with Tony caught in between. When his working relationship with Marc had run its course, it was to David that Tony returned. It was with David that Tony was able to stabilise his own talent, helping to solidify a star as unique and unforgettable as Marc had been – but taking it further, perfecting the art of adaptability, establishing artistry which was always a step ahead. The differences between Marc and David were as numerous as their similarities, actually. The

9

common denominator was Visconti, their facilitator and so-called 'enabler'. The very arrogance which dulled Marc's instinct and threw him off focus was the quality which crystallised David's creativity and paved his path for superstardom. The magic ingredient was sublimation.

To the many young pop fans seeking music with which to identify, to hide behind, to annoy our parents with, and in which to root for explanations to the universe and all therein, Bolan and Bowie were heaven-sent. Rock photographer Mick Rock, world-famous for his work with Bowie, Syd Barrett, Queen and others, described Bolan as John the Baptist to Bowie's Messiah. Inspired though this was, it was more complex than that. It was Bolan's metamorphosis from hippie to hip that provided young teens with a sex-toy via which to process pubescence. He was instant gratification. The Bowie thing, despite its wham-bam edge, was less physical, more obscure. Sexual-emotional conflict can be all-consuming at that age, if only subconsciously – certainly the case for we ridiculously bowler-hatted maidens incarcerated in all-girls' schools. To Bolan – raw, cute, compact – you kicked off your shoes and abandoned yourself to the beat. You chanted his nonsense rhymes while fantasising about getting naked with him . . . or at least lost in his hair. To Bowie – vampiric, angular, emaciated, no heart-throb – you sat around on stale rugs in common rooms, brushing and plaiting each other's manes while intel-lectualising over the lyrics. Both artists exploited androgyny, taunting the critics; but only with Bolan could we imagine getting our kit off. Looking back, Marc appeared to take his fans at face value. He tuned in to our fantasies.

What David did was deliver from a more perceptive and sophisticated angle. He played the long game. He knew that his younger fans would soon grow up. Many believe that Bowie would never have become a superstar if not for Marc Bolan. The competition between them was key to his creativity.

'They admired each other very much,' says Anya Wilson, who 'went out on a limb for' Bowie, 'adored' Bolan and promoted both, during her days as a plugger for UK radio.

'I believe that David Bowie would have happened anyway, with or without Bolan,' she adds. 'They both would have. But there is no question that they fed off and exerted some influence over each other. They were creating new music individually at the same time. Marc's glamour and David's strangeness were unique.'

Bolan flared in the early Seventies, faded mid-decade and was making a credible come-back at the time of his death, aged 29, in 1977. His moment was short-lived. But tragic though his demise, it was the best possible outcome in terms of rock immortality. As eminent psychiatrist Dr Cosmo Hallström told me when I interviewed him about Freddie Mercury, an early death could be deemed almost essential:

'Instead of becoming a fat, bloated, self-important old queen, he was cut off in his prime and is preserved at that age for eternity. For a rock star, it is not a bad way to go. They grow not old as we that are left grow old . . .'

I thought immediately of David Bowie, who turned 65 in January 2012. 'Isn't "sexagenarian rock star" an oxymoron?' John Entwistle used to joke. John died in 2002, aged 57, in Paradise, Nevada – which is exactly what he would have wanted. He once had a house on Priory Lane in Roehampton, a stone's throw from Barnes Common where Marc died, and where I sometimes stayed with him and his girlfriend Max. Those were the days. John and Marc had more than a few things in common – not least the fact that each had a customised Rolls Royce. John's was painted Harrods' green. He took an actual Harrods' carrier bag to the body shop to make sure that they matched the shade properly. It had been converted into a station wagon to accommodate his Irish wolfhound, Fits Perfectly. Marc's white Roller was really a Bentley with a Rolls Royce front, and was 'good for his voice.' The funny thing was that neither of them ever learned to drive.

It was John Entwistle who first took me to the Bolan tree.

Though not the only rock musician to lose his life in a car crash – his guitar hero Eddie Cochran had died the same way in 1960, aged 21 – Marc's death immortalised him as 'the James Dean of rock' thanks to a strange coincidence. The *East Of Eden* and *Rebel Without a Cause* star was killed in his Porsche Spyder in California on 30 September 1955, aged 24. It was Marc's 8th birthday.

Sometime in 1986, I spent a few days with Ken Russell and his then wife Vivian in Borrowdale, Cumbria, where they lived in an idyllic Lakeland stone cottage with ravishing views. We had arranged to talk about his horror flick *Gothic* (not that the director regarded it as a horror flick), and did some filming for something or other on Channel 4. Ken and I decided one afternoon to go out in a rowing boat on Derwentwater. We took with us what we could find in the fridge: a bottle of Laurent Perrier, two KitKats, a lump of Kendal mint cake and a head of uncooked broccoli. The cameraman was relegated to a second boat and was bringing up the rear.

I was, and remain, a huge fan of Russell's. His 1975 film version of The Who's rock opera *Tommy*, starring Roger Daltrey as the deaf, dumb and blind kid who sure played a mean pinball, is a minor masterpiece. On the back of its success, Ken cast Daltrey as Franz Liszt in his film *Lisztomania*, portraying the 19th century Hungarian composer and concert pianist as a fabulously sex-crazed degenerate. The movie, which also had a part for Ringo Starr and which was scored by 20th century keyboard wizard Rick Wakeman, was an extreme, flesh-filled romp-and-a-half which blasted Daltrey into the stratosphere, leaving audiences in no doubt as to his good points. What Ken cleverly served up in this feature, besides tongue-in-cheek sex, was one of the biggest rock stars in the world at that time playing the world's first-ever rock star. Lisztomania, or Liszt fever as it became known, was a 'medical condition' identified by Heinrich Heine in his 1844 paper on the Paris concert season, when fan frenzy during Liszt's intense performances was so hysterical – with women tearing his hair out, snatching his cigar butts and practically slaughtering each other for his gloves and handker-chiefs – that it was declared contagious. It also pre-echoed Frank Sinatra's bobby-soxers during the Fifties, Sixties' Beatlemania and Seventies' T. Rextasy. But by the time those phenomena came around, the world knew for sure that you couldn't catch it.

Sections of the media denounced Russell as a 'dirty old man' on *Lisztomania*'s release. 'Not dirty enough!' barked Ken.

Gothic was the story of Lord Byron and the Shelleys, or of an episode in their friendship, at least, when Byron invited his friends to Villa Diodati overlooking Lake Geneva, and challenged them to a drug-induced horror-writing competition.

It was the night that fellow-guest John Polidori created *The Vampyre* (who became Count Dracula), and when Mary Shelley, then only 18, pregnant with his child but not yet married to Percy, came up with *Frankenstein*. Gabriel Byrne and Julian Sands starred as Byron and Shelley in Russell's film, in which the late Natasha Richardson screen-debuted as Mary.

The discussion widened. Ken, who, as well as the many films he created, not least *Women in Love* and *The Devils*, had written novels about the sex lives of some of his favourite composers: Beethoven, Elgar, Brahms and Delius. But he seemed even crazier for poets. He'd started with a 1965 BBC film on Dante

Gabriel Rossetti, entitled *Dante's Inferno*, and he'd made *Clouds of Glory* about Lake District poets Coleridge and Wordsworth. He admitted to being 'a sucker for' 19th century Romantics. We agreed that the closest thing to mad, bad Bryon's relationship with Shelley, in rock terms, was David Bowie's with Marc Bolan.

'You *have* to make that film,' I told him, though it was obvious that he'd thought of it first.

'Yes, I do feel a special affection for Byron and his club foot – rather, his cloven hoof,' Ken mused.

'You realise that people regarded him as the devil.'

'I bet Bowie would love that,' I said, 'you must do it.'

'Trouble is,' replied Ken, 'I know too much. I'll have to wait until David is dead as well!'

Ken died in November 2011, that dream and countless others unfulfilled.

During a visit to the States in February 2012, my daughter Mia and I happened to see an enthralling exhibition on the life of Percy Bysshe Shelley at the New York Library. As I read of Shelley the intellectual waif being taken under the wing of the more robust and influential Lord Byron, and of how their explosive friendship developed, that conversation with Ken on Derwentwater all those years ago came back to me. The relationship between the two young Romantics was more significant than any other pairing in their lives. Each was the other's Yeatsian mask, projecting alternative aspects rather than opposites. Their intense conversations and interactions informed each other's poetry. There was rivalry and animosity; recklessness and emotional fall-out; boozing, drug-taking, complications with women; there was scandalous free love. Yet despite all this, the friendship endured, until Shelley died in tragic circumstances in 1822, at the age of 29.

When Shelley's body was cremated on the beach near Viareggio, northern Tuscany, Byron was present. Mythology attached to the circumstances of Shelley's death lingers to this day. Then there was Marc . . . who died in tragic circumstances in 1977, at the age of 29. When Marc's body was cremated in Golders Green, London, David Bowie was present. Mythology attached to the circumstances of Marc's death lingers to this day . . . It couldn't help but cross my mind how enchanted Marc might have been by all this.

'They *both* would', remarked Jeff Dexter, lifelong friend and confidant of Marc and David. Bedwell is still in touch with Jones.[3]

'The difference is, Deeb would take the coincidence with a pinch of salt and have a laugh over it. Marc would have actually "taken on" the belief that he was the reincarnation of Percy Shelley, bless him. Should I say, he would have given the *impression* of actually believing it. This was the line he would have fed the press . . . with his trademark wink to me, Tony Howard [Marc's manager], Keith Altham [PR] or anyone else on "his" side who might happen to be in the room. This was Marc's way of saying "*I* know that what I'm saying is a load of cobblers, and *you* know it's a load of cobblers, but no need for *them* to know. They're getting what they want: great copy. Why should they care if it's true or whether it's what I really believe or not?" He played them at their own game, the media, and he was brilliant at it. Ran rings round them. Who couldn't love him for that?'

Thirty-five years since his death, the music of Marc Bolan and T. Rex is as familiar to young fans as it was to those who loved him during his lifetime. Much of it is disseminated via commercials and films. Many were turned on to him by the soundtrack of the movie *Billy Elliot*: 'Children of the Revolution', 'Cosmic

Dancer', 'Get It On', 'I Love To Boogie', 'Ride a White Swan', all Bolan's. His records are played frequently on the radio, and not only by dedicated Sounds of the Seventies-style stations. Many younger musicians, from Marc Almond, Dr Robert of the Blow Monkeys, Morrissey and Boy George to Siouxsie Sioux, Lloyd Cole, and Toyah Willcox cite Bolan as their inspiration and pay homage to him in their songwriting and performing. Numerous contemporary artists, including Goldfrapp and Franz Ferdinand, draw from the infectious, distinctive sound of T. Rex. The tribute bands, the best of which is Danielz's T. Rextasy, are popular throughout the world. A number of Bolan pressings remain among the most valuable in record-collecting history.

Perhaps we shouldn't go back. The story's told. Yet much of what we 'know' about Marc Bolan is glorified gossip and speculation. So much received wisdom conflicts. Sensationalism is best filtered by those who are old enough to have been there, surely; who remember Marc Bolan for what he really was. But *who* was he?

Almost three and a half decades after his death, I still didn't know.

I had questions to ask. Would there be answers?

I

Music Out of the Moon

Marc Bolan was born Mark Feld on 30 September 1947. It was a vintage year for rock'n'roll, which he shared with a galaxy of future stars.[1] One in particular would turn out to be his consort, his co-star and even his adversary, but when all was said and done would remain his friend. David Robert Jones arrived eight months earlier than Mark, on what happened to be Elvis Presley's 12th birthday. He would become David Bowie.

Mark and David were baby boomers: a couple of the millions born during the post-war birth surge of 1946–64. They were the first generation of children to be exposed to the new American pop-culture, raised on Mickey Mouse and Davy Crockett. As history's first teenagers, they would buy rock'n'roll records and swoon over The King; they would also, if only their unsuspecting parents could have seen it coming, evolve into the hippies of 1960s' counter-culture – reacting in the extreme against an emerging consumerist ethos, growing their hair long, experimenting with drugs and, once girls were armed with the birth control pill, practising free love.

Mark's father Simeon Feld met his mother Phyllis Atkins at a munitions plant in London's Earls Court. Seventeen-year-old factory-worker Phyllis, the daughter of a Fulham greengrocer and a cleaning-lady, was a strapping, no-nonsense brunette. She had little in common with her diminutive blond suitor 'Sid', who was working as a porter in the same factory. His inflatable stories of life on the ocean wave were all it took.

Having been relieved of military duties on account of his poor eyesight, Sid had talked his way into the Dutch Merchant Navy, then sailed the North Atlantic and the sunny Caribbean Sea. He was seven years Phyllis's senior, with the gift of the gab and some to spare. Her family were what they called Church of England. Sid's were Jewish.

All Jews throughout the world at that time were preoccupied by the atrocities being committed against their people in Europe by Adolf Hitler's Nazis. Six million were murdered during World War II, a statistic too terrible to comprehend. A million were children.

While children born to a Jewish father and Gentile mother may be considered Jewish provided they are raised in the faith, this depends on matrilineal descent. Orthodox Jews, therefore, do not accept them as such. Nor is it possible to be 'half-Jewish'. Mark would become fascinated nonetheless by his dual heritage. He and his brother Harry were brought up to observe and respect certain traditions and customs of both cultures: Yom Kippur, Passover and Chanukkah as well as Easter, Whitsun (Pentecost) and Christmas. As he grew, Mark came to understand 'race' as a distinction referring to those with shared ancestry and common genetic traits – neither of which is required to be a 'Jew'. Most secular Jews considered their Jewishness to be a matter of culture or ethnicity. Certain foods, a few words of the Yiddish language and some holiday observances and rituals (while not regarding such practices as religious activities) were the extent of Mark's Jewishness. The most important trait that he took from his heritage was *chutzpah*: a Yiddish word referring to bold-faced arrogance, presumption, a brazen sense of self. It was *chutzpah* which gave him the nerve to seek fame and fortune. Although neither he nor his brother ever wore the *yarmulke* (traditional skullcap), Mark would be buried a Jew. For his funeral, his family observed to the letter the strictest requirements of the faith.

As a child, he loved to hear stories about his father's Russian-Polish grandparents, who had escaped to England from Eastern Europe in the late 1800s. They had been part of the mass Ashkenazic Jewish exodus following the assassination of Russia's Tsar Alexander II by the Narodnaya Volya (left-wing terrorist movement). Like many, they found their way into London's East End. North of the Thames and East of the city, the area had evolved from a cluster of villages in the marshes beyond old Londinium's walls. It was so overpopulated by immigrants and paupers at the turn of the last century that its future notoriety as a hotbed of crime and disease was perhaps inevitable.

Mark's parents were married in January 1945.

'A Jewish-Christian marriage was not nothing back then, especially during the war, what with all that was going on at the time,' comments Marc's elder brother Harry Feld, when I visit him and his wife Sandy in Southsea, Portsmouth. Rock photographer Steve Emberton put me in touch with Caron Willans and Danielz, and Danielz passed my number to the Felds. Despite many years of misrepresentation, and having even had their original photographs stolen by journalists and television producers, they agreed against the odds to be interviewed.

'Not that anyone in the family was racist, but eyebrows must have lifted. My father was one of six children, and had been brought up strictly Jewish. After he married Mum, who of course wasn't Jewish, the families just kind of went into themselves. Not that they all fell out, we just had different priorities and our own ways of life. We'd see the rest of the family rarely, at a wedding or at a funeral, say, but it was always friendly when we did. It was quite brave of my mum and dad to go in for a "mixed marriage", as it was regarded. We weren't religious as such, it was always more customs and traditions with us. Mum used to say that they just fell in love, and that nothing else mattered. I know that she and Dad were really close. They always seemed happy.'

Where should the newly-weds live? Only the run-down, bombed-out fringes of the East End were affordable. Even so, they couldn't manage more than a couple of cold-water, unheated upstairs rooms in a draughty Victorian house on Stoke Newington Common. Pregnant Phyllis was soon evacuated to a Yorkshire nursing home, where she could have the baby she was expecting in safety. When she and her husband were reunited that summer, VE (Victory in Europe) Day having been declared on 8 May, she presented him proudly with baby Harry.

So blasted in the Blitz was Stoke Newington that many of its residents had been made homeless. Although plenty of historic buildings survived the bombings, a high percentage of housing was damaged or destroyed.

The area would soon find itself consumed by frenetic post-war housing development and regeneration. In 1965 it would be absorbed into the London Borough of Hackney and acquire a progressive identity. Today, it boasts a rich mix of Afro-Caribbean, Irish, Asian, Jewish, Greek Cypriot and Turkish communities, and is a gentrified home to its share of artists, fashionistas and media types. In the mid-1940s, however, its overriding personality was Jewish. The number of strictly Orthodox Jews in Britain increased dramatically after the war. At first, this was due simply to immigration. While thousands of British Jews emigrated after the establishment of the State of Israel in 1948, many others migrated to London from North Africa and the Middle East, where they still faced isolation and persecution. The tendency towards larger than average families swelled their numbers. Ultra Orthodox Jews created tightly-knit and concentrated communities stretching from Stoke Newington, Tottenham and Stamford Hill to Hendon and Golders Green. A distinctive sight in their dark overcoats and black suits, their long, flowing sideburns curling down beneath black fedoras, they frequented the many synagogues, schools and specialist shops which served them, and kept themselves to themselves.

A familiar feature of Jewish East End and North London life had long been special activity clubs for young Jewish people, providing a means to keep kids off the streets and encourage decent citizenship, while offering a break from the poverty-stricken grind which most endured. As well as organising sports, drama, music and other pursuits, the celebrated Victoria Boys' Club would run weekend and summer camps, often on the Isle of Wight. One regular attendee, Lionel Begleiter of Brick Lane, made a modest name for himself when he began writing camp songs. Years later when he returned from the war, he rode past St. Bart's hospital on a bus one day, and was inspired to abbreviate his surname. It was as Lionel Bart that he would become the world-famous composer and lyricist of *Oliver!* – a musical based on *Oliver Twist* by Charles Dickens, which opened in London's West End in 1960 and in New York three years later. It was the first modern British musical to transfer successfully to Broadway. Despite the 17-year age difference, Bart and Bolan became good friends during the Sixties, and even discussed writing songs together.

There was little expectation of luxury in the post-war years. Most people didn't know what luxury was. Families simply got on with it, making the best of what they had. Wartime rationing was still in place, and would remain so until 1954.

One egg per person each week, two rashers of bacon, a quarter of butter, another of marge. You made do. Sausages, pies and corned beef were common fodder. Despite shortages, most mothers were able to rustle up a meal. Domestic coal fires contributed to the city's dense smog. Those without fireplaces and chimneys warmed their homes with paraffin heaters. Some families managed the odd get-away to Southend-on-Sea on the Thames estuary, in Essex, where they could stroll along the longest pleasure pier in the world and relieve their choked lungs. Horses still pulled milk carts around cobbled streets. Life was slower than it is lived today, and not only because hardly anyone owned a car.

Mark, named after his father's late brother, was born at the Hackney General on Homerton High Street, one of the munici-pal hospitals which had been built as Victorian workhouses for the destitute. Hospital births were just becoming the norm, most babies until then having been delivered at home with hot water and a helping hand. Not until the modern welfare state was created in 1948 in accordance with Health Secretary Aneurin Bevan's vision did medical treatment become free for all.

Sid, by now a lorry driver, was not present at Harry or Mark's births, because he was not permitted to be. Fathers were banned from hospital births at the time, and only allowed in during visit-ing hours. They were also prevented from holding their newborns, as it was considered 'unhygienic'. Even contact between mother and baby was mostly limited to feeding times, the two being kept on separate wards. There was little by way of post-natal support, and baby care at home was laborious. Terry-towelling nappies had to be hand-washed daily, dried in front of the fire, and were secured with safety pins. You had Dettol and soap, and baby powder if you were lucky. Many working class infants slept in wooden chest-drawers lined with blankets, as few families owned cots. Prams were handed down. Baby nightgowns and singlets were stitched from old sheets. Everyone knitted – matinee jack-ets, caps, booties, mittens – if and when they could afford any wool. Mark's babyhood was as humble as could be, but he had everything he needed. His parents adored him.

With nothing to lose, there was everything to play for. To the many children growing up in the 1950s, the seemingly deprived corner of London they called home was the most inspirational place on earth. Rich in immigrant cultures, a vast melting pot of heritages, and with a universal desire to Make Good, there was a magic about London's 'common' and 'deprived' neighbour-hoods which gave rise to infinite talent over the decades to come.

'We never felt deprived,' remembers Mitch Winehouse, former cab driver and father of late singing star Amy, whose family were long-standing friends of Eric Hall's clan.

'Mine, like so many others, was a typically working class Jewish family,' he told me, in an exclusive interview for the *Mail on Sunday* in May 2010.

'There would be twelve people living in a house at any given time. Men, women, kids, everyone worked. We lived in Stoke Newington like Marc Bolan's family, but when I was a little boy I spent most of my time in the East End proper, where my grandparents lived and where I went to school. My grandfather had a barber's shop on Commercial Street, and my grandmother had a hairdresser's behind that. They lived above the shop, which was not unusual. I'd come back from school at about 4 o'clock to find my mum Cynthia, who was a striking brunette, and her twin sister, my Auntie Lorna, who was a beautiful blonde, dancing. They were still only in their twenties, and they were just lovely.

'They'd put Sinatra on the radiogram in the salon when it wasn't busy and do ballroom dancing together. My mum and dad were fantastic ballroom dancers. People went dancing in those days to keep fit, the way they go to the gym today.

'My two uncles were brilliant tailors who had a factory making dresses and coats. Many Jewish people worked in *schmutter,* the rag trade, it was a long-standing tradition – tailoring, shoemaking, cabinet-making, cigar- and cigarette-making. Jews had always been makers,' reflects Mitch.

'But the thing I remember most about my childhood,' he says, 'is music: always music. The popular music of the day. At first, all that great jazz. Later on it was Adam Faith and Cliff Richard who we were mad for. All families like ours entertained ourselves, pre-television. Everyone had a piano. Even if you couldn't play, and even if the piano was off the back of a lorry and falling to bits, you had one.

'The other thing I always remember is mums and their obsessive cleaning. My mum was like a raving lunatic, manic with the cleaning. I think most of them were. In the cupboards, under the beds, everything. It was a pride thing with women: because other women judged you by how clean your home was. It didn't matter that you had nothing, no one did – but what you did have, however shabby, had to be spick and span, neat as a pin – all those funny little expressions. The childhood I had was exactly what I wanted to give my own kids. I grew up in a loving, respectable household where I felt very wanted, very secure.'

'So did I,' remembers Harry Feld, 'and so did Mark.'

'Yes, it was all many years ago, so it's hard to remember the details. But you are left with an overall impression of your childhood, aren't you? I've always looked back on it as a Golden Age. The bad bits get forgotten, it's the nice things that stick in your mind. Perhaps that's a self-preservation thing, I don't know. All I know is that when Mark and I were kids, we had everything we wanted. Our expectations were modest, we didn't ask for very much. Our parents did their best, and we loved them for it. We were a poor family, but so was everyone else, where we lived. We made do with what we had. We all did. There was a certain pride in that.'

★ ★ ★

Harry, who was just over 2 years old when Mark arrived, was delighted to have a little brother to play with.

'Mark and I were chalk and cheese in many ways', he says, 'but we mostly got on. We were very different to look at for a start: I was always bigger than him, being a couple of years older, but we were also built differently. Mark was like my dad, small for his age, quite fragile-looking, very wiry. I took after Mum, who was stocky and fit. My mum worked the markets, she was really strong. The Jaffa oranges used to come in big boxes, they must have weighed four stone each. She could pick one of those up with one arm and fling it onto the lorry, no trouble. That was quite something to see.

'The bedroom Mark and I shared was also our living room,' Harry says. 'We had a bath with a cold tap on it, and we heated buckets of water on the stove to pour in and have a hot bath. We did have an indoor toilet, though, unlike many.

'We played quite nicely together, but I was always chasing him, and he was always running away. He was so fast. We liked the usual things when we were little: Dinky cars and guns. Before we got a television, we just had a radio, and Mark did like to listen to that. You could almost see his little mind whirring as he sat there listening to programmes like the ghost stories. We would sometimes go to the cinemas on Stamford Hill and the Lower Clapton Road – Mum would save up, and take us when we had a bit of money. At first it was the usual kids' stuff, but when Mark got a bit older, he started getting into the horror films. They petrified him, because he wasn't that brave. At home, he didn't even like going upstairs on his own, and he was reluctant to go to sleep with the lights out. When we couldn't afford to go to the pictures, Mum read to us a lot, which she did really well. She had a good strong voice, a lot of character in it. All sorts, really. I can remember Bible stories. I think we had cowboys and Indians, and a book about dinosaurs. All little boys like dinosaurs, don't they? I know Mark did.'

2

Drop a Nickel In

In September 1952, a couple of weeks before his 5th birthday, Mark joined his brother Harry at the local Northwold Road state primary school. While his early school years are often referred to as having been idyllic and happy, contemporaries tell a different story.

'I was in the same class as Mark at school, from when I was about 7 until we took the Eleven Plus,' recalls Marilyn Roberts – whom I found by chance, after my friend Rick Wakeman introduced me to Marilyn's former husband, Rod Weinberg.

'He was a strange one. Not popular at all, I would say. He wasn't exactly what you could call academic, either. He couldn't really be bothered in lessons, his mind seemed to be always on something else. Always staring out the window dreaming, he was. I think writing and arithmetic and so on came quite hard to him. Probably wouldn't have done, had he concentrated: he certainly wasn't thick. He was the playground clown, really. You never saw Mark kicking a ball around, or joining in games with other kids. He tended to go around singing by himself, and then it was air guitar. He was always trying to draw attention to himself, like he needed our approval. We can be quite judgemental and cruel as kids, can't we? And none of us was very nice to

Mark. I feel quite ashamed to hear myself say that now. Yet I don't think he minded. It was as if he wasn't aware of any hostility – or maybe he didn't actually care what anyone thought. He did seem rather bold and self-contained for such a littl'un.

'All that singing did get on your nerves, though,' she laughs. 'No one thought he could sing, to be honest. The only one who thought he could sing was Mark.'

Nor did he enjoy close friendships during his few short years at primary school.

'I was far too young in those days to know what "ego" was,' admits Marilyn. 'But I now know that Mark Feld's ego was huge. You know those bit-of-a-loner kids who never really get in with anyone, who the pack don't like but they can't really tell you why? That was Mark. He had a few mates but, to be honest, most of the kids thought he was a little bit weird. Not in terms of his looks: frankly we all looked odd and badly turned-out. No one was cool, it was the clothes we wore.'

Mark would later remember wearing 'brown corduroy shorts (real hip kid I was) and a blue and white Snow White t-shirt.'

'Well, he was right in that there was no school uniform, just any old clothes,' grins his brother Harry, 'and they *were* old, some of 'em. Money was really tight.'

'We had been born into an area where there was a lot of deprivation,' adds Marilyn, 'and where childhood diseases were still rife.'

'At the end of Maury Road, on our corner,' Harry tells me, 'there was still a bombsite where we used to play, and where you could pick up all kinds. I'm not saying other kids weren't clean, but we were always well looked-after, my mother was a stickler for that kind of thing. But a lot of them were always getting infections. We knew kids with scurvy and rickets. It wasn't uncommon.'

The 1950s was the decade of mass disease eradication, with

smallpox, polio, tuberculosis and other illnesses on the priority target list. Comprehensive immunisation programmes would be introduced by the new National Health Service in the mid to late Fifties. Rickets, the bone-disease scourge of Victorian Britain, still plagued many – for which cod liver oil was given, and vitamin D added to milk. Scurvy resulted from deficiency in vitamin C.

'We'd get free orange juice from the welfare, which was very sweet and came in a medicine bottle,' remembers Harry. 'We also had free milk, at school – in a little bottle, at break-time. A school meal was a tanner – sixpence – in old money [the equivalent of 2.5 new pence]. It was the only thing you had to pay for, and you took your silver sixpence in every day.'

'And we all got nits,' says Marilyn, 'that was par for the course. But everyone got them, so you didn't feel ashamed. We were all in it together.

'I never got any new stuff, my clothes were my sister's hand-me-downs. It was the norm back then, none of us looked particularly smart or "together" when we were young. There wasn't much fashion sense going on, not the way young kids are today with their hundred-quid trainers, logo t-shirts and designer jeans. We didn't know any better, so it didn't bother us. This might well have had a bearing on Mark's obsession with image and clothes as he grew up, a reaction against poverty, against what he hadn't had as a kid. But who knows? It's easy to say with hindsight.'

One thing that Marilyn did notice was the uncommonly strong bond between Mark and his mother, Phyllis.

'Even more so because he was a boy,' she says. 'He was incredibly close to his mother, and she absolutely idolised him. You didn't see his father around that much.

'Mark's mum worshipped both her sons – and his brother was

lovely, I really did like Harry Feld – but her younger son was obviously the apple of her eye. Who wouldn't have an ego the size of a planet with a mother like that? The sun shone out of Mark as far as she was concerned. I did meet her a few times when she used to bring him to school, then come and get him at the gate of an afternoon, which she did until he got the hang of it. I never went to their home. We didn't really go to other people's houses for tea in those days, there wasn't enough food to go round! But I'm not sure I would have gone, even if they'd asked me. His mum seemed to me a big, imposing woman with a frighteningly loud voice. She probably wasn't that big or that loud at all, but she seemed that way to me. Mark did appear to take after her, in some ways. He got his dark hair from her, but in build he was more like his dad. Harry was the other way round, with his mum's heavier physique and his dad's blond hair. Mark seemed needier of her attention. I think that's why she lavished it on him.

'Mark wasn't likeable, I'm sorry to say,' says Marilyn, apologetically. 'He stood out from the crowd only because he didn't fit in. He rubbed a lot of the kids up the wrong way. He was different. Funny thing was, he didn't appear to mind.'

'Neither of us liked school,' remembers Harry Feld. 'We weren't what you could call swots. You went to school because you had to, but we didn't get an awful lot out of it. Most of us were marking time there, it was the same old routine, day in, day out. We went through the motions. I was just bored, most of the time. I wasn't particularly good at anything, and I always felt we learned more at home anyway, listening to Mum and Dad.

'Mark had something I didn't have, which was this ability to take himself off into other worlds in his head. He did it when he didn't like or couldn't get into what was going on around him. I had no idea then, but I realise now that that's a gift, something few people have. There was definitely something special about my brother. Even at that age.'

The nation stopped what it was doing on 2 June 1953, when Elizabeth II was crowned Queen of the United Kingdom, Australia, Canada, New Zealand, South Africa, Ceylon and Pakistan, and was confirmed Head of the Commonwealth. The ceremony took place at London's Westminster Abbey, the first ever coronation to be televised. It was also the world's first major broadcast event.

'I remember watching it,' says Harry. 'We had to. My mum insisted. People saw the service in church halls and so on, all gathered round one tiny television set. There was a big children's tea party along the street, us all sitting out there, people doing pretend coronations and stuff. You had fancy dress, some of the kids were done up as little John Bulls. There was bunting every-where, and a lot of princesses, that day. I think Mark was one of them! He had such beautiful hair, he could have passed for a girl. I don't think he minded that, either!'

By 1955, when Mark was nearly 8, he was already jumping on the number 73 bus from Stoke Newington after school, and heading up west to join his mother on her Berwick Street Market grocery stall. It was there that his pennies began to drop.

Soho, as he would soon discover, was the hub of the UK film and music industries. Denmark Street off Charing Cross Road, a short stroll from the Soho street markets, had long been known as the British Tin Pan Alley thanks to the music publishers and songwriters who congregated there. Donovan, Jimi Hendrix, The Rolling Stones and the Sex Pistols would all record in its basement studios, while Elton John would compose his 1970 breakthrough there, 'Your Song'. This was where, in the late 1950s, Lionel Bart first heard the new American R&B which was coming in off the ships with the Merchant Navy seamen, and began writing the earliest British rock'n'roll songs for Denmark Street's publishers. He had a hand in the discovery of Tommy Steele and Marty Wilde, wrote 'Living Doll' for Presley-esque Cliff Richard and 'Little White Bull' for Steele. Shirley Bassey had a hit with a Bart composition 'As Long As He Needs Me' from the musical *Oliver!*, as did Matt Monro, with his theme of the 1963 James Bond film *From Russia with Love*. Between 1957 and 1960, Bart landed nine Ivor Novello Awards, and once said that his favourite recording artist was Adam Faith. Adam enjoyed Bart-penned chart successes with 'Easy Going Me' and 'Big Time' – the latter from Lionel's hit musical *Fings Ain't Wot They Used T'Be*.

'Adam's thing was – the *terrific* thing – that he couldn't really sing!' Bart once observed. 'The whole appeal of his throwaway delivery was that people listened to it, kids listened to it, and said "well, I can sing as well as that!"'

It was the secret, in a nutshell, of how to make pop music popular.

Despite its seedy nocturnal reputation as London's red light district, most visitors to Soho in the late Forties and early Fifties came for the live jazz. Club Eleven had opened on Great Windmill Street in 1948, with Johnny Dankworth and Ronnie Scott fronting the house bands. The club played an important part in the evolution of British bebop – a pacey, US-born fusion of jazz, improv and instrumental showing-off, basically, which was taking Soho by storm. The term would hit the mainstream with American rockabilly star Gene Vincent's 1956 hit 'Be-Bop-A-Lula'. Club Eleven moved to Carnaby Street in 1950, and was closed down following a police raid. Plenty of others sprang up to take its place, with London's first skiffle club opening in Wardour Street's Roundhouse pub in 1952. Once the Beatniks began moving in on Soho, the Fifties scene kicked in. Beatniks were a spin-off of America's Beat generation, popularised by writers Jack Kerouac and Allen Ginsberg and their ilk, and comprising New York's disaffected intellectual youth and downtrodden hipsters who were the forerunners of the global hippie movement.

With the beatniks came the coffee bars, where they gathered to indulge in poetry readings, discuss French and Italian art films, compare and swap records, trawl through Italian magazines in search of style ideas, and to debate and jive-dance to records played on jukeboxes. Some coffee bar owners even kept back space on the jukeboxes for customers to play their own records on them. Coffee bars appealed to young people because they stayed open into the early hours – unlike pubs, which closed promptly at 11pm, according to regulations at the time. The 2i's on Old Compton Street which opened in 1956 was the most famous. Nick-named for the Irani brothers who owned it – 'the two 'I's' – the bar was later dubbed 'Europe's first rock club'. It was in the 2i's in 1958 that Ian 'Sammy' Samwell met Harry Webb, who became Cliff Richard and for whom he wrote 'Move It' – a chart breakthrough for Cliff and The Drifters, of which Samwell became one. The Marquee Club opened on Wardour Street that year, where the Stones would perform their first gig in 1962. Brian Jones, Eric Clapton and a host of other young musicians began taking up residence in the neighbourhood. It was all happening.

'Stock Records on South Molton Street [beyond Soho on the other side of Regent Street] was the place to be in the Fifties,' remembers BBC Radio 2 producer Phil Swern.

'They had all the imports. R&B, blues, rock'n'roll. Little

Milton, "Queen of the Blues" Koko Taylor, Chuck Berry, Bo Diddley, Fats Domino, John Lee Hooker, Elvis. We were like kids in a sweet shop in there.'

Little wonder that the young Mark Feld became intoxicated by the hip-an'-happenin' Soho scene. Barely a day went by when he didn't join his mother on the Berwick Street stall, always keen to nip round the corner to get the coffees in at the 2i's so that he could drop a couple of discs on the jukebox. His favourite was Elvis Presley, the young Mississippi-born rocker who had recorded his first single 'That's All Right' at Sam Phillips' Sun Studios in Memphis the year before, and had embarked upon a debut US tour which would change everything.

On his 9th birthday in September 1956, Mark's parents presented him with his first guitar. The £9 instrument cost double what his father was earning a week, but a hire purchase agreement made it possible. Not that Mark needed to know about that. The first song he practised, remembers his brother Harry, was Elvis's 'Hound Dog' – but only because it happened to be in the charts at the time.

'He was hopeless, really. He couldn't play to save his life', laughs Harry. 'As they say, it could only get better, but you had to admire his energy and enthusiasm. He was always at it, there was no stopping him. It got him in with the girls, too, because they were impressed.'

At 9 years old?

'Oh yes!,' laughs Harry. 'He was very grown-up for his age, was Mark. He'd already had his first encounters, shall we say!'

A heap more pennies landed the following summer, when Mark, not yet 10, became obsessed with the American musical movie *The Girl Can't Help It*. Conceived as a vehicle for the blonde bombshell actress Jayne Mansfield, its tongue-in-cheek sub-plot focused on American teenagers and their passion for rock'n'roll.

Jayne's abundant charms aside, it would achieve legendary status as the 'most potent celebration of rock music ever captured on film'. The original score features a title song performed by Little Richard. Ray Anthony, the celebrated band-leader and trumpeter who had played for Glenn Miller in the early Forties, earned a credit in the film for his tune 'Big Band Boogie'. Fats Domino, Eddie Cochran and Gene Vincent & His Bluecaps all performed cameos in this timeless piece.

Was this the first time young Mark heard the word 'boogie', which would inspire his future songwriting as well as name his 1972 performance flick (*Born to Boogie*)? It's possible, although it would have been familiar to his mother (and therefore to him) from The Andrews Sisters' massive 1941 war-time hit 'The Boogie Woogie Bugle Boy From Company B'. What did 'boogie' mean? Any number of things. Its most likely source was America's black ghettoes, where it referred to all kinds, from low-grade marijuana to ghetto folk themselves. Like its counterpart expression 'rock'n'roll', it was also used to describe energetic dancing, get-going and red-hot sex.[1]

Elsewhere in England that summer of 1957, *The Girl Can't Help It* was working its magic on a couple of other working class lads destined for stardom ahead of Mark. In Liverpool, 16-year-old John Lennon was mesmerised by the moving images of his American rock'n'roll idols, having hitherto known only how they sounded. In July, Lennon performed at a local garden party with his group The Quarrymen, where he was introduced to 15-year-old Paul McCartney. Paul so impressed John with his rendition of 'Twenty Flight Rock' – performed by Eddie Cochran in the film, and released as a single – that he invited him to join the group. The following year was Elvis's turn, with the future King's legendary performance of 'Jailhouse Rock' in the eponymous film sometimes referred to as the world's first rock video. It bears an uncanny resemblance to the 'Rock Around The Rockpile' sequence in *The Girl Can't Help It*.

It was even said that Elvis copied his signature leg movements and hip-swivellings from actor Edmond O'Brien, who performed said moves in the film.[2] Better, the producers of *The Girl Can't Help It* had wanted Elvis for their film but the budget wouldn't stretch to the demands of his manager Tom Parker.

Back in the family manor, Mark had caught the attention of Helen Shapiro, a local Jewish council estate girl destined for stardom in her early teens thanks to her precociously adult and beautifully mellow voice. Marc would recall that the band they were in together was called Susie and the Hula Hoops, although Shapiro has said that she doesn't remember the name. Shapiro, who became the youngest-ever female chart topper in the UK, had her first hit at fourteen with 'Don't Treat Me Like A Child', before scoring two Number Ones with 'You Don't Know' and 'Walking Back To Happiness'. When The Beatles first toured the UK in 1962–63, they were Helen's support act. She later took the role of Nancy in Lionel Bart's *Oliver!*

When Eddie Cochran achieved his breakthrough in August 1958 with 'Summertime Blues', 11-year-old Mark knew exactly what he wanted to do with his life. This was the good news. The bad was that he had failed his Eleven Plus. It came as no surprise to his family, who suffered no lasting disappointment. The annoying part, as far as Mark was concerned, was that there was no getting out of another four years of school.

3
No Dice, Son

We tend to remember the things that happen around the time we start secondary school. In Mark's case, 1958 was anything but a boring year. Swash-buckling Tyrone Power, the 'world's greatest movie star', dropped dead in Spain aged 44, on the set of *Solomon and Sheba*. His co-star Gina Lollobrigida kept calm and carried on with Yul Brynner. Members of the Manchester United football team were killed in the Munich air disaster. Britain's first stretch of motorway, the eight-mile Preston bypass, was opened. Boris Pasternak's classic novel *Doctor Zhivago* was published, and the Broadway musical *My Fair Lady* starring Julie Andrews debuted in London – with black-market tickets selling for as much as £5 (more than five times their original price). General de Gaulle was elected President of France; youths staged one of the first anti-nuclear demonstrations in Trafalgar Square, and danced at the Albert Memorial; and the Lord Chamberlain of Great Britain lifted the ban on the portrayal of homosexuality on the stage – despite the fact that the Sexual Offences Act, decriminalising homosexual behaviour between consenting adult males over the age of 21, would not be passed for another nine years, in 1967.[1] This was also the year when TV producer Jack Good, of BBC *6.5 Special* fame, launched the UK's first-ever pop music show *Oh Boy*, broadcast live from the Hackney Empire on Saturday mornings. Featuring home-grown stars such as the likes of Cliff Richard, Marty Wilde, Billy Fury, Lonnie Donegan, Adam Faith and Shirley Bassey, the series also welcomed visiting American stars. When his guitar hero Eddie Cochran appeared on the programme, Mark claimed to have carried Eddie's Gretsch guitar out to his car for him.

But perhaps the most momentous occurrence of 1958, as far as locals were concerned, was the fire which destroyed their beloved Collins's Music Hall on Islington Green. I lived in that part of Islington for nine years, during the Nineties, and the place was still legendary.

'The Green' is a triangle at the meeting point of Upper Street and the Essex Road (formerly Lower Street) which was once a patch of common grazing land. In the 1950s, with little else to do after school, local teenagers congregated and hung out there. Well-known today for its Screen On the Green independent cinema, the Green was famous during Mark and Harry's childhood as the site of the now legendary music hall, where their parents Sid and Phyllis loved to go. So great was its loss to the community that neighbourhood folk wept openly in the street as they watched it go up in smoke.

Music hall, like pantomime, was a uniquely British institution. It had begun with drinking and singing parties in pubs, where the best performers were paid with free ale. The trend spread, and soon concert rooms were being built onto pubs to accommodate the many enthusiastic participants. By the late 1800s, there was barely a town in the land without a music hall. Artists would tear from venue to venue, performing up to five times a night in an effort to earn a crust. They often adopted exotic names to ensure that audiences remembered them. Although essentially working class entertainment, music hall achieved a

37

modicum of respectability when the Prince of Wales, later His Majesty King Edward VII, developed a penchant for it.

Collins's began life in the 1800s as the Lansdowne Arms public house. The Lansdowne was converted by Irish entertainer Sam Collins, who opened it in 1863 and ran it as a venue until his death two years later. Hoxton-born Marie Lloyd, racy darling of late 19th century music hall, consolidated her fame there. Her 1922 funeral was attended by more than 100,000 mourners.

Marie Lloyd Junior famously performed a tribute to her mother's Edwardian act there, in 1944.

Music hall entertainment declined in popularity after 1902, when the sale of alcohol in theatres was banned. Collins's changed hands, evolving into a 'temple of varieties' featuring singers, dancers, trick cyclists, jugglers, contortionists, comedians and 'tellers-of-tales'. It was a local hub offering relief from the daily grind, where the workers could let down their hair and join in the singing of popular old songs. 'Any Old Iron', 'Boiled Beef & Carrots', 'Daddy Wouldn't Buy Me a Bow-Wow', 'I Do Like To Be Beside the Seaside' and 'Burlington Bertie From Bow' were the colourful ditties of Mark's childhood, the songs often sung around the home. It also became a mecca for the early talent scouts and agents. This was where Charlie Chaplin, Tommy Cooper, Norman Wisdom, Tommy Trinder and Benny Hill all 'had a start'. By 1950, Collins's was featuring Easter parades and Barry Snow & his Hammond Organ. The 'good old days', 'something for everyone' flavour of Collins's and music hall in general was the genesis of variety television.

By the time Mark arrived at the Palatine Road annex of the shabby William Wordsworth mixed secondary modern school in September 1958, with 'Summertime Blues' still ringing in his ears, his brother Harry had progressed to the main building on Albion Road, which ran up to Islington Green.

'School seemed pretty pointless to both of us by then', recalls Harry. 'I think we'd both had enough of it, but it wasn't for too much longer. In those days you could leave once you'd turned 15, which is precisely what both of us did: me in 1960 and Mark in 1962.

'I don't think Mum and Dad had any great expectations of us as scholars. But Mum didn't worry. She knew we'd get by on our wits.'

It has long been assumed that Mark's inability to spell and write correctly according to conventional educational expectations were the result of chronic dyslexia – these days a recognised learning difficulty often referred to as 'word blindness'.

'He wasn't dyslexic,' insists Harry, 'he just couldn't be bothered.'

Diagnosis was not available at the time. Although the first recorded assessment was made in the UK in 1896, it was not until 1970, long after Mark had left school, that the affliction entered the mainstream when it was recognised by Parliament in the Chronically Sick and Disabled Persons Act. While a popular image prevails of many famous achievers having been learning-disabled – Leonardo da Vinci, Albert Einstein, Thomas Edison and Walt Disney among them – eccentricities in learning habits and routes to greatness were not 'proof' of dyslexia or anything else, but were merely conjecture. It is doubtful that Mark ever considered himself dyslexic, though quite possible that he was.

'His shortcomings were more the result of a poor education, really,' reflects Jeff Dexter, his lifelong friend. 'I've got hand-written stuff from him I still can't make head nor tail of. He'd often misspell or mis-hear things, but it never bothered him. *He* knew what he meant.'

'I always had trouble in school,' was Mark's own take. 'I wanted to find out about things that you couldn't just look up in books.'

Not that he was averse to literature. At one point he became fascinated by the Cumbrian Romantic poet William Wordsworth, who lent his name to Mark and Harry's school. Mark found himself relating to all kinds of facts about Wordsworth's early life. As a child, he learned, Wordsworth had 'heard the moors breathing down his shirt collar'. He imagined cliffs pursuing him across the water as he rowed his boat on the lake. Once, as he lingered on the hills beyond Penrith Beacon, close to the execution site of a local murderer, he became so terrorised by the 'echoes' of what had occurred there that he fled all the way to the beacon summit. Wordsworth understood from a relatively young age that his psychological awareness and emotional fragility were keys to his creativity.

Another character which captured young Mark's imagination was the subject of Carlo Maria Franzero's book *Beau Brummell: His Life & Times* which was published the year Mark started at secondary school. Brummell was a famous Eton and Oxford-educated Regency poser who became a kind of fashion court jester, impressing royalty with his wit, manners and style and achieving a profile as one of the original dandies. Brummell claimed that he took five hours to dress, and that he polished his boots with Champagne. He died penniless and insane, but not forgotten. A statue of him by sculptor Irena Sedlecka takes pride of place on London's fashionable Jermyn Street.[2] Brummell was the subject of a silent 1924 movie starring John Barrymore and Mary Astor, which was remade in 1954 with Stewart Granger and Elizabeth Taylor. Mark saw the remake, and was transfixed.

From then on, having identified an easy way to stand out from the crowd and impress (or annoy) his peers, Mark became obsessed with clothes and style while continuing to strum his guitar and soak up the latest pop hits.

'I never liked school very much, so I started getting into clothes when I was about 12,' Marc told *Honey* magazine in 1970.

'Clothes were then, I suppose, wisdom and knowledge and getting satisfaction as a human being. In those days, all I really cared about was creating a sort of material vision of what I wanted to be like.'

In February 1959, Mark reeled in shock along with music fans all over the world at the news that Buddy Holly, Ritchie Valens and J.P. Richardson ('the Big Bopper'), friends of his idol Eddie Cochran, had been killed in a plane crash while touring the US.[3]

'We met in Connick's Junior Man on Kingsland Road in the wastes of Dalston,' remembers Jeff Dexter.

Jeff and I were introduced by two mutual friends: Songlink International publisher and drummer David Stark, and musician/impresario Tony Moore. Jeff cancelled our first five appointments, so reluctant was he to talk to me. Once we'd set eyes on each other and he felt comfortable about opening up, I returned to his home to interview him on six further occasions. A long-term illness precludes him from getting out much at the moment, but there's a constant stream of rock'n'roll types. His phone rings constantly.

'I was 13, he was 12,' says Jeff. 'He was looking through a pile of things on one side of the shop, and I was on the other, talking to Gerry Connick. We really just glared at each other, the first time we met. I was from south London – the Elephant. He was from north London – Stoke Newington. I suppose we were just sussing each other out.'

Jeff, who started life as Dexter Bedwell in 1945, would become known as 'the man who taught Britain to twist' at the popular Lyceum Ballroom, off London's Strand. He would go on to achieve fame as a festival promoter, music business manager, influential club DJ and arbiter of style throughout the Sixties and Seventies, getting the Beatles booted and suited and working with every major act from The Who to The Rolling Stones.

What was the attraction between him and Mark?

'We were not close friends at first,' he admits. 'But we got that way. We had a lot in common. We loved clothes. It was after seeing us in his shop several times at the same time that Gerry Connick said "you two are like two little midgets together!"'

'"Midgets!" one of us cried. "We're in proportion!" shouted the other one. I was four foot eight at the time, and so was Mark. You hit it off, you became mates, and that was that.

'We used to talk about little else but clothes. We did have one very frank early discussion about sex: he told me quite matter-of-fact one day that he'd been doing it since the age of 9. "Oh well, you started late, didn't you!" I retorted. I'd been at it since I was 6, when I got in a clinch with a cousin of mine. Liked it, too. There was no way back, was there?

'Cut to a couple of years later, I'm learning tailoring at a school in Hoxton. Before long, I could buy a shirt for eight bob from Woolworth's and turn it into something that looked like it had come out of Jermyn Street. There were few shops in those days that catered for young people who didn't just want the stuff that normal schoolboys wore, or that made you look like a younger version of your dad.'

Connick's was an unusual store for its time and location, reflects Jeff, because it was importing complete ranges of interesting clothes for boys from France and Italy.

'It was also very close to my school in Hoxton. So before I hopped on the Number 35 bus and went back home to the

Elephant, I'd walk up and go in there first. If I'd earned some money that week, I'd go in on a Saturday. How did I earn money? I worked on a fruit stall, in the surplus store, the hardware store. I did three paper rounds. All kids like us worked, most of us did something. No, it wasn't Dickensian, no one was stuffing us up chimneys. Even if you were just delivering newspapers, it was all about buying yourself a bit of independence. I used to get up every morning, arrive at the kiosk at a quarter to seven, seven o'clock, and take the papers out before school. You did it. My father was a dustman, my mother only worked part-time. We had nothing. If you needed things, if you wanted a few bob in your pocket, you had to work.

'Mark and I were just two little blokes who wanted to dress up. Eventually I got to work at the Lyceum – where I shouldn't have been, because at 14 I was far too young to go in there – and then it became all about music and style. And of course ballrooms were packed with young birds, who were impossible to resist.'

'There weren't many places where you could go in London at that time to hear "new" music,' Dexter says.

'It was mainly the ballrooms. One of the most important figures on the scene at that time was Ian "Sammy" Samwell: the guy who wrote "Move It" for Cliff Richard. He was the first proper super-jock in the London ballrooms. I really admired him. Not that I wanted to be him – he still had a quiff in his hair! But he certainly knew his music, and was playing sounds we'd never heard before. Stuff rooted in far-flung cultures we knew nothing about. He came from the "rocker" side, but his true love was country & western, rhythm'n'blues. We weren't hearing all that indigenous American music at that time. Fifties rock'n'roll was very new to us then.'

Not that much original American music was making its way into the ballrooms at first.

'We got some from source, sure. But every publisher was onto it. As soon as something was published in America, the sheet music would arrive in UK and you'd have an ersatz British version of it before you could say "boo". Everything coming in from the States was covered by a British artist here. And of course at that time, having needle-time restrictions on radio, there wasn't an awful lot of recorded music. Most of it was live. To keep the Musician's Union happy and the business side happy, you had to use the home-grown version.'

The year of 1960 was when compulsory military call-up in Britain ended, so no National Service for Jeff and Mark. They saw, instead, the dawning of the so-called counterculture of the Sixties (1960-73), which started as a reaction to US military intervention in Vietnam. As the American Dream was challenged and found wanting, young people began to ponder and re-evaluate the notions of 'ambition' and 'success.' Youth culture and then hippie culture caught on and became widespread, riding the crest of a tidal wave of change. Musicians, more than any other cultural group, responded to this call. Thousands of singers, songwriters and groups, primarily in Britain and America, recognised opportunity and began to take advantage of the shifts in mood.

It was also in 1960 when Mark's old infant school classmate and playground adversary caught up with him again.

'When I was about 13,' remembers Marilyn Roberts, 'I started hanging out with my friends on Stamford Hill [a sort of Jewish-London promenade, where youngsters would gather, pose and flirt with each other] at about the same time as Mark started hanging around the *Schtip*, also known as the *Schtip* House.

'This was the Fairsports amusement arcade so-nicknamed because they took all your money. The Yiddish word literally means "to take, to take". I was surprised to see that he really had a look by then,' she says. 'Quite the dandy. He was the first one in a Crombie overcoat, for example. He even wore it with a bowler hat and a rolled-up umbrella, like a business man. It was like he was in fancy dress all the time. Most people thought he was a prat, basically. But he had his small group of cronies – Eric Hall [later a record promoter and DJ] and Gerry Goldstein [who worked in the rag trade], all those guys – and he was tremendously confident in himself.'

That, says Marilyn was when Mark turned into a mod. This short-lived 'movement' (to be revived in the 1970s) originated largely among the Jewish East End working class, and was effectively an extension of beatnik culture. The term 'mod' derived from 'modernist', denoting modern jazz musicians and their followers. Mods were obsessed with sharp fashion, distinctive musical styles (Jamaican ska, British beat, Afro-American soul, R&B) and favoured customised motor scooters, which they took to riding round in gangs. Mark never had a scooter, but Harry did. This habit gave rise to the notorious 1960s' bank holiday bashes in seaside towns such as Clacton, Hastings, Margate and Brighton. Scooter-mounted mods clashing with black-leathered rockers on motorbikes guaranteed mass police arrest. These aggressive subcultures melted into the more caricaturist love-and-peace-hippies-versus-chippy-but-relatively-harmless-skin-heads theme by the end of the decade.

'Mark was dressing himself at the high-end cost bracket of fashion when I got to know him again during our teenage years,' remembers Marilyn. 'How did he afford it? No one knew. I knew that he was working a bit on his mother's stall and eventually he started doing a bit of modelling. Magazines, fashion shops and stuff. His mother also indulged him, the sun kept on shining out of Mark. Someone went around saying that he even used to nick money from the takings on her stall. If he did, knowing her, she turned a blind eye to it. Mark, stealing? Don't go there. She would never believe anything bad about her Mark.

'The funny thing is, had we known then what was to become of him later, we wouldn't have considered him such a jerk.'

Still not likeable, then?

'No he *wasn't!*' she laughs. 'Mark rubbed a lot of people up the wrong way. I saw him picked up and literally thrown out of the *Schtip*, more than once. But there was something about him that I had to admire. He had this amazing self-belief. It was intrinsic in his personality, and I can see now that he was born with it. On top of that, his mother led him to believe that he was brilliant and could do anything he wanted, which was a huge part of the character he became. She was such a formidable person in so many ways. That is very much what mothers in the East End were like in those days. It was fairly obvious that Mark's ego was being groomed at home. Let's face it, that's half the job done. If you can sing, it's a bonus.'

Musical talent proved short-lived salvation for Marc's hero Eddie Cochran, when he was killed in a road accident in Wiltshire during his British tour that April. A passenger in a Ford Consul mini-cab, en route to the airport for a brief, mid-tour visit home to the US, Cochran was just 21 years old.

'I didn't get into the Jewish Free School. I was downgraded for being too naughty, and was despatched in shame to the local comprehensive, William Wordsworth,' recalls Richard Young.

'That was where I met Mark Feld. We sat next to each other in class, and became partners in crime. It was all downhill from there.'

I had known Richard professionally and socially for 27 years, yet never knew he had gone to school with Marc Bolan. It was only when I called his wife, Susan, to enquire about a picture, and got talking about this book, that she mentioned it.

'You never said!' I accused him, when we spoke to arrange the interview.

'You never asked!' Richard laughed.

Young, named by *The Times* in 2006 as 'one of the most important photographers of the 20th century', has spent forty years photographing the great and the good: from Her Majesty Queen Elizabeth II, the late Diana, Princess of Wales and Fidel Castro to Elizabeth Taylor and Richard Burton, Paul McCartney, Mick Jagger and Bob Marley, Andy Warhol and Marvin Gaye. He would travel to Romanian orphanages with Michael Jackson, and all over the globe with Freddie Mercury and Queen. I recall hair-raising exploits with Richard on the band's Magic tour in Hungary in 1986, which we were both covering for the British press. Richard was by then a star himself.

'We played truant all the time. It didn't go down well at school,' chuckles Young. 'We were hopeless. We didn't want to play games with the other kids, who we thought were right turkeys. So we'd duck out of school and get the 73 bus to Soho, where my father also had a stall selling ladies' lingerie and hosiery. Even as a boy I could tell a 15-denier stocking from a 20-denier!'

Richard describes Mark Feld as 'one of the biggest influences on my life'.

'Because of the way he looked, primarily. He was the only kid who came to school in handmade clothes and shoes . . . at the age of 12. No one knew where he got the money from. He'd help his mother a bit on the stall, and pick up money from his parents. I know mum gave him pocket money. But it was mostly a mystery. I knew not to ask too many questions, but I've always wondered about it. We are talking 1961, 1962, money too tight to mention.

How *does* a kid get the dough together to get handmade shirts in the East End? However he did it, Mark always looked fantastic.'

Thanks to Mark, says Richard, he has always taken pride in his own appearance.

'His influence has stayed with me all my life. I did covet his style, I have no shame in admitting it. I tried to copy it, but usually failed. I remember going to great lengths to have a suede jacket just like his. My mum did get me one, but I was dreadfully disappointed when I found out it wasn't real suede, only suedette.

'He was wonderful,' Richard adds, 'a real visionary. He had so much style and intellect: not what you'd call an academic intellect, but a sort of instinct, which lifted him above the kind of kids who always had their noses in books. Whatever they were trying to teach us at school had no lasting effect on my life – nor on Mark's. We both thought school work was ridiculous, a complete waste of time. We couldn't wait to get out there in the world and make our mark, so to speak. I was always spurred on by his enthusiasm to make something of myself. He was special. If other kids "didn't like" him, it was because they didn't get him. People are always threatened by someone who dares to be different, and their unease manifests itself in dislike. Mark was adorable. I say that as a straight man! It was such a joy to be around him, there was never a dull moment – all the clichés. In all the years I've been taking pictures of famous people, I promise you, I have never met anyone else like him.'

When Richard left school at 15 going on 16, his mother got him a job in a boutique on Old Compton Street, Soho, called Sportique, selling the most fashionable clothing in London at that time.

'Our customers were people like David Hockney, Francis Bacon, Bob Dylan, The Beatles. When Mark Feld became

Marc Bolan, I used to kit him out too. By 1969 I was doing other stuff in the fashion business, and he was busy becoming a star. We simply lost touch for a while at that point, as friends do. But not forever.'

Another close friend of Mark's in those days was Eric Hall: a good Jewish boy who became a singer, publicist and record plugger. Eric promoted 'Bohemian Rhapsody', and claims that his dear friend Freddie Mercury wrote 'Killer Queen' for him – because he kept his Moet & Chandon in a cabinet in his office at EMI. Hall was also a showbusiness and football agent along the way. He is perhaps best-known for having organised for the Sex Pistols to appear on Thames Television's *Today* programme in 1976, when presenter Bill Grundy lost control of the show as the punks proceeded to swear their way through the interview. The studio switchboard was jammed with complaints. Grundy was suspended for 'sloppy journalism', while Thames TV was accused of 'a gross error of judgement'. Hall knew it was publicity that money couldn't buy.

I have known Eric since I was a teenager, when Eric was looking after a nightclub for Terry Venables, a family friend.

'We'd go in the *Schtip* and play the machines for want of something better to do,' says Hall. 'Mark and I had a lot in common, being both East End/North London Jewish boys. We knew each other like the back of our hands.

'We used to get in there mainly on a Sunday, but also during the week – there'd be me, Mark, Mickey Simmonds and Peter Sugar of the Stamford Hill boys. They were a bit older than us. Very smart boys. Mods. They were our friends, we looked up to them. We all became a bit of a rat pack. All meet there, then get on the 653 bus to the El Toro Club in St John's Wood. All the Jewish girls and boys went there, we called it the "let my people go-go" club. Mark had more girls after him there than you could ever wish to meet. He loved all the attention, he lapped it up. We weren't religious, our Jewishness was our culture. We weren't the pious lot, we just had Yiddisher roots. We'd go out, have some soup, a bit of chopped liver, some fish, some chicken together. We were proud of being Jewish, and it's easier to stick with your own.

'Mark and I were similar ages. We shared history, we both loved music, and we stayed friends for life. He was always going to be a star, no question. He had charisma, and he had talent. We could be twenty five guys out, of a night, and he was the one. Monster, monster star quality. He looked like a star at 13.'

By now, Marc and Jeff Dexter were more than familiar faces to each other in the fancier menswear stores.

'We'd been shopping acquaintances for quite a long time, but then it developed into something more,' Jeff says. 'It wasn't really until 1961 that we'd begun to go shopping together in the West End and then hanging out in Soho. We'd started skipping off school and doing things we shouldn't be doing during the day. We hung out together because we got each other. We both wanted a different kind of education. A street education.'

Times were starting to change towards the end of 1961. While American folk singer-songwriter Bob Dylan worked on his civil rights/anti-war stance and released his eponymous debut album, predicting the route that contemporary popular music would take, the Felds of Stoke Newington were on the move. The large Victorian house in part of which Mark's family had lived in a flat for many years was purchased by Hackney Council, cueing their turn to be re-housed. Not elsewhere in the neighbourhood they knew and loved, but all the way across the capital and out the other side, in a south-western corner of a foreign field that might just about still be England. Their new home was a nowhere-land run by Wandsworth, behind Summerstown – east of Wimbledon, west of Tooting, south of Earlsfield and north of Colliers Wood. This fragment of a place divided by two main roads was once a damp hamlet of dwellings for workers in the Wandle mills. It had been rejuvenated, if that's not too strong a word, by the construction of a bunch of Sun Cottages. These Scandinavian-manufactured 'portahomes' were a variation on the theme of the two-bedroom pre-fabricated houses thrown up all over Britain after the end of the war, to house those made homeless by enemy bombing.

They were built to last between ten and fifteen years (although some tenants would still be living in them decades later). The homes were factory-made, mass-produced, transported by road and assembled on site. Although the prefabricated house has made something of a trendy comeback in recent years – the stylish German Huf House being a prime example – the 'prefab' acquired a pejorative connotation during the 1960s, when 'more respectable' home-owners looked down their noses at those who still lived in them. There remains no trace of those cottages in Summerstown today. There remains not much of anything, actually, save a few old buildings which have survived against the odds, and the imposing Romanesque, grade II-listed St Mary's parish church.

'It didn't matter to us what other people thought,' insists Harry Feld. 'My mum loved it. The cottage was made of aluminium, in two halves, bolted together on concrete stilts with little steps up to the front door. These were more modern than the early post-war prefabs and it was quite something to get one. The cooker, the sideboard, the beds, everything was fitted in. We had hot running water, a proper bathroom, indoor toilet, the works. Mark and I had a little bedroom to share, as opposed to sleeping in the living room which we'd always done. All you had to do was supply your bedsheets. Maybe it wasn't much, looking back, but my mum and dad were so proud of that prefab. It was a step up, as they saw it. I'd go as far as to say that it changed our lives.'

For Mark, the changes were mostly negative. Removed from his Stamford Hill stomping ground and estranged from his mob – the very mob with whom he had appeared in a somewhat condescending feature on mod culture, 'Faces Without Shadows' for *Town* magazine, published in September 1962 – he dragged his heels around the playground of his new school Hillcroft on Beechcroft Road (now Ernest Bevin College) for a couple of months while wondering what to do next. He needed, he knew, to focus on how he was going to make his mark on the world. His mother might have given up her Berwick Street market stall, but her younger son had not given up on Soho.

'It was more of a home to Mark than Wimbledon ever was,' explains Eric Hall. 'Stamford Hill and Soho were where he did his growing up, they were the places that shaped him.

'When you've got charisma like he had, you're a good-looking boy, you start hanging around Carnaby Street, you've got the poses. By the time he was 15, Mark was striking one hell of a pose. See, he could have been a butcher, a cab driver, which is what half the family were. He'd still have been the *best* butcher, the *star* cab driver, know what I'm saying? He had something which set him apart from the rest. I think he knew it, too, though he didn't used to say it. He didn't boast. Not at that stage. For one thing, he wasn't sure yet what he was going to be a star *at*.'

In June 1962, The Beatles completed their first recording session with producer George Martin at the EMI studios on Abbey

Road. When they landed in London from Hamburg via Liverpool, it was Mark's old friend Jeff Dexter – now 16 years old and already a professional dancer, singer, DJ and fancy fixture at the Lyceum Ballroom – whom their manager Brian Epstein consulted regarding their image.

'Yes, it was me who got them to Dougie Millings, who made their classic collar-less Beatles suits,' Dexter confirms. 'He was the rock'n'roll tailor of the day. He was also my tailor; I didn't have the time to sew anymore. Ian "Sammy" Samwell was getting suits made by him, as was Cliff Richard. Funny thing happened when we got George, John, Ringo and Paul in there: Dougie said to them, "You do know who Jeff is, don't you? He's the Milky Bar Kid." As it happened, I *was* the Milky Bar Kid, for one show – or rather, one at the Lyceum and one in York. This was because the actual Kid was too young to be out in the ballrooms, so I had to dress up and be him for a couple of nights, as I was small enough. The Beatles ran off saying, "We know the Milky Bar Kid!" Everywhere I went after that, thanks to the Fab Four, I was being stopped for autographs.

'They also picked up on my après-ski boots from the dance footwear store Anello & Davide – easy on, easy off. We called them "après-ski" because the "piste" was what the dancers called the dance floor – as well as "rug", as in "cut a rug". Actually, I think The Beatles bought Anello's Baba Boot first. I also took them to Star Shirtmakers on Wardour Street, direct from Dougie's workroom.'

The Fab Four's first single 'Love Me Do' was released on 5 October that year. Early stirrings of Beatlemania were felt throughout the land.

In 1961, after the Russians installed ballistic missiles on Cuba, ninety miles off the Florida coast, the world found itself on the brink of nuclear war. Folk music evolved into protest music, the antidote to which was The Beach Boys. Marilyn Monroe was dead at 36, having apparently overdosed on pills. Andy Warhol became famous for more than fifteen minutes, on account of a can of soup. Movie-goers flocked to see *West Side Story* and *Lawrence of Arabia*. On Mark's 15th birthday, brave African American James Meredith changed the course of civil rights history when he defied racial segregation to register for classes at the University of Mississippi. Meanwhile, in another far-flung corner of a London suburb – Bromley, in Kent – another frustrated mod poser with stars in his mismatched eyes was, like Mark Feld, also wondering what to do next.

4

Call Him a Man

'You didn't leave your parental home to live in a flat in those days,' says Marilyn Roberts. 'You left home to get married. You married young, and you started your own family. Most people did', adds the woman whose first husband Rod Weinberg would go on to make it big in the entertainment business as an agent, promoter and producer for artists such as Rick Wakeman, Marvin Gaye, Billy Ocean and The Damned; as a director of the world-famous Rainbow Theatre, and most notably as a manager of The Animals.

'So for Mark to go and do just that was ahead of its time. The London gay scene, Carnaby Street, all that, flew in the face of his classic Jewish upbringing – which you'd have to say it was, even though his Mum wasn't Jewish. He and Harry were raised as good Jewish boys. There was Harry toeing the line, leaving school, getting himself a job, finding himself a nice girl, sorting himself out and starting to settle down. And there was Mark – who didn't seem to know what on earth to do with himself.'

It was a huge dilemma for him, as Marilyn recalls.

'He looked around, saw what everyone else was up to and especially what his brother was doing, and didn't want that for himself,' she says. 'Mark wanted more. The world was changing rapidly, and you could tell he was anxious not to get left behind. He didn't want his life to stagnate, as he'd put it, he needed to get in on it all. When you are as selfish as I believe he was, it probably doesn't matter that the lifestyle choices you make could be regarded as an embarrassment to your family. "Why should our parents know everything about what we do anyway?" was his attitude all along. He couldn't see how disrespectful that was – which it really was, in those days. What you always got loud and clear from Mark was that his own pleasures and goals in life ranked highest for him.'

Achieving a sense of identity is the primary task of teenagers, not that the vast majority go about this consciously. Suspended between childhood and maturity and with no one but his rock'n'roll idols to look up to and try to emulate, Mark's mid-to-late teenage development was blighted by obsessive self-awareness and an over-inflated sense of his own importance.

Before he could begin to navigate his adult life, he needed to know who he was – or at least who to pretend to be. That was the rub.

'For adolescents who never achieve an integrated identity, all the world's a stage,' explains Dr Stephen A. Johnson, doctor of psychology and theology.

'In their adult years, they will play the part of human beings who change roles to please whoever happens to be watching. Their clothes, their language, their thoughts and their feelings are all part of the script. Their purpose will be to receive approval from those they hope to impress. Life will become a charade, and the players will never enjoy the security of personal identity, or experience the strength that comes from a sense of self-worth.'

Mark felt compelled, in other words, to project himself beyond the limits of his capabilities, because deep down he feared that the real him would never be good enough. Today, he might be diagnosed as an extreme narcissist: someone who displays unreasonably egotistical preoccupation with himself, his personal preferences, needs, aspirations and successes, and with the impression he makes on others. This self-absorption leads the narcissist to believe that everyone else is merely there for his benefit, simply to be used. It usually begins during childhood, as the result of either a traumatic separation or a disproportionately profound attachment, such as Mark had forged with his mother. As if frozen in time, he becomes emotionally 'stuck'. He then proceeds through life indulging in relationships which emulate the one which originally caused either the loss or the dependence, and in which the extreme narcissist is the object of adulation and even worship.

Mark's women, in their various ways, would all be maternal figures: putting him first, administering lovingly to his needs and providing an exclusive round-the-clock ego boost. In order to survive, the extreme narcissist must also build a barrier between himself and the outside world, protecting him from 'ordinary people'. This barrier is known as 'the false persona'. The identity he presents is fake, and in no way reflects the true individual within. Although obviously never diagnosed, such specialist psychology having yet to become fashionable, it seems probable that Mark was the kind of narcissist referred to today as 'success-orientated'. He would remain your friend and keep you close for as long as you were useful to him. Once you had nothing further to offer and he'd sucked you dry, you would be history.

'That's for sure,' affirms Jeff Dexter.

'No doubt about it. Extreme narcissist? That was the Mark I knew, all right! That was him all over. But not *just* him. Show me a star who isn't that way. A well-adjusted rock'n'roll star is a contradiction in terms. I've seen enough of it all to know that superstardom is a killer: of real life, of music, of creativity. Very few people get it right. Many who seek it wind up wishing they hadn't, and most who succeed eventually become casualties. However long that takes.'

No longer a schoolboy but by no means yet a young man of independent means, 15-year-old Mark now found himself at a crossroads. Without the luxury of stepping-stone college years during which to try on a few personalities while preparing for the workplace and the world, he had no idea how to begin. Phyllis would indulge and bankroll him for a few more years, turning a blind eye to his long lie-ins and habit of sitting around, eating her and Sid out of house and home. His parents were out working all day – his father a van driver at this stage, while his mother, with her head for figures, had become a bank clerk. There were a couple of half-hearted attempts at holding down a 'normal' job – first as a shop assistant, then as a burger bar kitchen washer-upper – but Mark was never going to make mainstream employment material.

He did the only thing he felt he could do, which was to set about expanding his intellect and broadening his mind while awaiting some flicker of inspiration. He became, in the mildest sense, a layabout autodidact, finding unexpected enthusiasm for the kind of literature which had left him cold at school. In particular and out of nowhere he developed an interest in 19th century English poetry.

'I think someone might have told him he reminded them of one of these old-fashioned poet types – whether it was the face, the profile, his hair or his colouring,' Harry strains to remember. 'That's all it would have been with Mark. Give him a sliver of an idea and it was a ball for him to run with. He liked the sound of something, he'd go to the library, get books out. He never looked all that deeply into things, but enough to have you thinking he knew more than he really did. That was Mark. Making the right impression was very important to him.'

'I'm never surprised by anyone with negligible education turning out to be enquiring and brilliant,' counters Simon Napier-Bell, who became the future Marc Bolan's manager. When he first met Mark during the early Sixties, debonair Simon was one of the industry figures whose attention young hustlers craved. A loaded chap-about-town and a successful songwriter thanks to hits he had written for Dusty Springfield, Simon would achieve fame as manager of Bolan, Japan, Wham! and George Michael.

I struggle to remember the when-where-why of how I met Simon. He assures me that I was 'about 15', but is undoubtedly flattering me. We have certainly been partners-in-crime for as long as I can remember. He has lived for years in Thailand, yet we still seem to manage two or three all-night dinners a year.

'I'm no lover of formal education,' Simon elaborates. 'I have never felt that it made anyone more able to understand people or the world around them, it just gives them a base knowledge. In some case it teaches people how to learn for themselves. But in my case, and I'm sure in Mark's, it was leaving school that freed him up to start learning about the world. But I've no idea what set him off on his reading, other than the delight of learning.'

Who knows how he discovered the relatively obscure Jean Nicolas 'Arthur' Rimbaud, the glamorous but doomed French-born Romantic poet who wrote his most celebrated works while still in his teens. Dubbed 'the infant Shakespeare' by Victor Hugo, Rimbaud abandoned creative writing altogether by the time he was 20, and was dead at 37. It is easy to see why Mark was so taken by his live-fast-die-young existence. With Charles Baudelaire, Paul Verlaine, Oscar Wilde, Aubrey Beardsley and their set, Rimbaud became an important figure in the Decadent Movement of art, music and literature. He was also a self-confessed Libertine with a passion for sensual delights, and ran with a like-minded pack: Byron, Baudelaire, Casanova and the Marquis de Sade. Mark was enchanted by all this, and would rave about Rimbaud in future interviews. He read up on the poet and devoured his works – leaving him further inspired to explore classical Greek and Roman mythology.

Mark also read Khalil Gibran – the Syrian-born American writer best-known for his 1923 book of inspirational fiction *The Prophet*, which was enjoying a revival during 1960s' counterculture.

Gibran, he learned, was (and remains) the third best-selling poet of all time, behind William Shakespeare and Lao Tzu, a philosopher of Ancient China and author of the *Tao Te Ching*, the classic text outlining the principles of Taoism. Mark quickly developed a superficial interest in 'trendy', 'mystical' world philosophies and religions, including Buddhism and Taoism. Dipping into literature on ancient civilisations, he vowed to one day explore some of the planet's most fabled locations: Egypt's pyramids; Petra, in modern-day Jordan, the 'red-rose city half as old as time'; Nepal, and Tibet – about which he couldn't stop fantasising after seeing Frank Capra's famous film *Lost Horizon* (based on James Hilton's 1933 novel) set in mythical Shangri-La; and the Makli Hill Tombs of Sind, one of the world's largest necropolises. Mark discovered Makli Hill while reading about the Vedic civilisation which thrived in the region of southern Asia now known as Pakistan. He was fascinated to learn that British rule in India ended in 1947, the year of his birth, and that one of the last great legacies of the British in the colony was the creation of a legendary railway through an all-but-forgotten gateway into India. It was called the Bolan Pass.

Literature and poetry were all very well. There was still prosaic reality to contend with, as well as the need to earn a crust. Mark was soon tapping his mother for funds in order to buy himself a short course of basic modelling lessons. He put his tuition to fair use on some minor catalogue and brochure assignments, but interest soon waned in the unedifying pursuit of posing for pictures in clothes he would never normally wear. Nor were the rewards phenomenal. What he earned at least afforded him a new guitar.

There came turning points in 1963. The first was when his folk idol released the album *The Freewheelin' Bob Dylan*. The track 'Blowin' In The Wind' was a huge hit for Peter, Paul and Mary, and Dylan sang with them at the Newport Folk Festival on Rhode Island that summer. Dylan also began a high-profile romance with Joan Baez, appearing at her concerts, and head-lined at the Carnegie Hall. Mark lapped all this up, resolving to perform at the hallowed Manhattan venue himself one day. The other was when his old partner in crime Jeff Dexter dragged him along to a screening of Cliff Richard's new film, *Summer Holiday*.

'I wasn't spending too much time checking out and listening to music with Mark at that point, because we were too busy shopping for clothes,' Dexter remembers. 'But we did go to movies together. When they opened *Summer Holiday*, I was keen to see it because I'd been offered a part in it, but I got rowed out of it. That came about through Sammy Samwell, who had worked on Cliff's previous film, *The Young Ones*. Sammy had become my mentor and close friend. He was the one who showed me the ropes in terms of DJ'ing. I was a bit too busy for filming,

I'd have had to drop everything. I was also dancing at the time, and occasionally singing in Cyril Stapleton's band, and running a record promotion company with another DJ, Tony Calder. Mark used to come up from his mum's stall round the corner to our office at 15 Poland Street.'

Dexter was keen to see the film primarily to find out what he had missed. He invited Mark to accompany him to a screening.

'I had passes, and took Mark with me to a matinee show just after the premiere,' he says.

It was a big deal and a huge box office hit, spawning four Number One hit singles that year.

'When we came out,' Jeff remembers, 'he went, "That's *it*! I'm gonna be like Cliff Richard! I'm gonna be a real big star!"'

'I went "Mark! You're *not* gonna be like Cliff Richard! You can't even fuckin' sing!"'

'He kind of took that to heart,' says Jeff. 'I didn't believe that he could do it, but perhaps I should have kept my mouth shut and my opinion to myself. What I said ended our closeness at that time. I didn't really see him again until about four years later.'

The world at large had bigger things to worry about, after President John Fitzgerald Kennedy was assassinated in Dallas, Texas, in November 1963. Everyone remembers where they were when they heard the news: of a defining moment in history as well as the subject of everlasting conspiracy theories. It was the day when America lost its innocence, not to mention much of its hope.

When popular teatime television show *The Five O'Clock Club* with Muriel Young and Wally Whyton debuted in 1963, Mark was one of the first to pitch up seeking work as an extra. David

Bowie was another, as 'Club' regular Allan Warren recalled Warren and Mark began hanging out together, and eventually the former invited the latter to share his Earls Court flat. It was Mark's first experience of living away from home, and it is not on record what his mother and father made of it.

In his quest for the big time, and inspired by the success of The Beatles in America – they had kicked off the 'British Invasion' in February 1964 with an historical coast-to-coast appearance on television's *The Ed Sullivan Show*, watched by 73 million viewers – he began to work earnestly on his music, writing and rehearsing for several hours a day with the curtains closed. His theory was that if the Fab Four from Liverpool could do it, anybody could – despite the fact that they'd been putting in their 10,000 hours at clubs like the Star-Club and the Kaiserkeller on the Reeperbahn in Hamburg for years. Mark began to follow their progress closely. He paid particular attention to their meeting with Bob Dylan in New York that August, when Dylan, who had become a virtual recluse as a result of fan pressure, introduced The Beatles to cannabis.

Impatient to make a name for himself, it is recorded that Mark persuaded his flatmate Warren to manage him. Studio time is said to have been booked, during which Mark took his first baby steps into the realm of recorded music. This has long been believed to have been towards the end of 1964, just as Dylan's *The Times They Are a-Changin'* was making him a hero of the protest movement. Accounts conflict as to exactly what, where, when and who else was involved in Mark's musical debut – Regent Sound Studios in Denmark Street are cited, as are Maximum Sound on Dean Street.

But it turns out that Allen Warren was not Mark's first manager after all. According to lifelong Bolan fan Caron Willans and her husband Danielz,[1] Mark's first manager was a wealthy, mixed-race, homosexual barrister by the name of Geoffrey Delaroy-Hall.

'Geoffrey Delaroy-Hall began managing Mark in 1963, after meeting him at a party in London,' Caron confirms. 'He owned a property at 25 Manchester Square, where Mark later lived with Mike Pruskin.

'Delaroy-Hall and Mark had a relationship. At 15, Mark was too young to sign a management contract, so it was signed by his mother, Mrs Phyllis Feld. Mrs Feld didn't like Delaroy-Hall because she thought he was bedding Mark, which he probably was.'

According to records, Delaroy-Hall paid for a recording session at IBC Studios on 28 August 1964. Mark recorded a track entitled 'All At Once', written by George Bellamy. This, and not anything cut with Warren, was most likely Marc's first-ever recording.

'Geoffrey gave Danielz and me the tape a few years ago,' says Caron. 'We subsequently released it as a 7" single on Madman Records.[2] He also showed us contracts, letters and photos from Mark, which he had kept. He died of cancer in 2002. We had kept in touch with him, and we attended his funeral.'

Perhaps even more intriguing is the mystery attached to the composition Mark recorded for Delaroy-Hall. Convinced that the 'George Bellamy' referred to in documents was the Sunderland-born guitarist of The Tornados,[3] Caron sent him a copy of the single. She received a letter from Bellamy by return, denying involvement.

With Warren, in any case, there was now audible proof that Mark Feld, who changed his name briefly to Toby Tyler (the name lifted from a 1960 Disney feature) had absolutely no idea about who he wanted to be or what he wanted to sound like. It is clear that he was striving for a Dylan-esque vocal style with his versions, for Warren, of 'Blowin' In The Wind' and 'The Road I'm On (Gloria)' – an obscure Dion 'The Runaway' Dimucci B-side.

His guitar- and harmonica-playing left everything to be desired. Despite all this, pressings were made and despatched to relevant industry figures, along with specially-commissioned publicity pictures. There were no takers – not even at *The Five O'Clock Club*. He and Warren did get in to see the A & R folk at the mighty EMI, however, which led to an audition with John Burgess for Columbia at EMI's studios on Abbey Road. Remarkably, John, George Martin's partner at AIR Studios years later, recalled the event. Little impression was made, alas, with Burgess hearing nothing in Mark's vocal style or instrumental ability that he hadn't heard before. Warren and Mark left empty-handed.[4]

Warren would later claim that Mark experimented energetically with his sexuality while living under his roof, entertaining a steady stream of male and female friends.

'If he did, then it would have been done in the spirit of the age,' reasons Keith Altham, a popular music journalist who became an acclaimed rock publicist.

'The edges were blurred back then. If you weren't married, everyone went to bed with everyone else. Gender was almost irrelevant. A lot of men in the music business and in the wider entertainment business were homosexual – then as now. If you were hustling to get somewhere in the industry, it was all part of the game: flirt a bit, lead them on, let them think they were onto a good thing with you so that you'd get what you wanted, which in Mark's case was exposure and a record deal.

'Old queens love nothing more than to be seen out with pretty young boys,' says Keith, 'it was common. I don't believe that Marc had biologically gay tendencies nor that he was ever into full-blown gay sex. It would only ever have been a bit of messing about with him. Put it this way, there was always a female love interest around . . . which you just don't get with a gay man. Marc was only going along with it all, a means to an end. Hard to imagine such permissiveness in this post-AIDS age, I know, but that's the way it was.'

'I'm sure Mark never had sex with another man,' Eric Hall insists. 'He had more girls than you could ever wish to meet. The men who've said they did it with him, that was wishful thinking. If he did go with any of them, which I doubt, then in those very early days it would have been to try and get on. To curry favour. But I knew him from the age of 12, 13, and I never saw any inclination. He never behaved that way on Stamford Hill. When I was promoting him years later, there was never any sign of him being gay.'

Simon Napier-Bell reckons that Mark was attracted by the gay scene as much as by gay sex.

'Gay men had freedom, they had nice flats, they had good cars, they had disposable income,' he points out. 'No silly wives and children. Every young straight guy in the Sixties wanted to live like gays lived but without the sex. This made it very easy for gays to pull straight boys. But who knows what it was like for ordinary people. I had a Ford Thunderbird. I managed a major rock group [The Yardbirds]. If I fancied a young guy he would almost certainly be flattered, though wary too.

'By the time I met Mark, he'd been around the gay scene for a while. He first came to my flat in 1966, so he was already 18 or 19. He'd been around London, as a male model, and then as a pop singer for Decca (managed by Jim Economides) since he was 15. He was *totally* familiar with gay sex. In fact, it never occurred to me at the time that he was anything *but* gay.

'This was all to do with the intrinsic nature of the Sixties,' Simon elaborates. 'There was a great sexual freedom – but only in the doing. I don't think there was ever a period when young straight guys were more interested in sexual experiment. The Pill had OK'd it in a blanket sort of way. Yet sex was never talked about. In public, on the radio, on TV, it would be unthinkable to mention oral sex, or even masturbation. Perhaps it was because a sexual experiment would never be talked about, that people were so ready to try it. Whereas now, when bisexuality is so readily accepted, it's also talked about all the time. Do it and everyone will know. So people are *more* cautious, not less.'

It's a paradox all right.

Jeff Dexter remains adamant that Mark was not attracted to homosexuals.

'A few men have said, written and implied down the years that they shagged Marc. I know they didn't,' he says, 'he wasn't into blokes! Put it this way, I slept with him enough times! We cuddled, it was affectionate, it was TLC, but nothing went on. If ever it did, there was always a bird in between!

'He wanted people to believe that he did all that,' insists Jeff. 'Why? Because most of the men who controlled the music industry and the media – TV and radio – even in those days, were poofs, which is what we called them: the term "gay" was not yet in use. So if you camped it up, you'd get more attention. People would live in hope, so to speak. I think it's virtually impossible that Mark ever had sex with another man.

'He would lead people on when it suited him, sure, but he would definitely never go that route. He loved women. He might have given the odd bloke here and there a hug, but he wouldn't have held his cock. Or done much else. He liked pussy. Far too much. Too much for his own good, a lot of the time.'

The odd job here and there had to be found if Mark was going to feed himself. He put in the hours as a club cloakroom attendant, carefully stashing his tips. He kept at it with his music, convinced that he was on the verge of a breakthrough, until along happened Scottish singer-songwriter Donovan in 1965, with his single 'Catch the Wind'. It soared to Number 4 in the UK, and to Number 23 a few months later on the US chart. Donovan became a huge favourite on the popular TV show *Ready, Steady, Go!* and re-recorded the song for his album *What's Bin Did, What's Bin Hid*. As far as Mark was concerned, 'the British Bob Dylan' looked and sounded just like Mark Feld. Even when he contrived to get a closer look at him, joining a Ban the Bomb CND rally in London in which Joan Baez, Tom Paxton and Donovan were marching, he couldn't see what all the fuss was about. Donovan Leitch from Glasgow, star quality? They were having a laugh.

It was clearly time to take stock for a bit. He went home to Mum.

Then came The Wizard. American actor Riggs O'Hara had no way of knowing, when he and Mark were introduced by Alan Warren, what an important part O'Hara would play in the development of Mark Feld the musician. What began as hero-worship, with Mark writing copiously in his diary about this cool Yank dude who took his reason away, erupted into full-blown fantasy. The poetry and songs which followed created another turning point in Mark's artistic progress. His imagination was awakened by this older, worldly-wise, larger-than-life figure who had lived, was cool, seemed cultured and said the right things. Whether Mark believed that O'Hara could open doors for him, or whether he was just blindly besotted, the pair were soon inseparable.

Riggs O'Hara, not his real name, hailed from the Irish quarter of New York's blue-collar Bronx. He arrived in London during the late Fifties as one of the cast of the musical *Guys & Dolls*, and never went back. He worked as a theatre director and took bit parts in films, most notably *The Virgin Soldiers* in 1969.[5] When he met Mark late in 1964 or early 1965, he was flat-sharing in Barnes with another actor, Likely Lad James Bolam.

Mark wasted no time in responding to the inevitable invitation, and moved in. Their brief sojourn in Paris has become the stuff of legend – fuelled, no doubt, by Mark's inability to resist spinning a sensational yarn where a factual postcard account would do.

'Mark and his pal Riggs take a little trip across *la Manche*, do the *Tour Eiffel* and a *bateau mouche* on the Seine, suck on a few *escargots* and some *cuisses de grenouille* and swallow their bath water in *rosé*' becomes in Marc's mind an exotic ensconcement in a forest *château* involving spells, potions, cauldrons and the ritualistic sacrifice of cats. The unsuspecting arc levitated, the innocent corrupted by cannibalism, and spirits are summoned to do their darkest in circumstances unimaginable to right-thinking folk.

Mark banged on for years, well into his fame, about his experiences of occultism and witchcraft among the French. As he warmed to his theme, he embellished it every time it was asked about. When eventually he saw fit to dismiss it with the explanation that he himself had been the victim of exaggeration and invention, the media were ironically more inclined to believe the fiction. Nobody wanted to hear the boring truth that there had been no wizard. Fantasy makes better copy, after all.

'Mark told me about this man he'd had an affair with: Riggs O'Hara,' recalls Simon Napier-Bell.

'A wonderful name – oil wells, Irish, a world traveller – you can hear it all in the name. One day, many years after I stopped managing Marc, I was in a gay bar and I heard the name "Riggs". I turned round to see an astonishingly camp queen talking much like Kenneth Williams. I asked if he was Riggs O'Hara and yes, he was. But because of the sound of his name, Marc had seen someone quite different. He wrote a song called 'The Wizard', about a magician who lived in the woods. He told me how he'd hitch-hiked to Paris and had an experience with this man who made wicked potions and lived in the forest. But later he confessed that he'd met a conjurer in a gay bar in Paris, and had gone home with him. The rest had come from his imagination.'

Not quite the facts of the fantasy, as it were, but you get the drift.

And yet, Marc's 'Wizard', who inspired much of his songwriting, was not the first nor the last fictitious sorcerer to invade popular culture as a plausible character. There had long been Llyr, Merlin, Gandalf and the Wizard of Oz. There would soon be Albus Dumbledore, the head of Hogwarts – 'real' to millions of children thanks to J.K. Rowling.

'Mark was always telling the tale of "The Wizard", recalls Keith Altham, who knew Mark long before he made it, and whom I have known since my earliest days as a rookie rock hack.

'It turned out to be nonsense, of course, but then again . . . It was all part of what he did as an extension of his imagination. He *did* know some bloke he went to France with, who maybe did a bit of sleight of hand, a few tricks, a bit of conjuring. Maybe he did have some dubious relationship with him which left a lasting impression on him. What's certain is that he came back going, "I met this Wizard in France, who changed my life." Something did happen to him there, either emotionally, or some kind of sea change in his attitude to what he was doing with his life. Something that gave him a deep sense of self-belief. I was very wary of laughing about it too much.'

'There *was* a Wizard!' insists Jeff Dexter. 'In the metaphorical sense, at least. Mark had a profound, uplifting experience when he travelled to Paris with Riggs O'Hara – and I don't just mean because it was the first time he had ever gone abroad.

'Mark found another place with Riggs. A new aspect of himself. That person, who might otherwise be just a simple actor, did become his "Wizard" for that moment in time. From then on, The Wizard comes through as a motif in various guises in his songwriting, as an expression of "something more". There is that thing in life where something comes along and takes you out of yourself. It elevates you to another plane, and you don't know how to explain it. It's like a portal into a further dimension, which is nigh on impossible to articulate.

'"The Wizard", in Mark's life,' explains Jeff, was a device. 'It became his way of processing these big experiences which an ordinary little bloke of bare minimum education finds overwhelming and difficult to comprehend, let alone share. This is no different from the myths of the ancient Greeks and Romans, or those who lived in Biblical times, who invented characters, creatures and scenarios to record and explain the big events their limited intellect didn't allow them to understand. Look at some of the books of the Old Testament.

'It's about what it represented, rather than what it actually was.'

5

Faces Like a Poem

As for the name, there was nothing mysterious about Mark's decision to opt for something different, simply an inclination to follow an old music hall tradition he'd been aware of since his childhood; a tool which would allow him to stand out from the crowd. He was in good company. Many of Mark's contemporaries were distinguishing themselves with stage names at that time. Richard Starkey posed as Ringo Starr, Robert Zimmerman self-reinvented as Bob Dylan and Elton John had started life as Reginald Dwight. Iggy Pop was once James Newell Osterberg. Cat Stevens was originally Steven Georgiou (and was soon to be Yusuf Islam). As for David Bowie, he might never have been so memorable as a Jones . . .

Conflicting theories abound as to why Mark Feld became Marc Bolan. Nothing is proven. He simply Gallicised his first name, it seems, to become what he called a 'French Cockney' following the 'Wizard in Paris' experience. Having explored a little Roman mythology, he had learned enough to know that his name derived from Mars, god of war (in Greek, Ares), and that it would be Marcus (which he abbreviated) or Marquis, in French. He appears never to have felt inclined to divulge the inspiration behind 'Bolan', however. He once alluded, in an interview, to an early occasion when Decca Records got his name wrong on a demo label – inexplicably calling him 'Bowland'.

It has elsewhere been suggested that the name may have been a variation on the theme of Marc Bohan, a French couturier. Jeff Dexter and Mark were estranged at the time of the metamorphosis. When their friendship resumed, the deed was done, and Jeff never thought to ask. Harry Feld can't be certain, but favours speculation that his brother pinched the surname of Riggs O'Hara's flatmate, James Bolam, switching the final letter to an 'N'. From what we know of Marc, however, this seems too mundane.

A peek into the history of his family name offers no clues. 'Feld' has medieval roots, denoting a person who lived or worked on cleared forest land. Its first recorded spelling anywhere in the world is believed to have been that of Robert de Felde in 1185, on a list of Knights Templar in England's Gloucestershire (where oaks were 'felled').

The surname spread widely throughout Prussia, and appeared variously as Feld, Feild, Velde, Delafeld and Feldmann, to name a few. Intriguingly, among the first settlers to the new colony of Virginia in America was one James Feild, who arrived on the ship *Swan of London* in 1624.

Did Mark really, as many assume, simply swipe the adopted first name and family name of his folk idol Bob Dylan, cut out the middle three letters and push the first two and last three together? I have long preferred to think that there was more to the process than that.

'There certainly *was*,' declares Simon Napier-Bell.

Although he loves, Simon says, the idea of my romantic novelist's approach to discovering the source of Marc Bolan's name, the truth 'is so much easier, and more mundane. Though perhaps even more romantic.'

Marc's most cherished heroes of all, he reveals, were James Dean and Chet Baker – the celebrated Oklahoma-born jazz trumpeter, singer and flugelhornist born Chesney Henry Baker, who had matinee-idol looks and a much-publicised heroin habit.

'Mark adored them not so much for their names, but for their incredibly cool images,' says Simon, 'with which he became obsessed. Very fall-in-love-able with . . . and he certainly fell in love with Chet. This had happened before I met him, of course, which I didn't do until 1966.

'Coming into the Chet Baker Quintet in 1955 was an unknown Belgian pianist. With his arrival, Chet changed the style of the group slightly, and took to singing as well as playing the trumpet. He recorded an EP, *Chet Baker Sings*, released in 1956. Mark had fallen completely for Chet's picture on the sleeve. He obviously discovered it quite a while after its original release, on one of his second-hand record shop trawls. It was one of his gems. He carried a copy of that EP around with him – a common practice in those days.

'I had it in my record collection too. He saw it in my flat. He happened to mention in passing one day that it had been the inspiration for the name he had chosen. I didn't twig at first, but then I got it.

'The name of the Belgian pianist who helped Chet Baker find his singing voice was François "Francy" Boland. Mark, on an earnest quest for a "star name" of his own, adopted Francy's surname and dropped the "D"' – which, when you say it in a French accent, I add, you don't really hear anyway. It's as good as silent. While Marc liked to hear it as BollON rather than BEAU-lann, he obviously became fond of the Cockneyfied pronunciation.

He apparently liked the way the Americans said it, too, which was more like BOLL-an.

'Exactly!' Simon agrees. 'It doesn't surprise me one bit that he never explained the name,' he laughs.

'He understood the game, you see. An important aspect of stardom is the ability to keep them guessing. Once your fans know everything about you, once they realise that you are only as human as they are, they start losing interest. Fans *want* you to be remote, enigmatic and unknowable. They can hardly worship you if you are obviously "only" one of them. Marc got this. It is vital to maintain a little mystery, to keep them coming back for more.'

Marc would discover, thanks to his interest in all things Eastern, that Bolan was also a popular first name for Chinese baby girls, meaning 'to go together like waves'. In Mandarin, it also signifies 'to read voraciously'. It was music to this born-again bookworm's ears.

Marc Bolan's first encounter with David Bowie in 1964 was an unceremonious affair. It happened soon after 18-year-old Mike Pruskin, an up-coming independent publicist who became one of Marc's early managers while doubling as his flatmate, introduced his charge to Leslie Conn – a talent scout for the Dick James Organisation and the caretaker of Doris Day's music publishing. Dick James, a high-profile Eastender, former dance band singer, close friend of Beatles' producer George Martin and co-founder, with Brian Epstein, of their publishing company, Northern Songs, also handled the careers of Billy J. Kramer and Gerry and the Pacemakers, and would sign Elton John in 1967.

No wonder Marc believed that he was getting somewhere. He wasn't, though. While Conn and James agreed that Jones had potential, they couldn't see what on earth they could do with Bolan. It was a No from them.

Bowie – Brixton-born, Bromley-based, still known at the time as Davy or Davie Jones – had much more going for him. He was already a veteran band member when he came contract-seeking at DJM. He had joined his first group The Konrads at the age of 15, while still at school. He was a strange-looking thing, on account of damage to his left eye, sustained in a fight over a girl-friend with his classmate George Underwood who would go on to create artwork for the early albums of both David and Marc, so no hard feelings. David quit The Konrads for the King Bees, with whom he was so determined to make it that he even wrote to washing machine magnate John Bloom, imploring him to become the group's Brian Epstein. Bloom did not respond, but he did tell his friend Leslie Conn about them. Conn in turn was so taken with Davie Jones and the King Bees that he booked them for someone's wedding anniversary bash – but had to halt their set after only a quarter of an hour because their heavy R&B sound was way too loud. They got a management contract out of him, however, as well as a single. 'Li'l Liza Jane' on Decca's Vocalion Pop label was David's debut release. It flopped. He quit a month later to join The Manish Boys, a folk-soul-blues outfit – for whom, he recalled later, he was going to be their Mick Jagger. Their single 'I Pity the Fool' died a death too.

David moved on to join the Lower Third, a blues trio heav-ily influenced by The Who. They too released a single, 'You've Got a Habit of Leaving'. This also failed to chart. Conn felt he had done his best, and killed the contract. David announced that he was quitting pop to 'study mime at Sadler's Wells'. He kept on with the Lower Third, however. His new manager Ralph Horton then saw him into another group, The Buzz, another flop single, 'Do Anything You Say', and on into The Riot Squad. In 1966, Horton introduced David to Ken Pitt, who became David's first manager (as a solo artist). Fed up with his dull stage name, not least because it confused him with Davy Jones, frontman of The Monkees, he half-inched the surname of 19th century slave trader, pioneer and American folk hero James 'Jim' Bowie, who had lent his name to a popular curve-point knife.

Marc and David took to meeting for regular coffees at La Gioconda, a popular music biz haunt on Tin Pan Alley, where Marc would sit and pester his new friend for tips on how to get signed. Also moving and shaking on the Denmark Street scene at the time was Marc's old mucker from their Stamford Hill days, Eric Hall.

'Like Mark, I left school at 15 and didn't know what to do next,' admits Hall.

Hall's uncle, Tony Hiller, had been a song and dance man and half of The Hiller Brothers, who went on to write songs recorded by over three hundred artists.

'Uncle Tony worked at Mills Music on Denmark Street. I wanted to get into the music business, so I pestered him to get me a job in his office. Teaboy, runner, I did everything. Our other teaboy was Reg Dwight, who became Elton John. We worked together every day. We were just kids.

'I talked my way from there to there to there. I worked for Don Arden for years – the Al Capone of the pop business, Sharon Osbourne's dad and Ozzy Osbourne's father-in-law – until EMI poached me to be head of promotion.'

In those days, remembers Hall, the Alley hummed with a diverse and louche crowd.

'The football lot – Terry Venables, George Graham, Johnny Hollins and the rest – used to love to come down to that bit of Denmark Street and drink with music people like Matt Monro and Tommy Steele. We had the Showbiz XI, a charity football team which had been going since the late Fifties. The players were pop stars, TV personalities, ex-footballers like your dad [*Mirror* and *Independent* sports writer Ken Jones]. Des O'Connor,

Mike and Bernie Winters, John Burgess [the A&R guy at EMI who turned down Mark], Ziggy Jackson – who was A&R at Melodisc Records – Bill Cotton, Chad McDevitt – one of the originators of the 1950s skiffle craze. Even Sean Connery would play. 007! These guys all used to pop into Mills Music, and come with us to the Tin Pan Alley Club. As far as Marc and I were concerned, Denmark Street was our new Stamford Hill.'

Such was the London scene during the so-called Swinging Sixties that everyone in the music business knew everyone else. The acts were playing the same venues, hanging in the same clubs, swilling the same coffee in the same handful of places, as were all the music business folk. Leslie Conn may not have seen a future for Marc, but others were champing at the bit to bring him on board.

As a young teen, Mike Hurst was a precocious guitarist and singer-songwriter who was singled out by rocker Eddie Cochran when he auditioned on Jack Good's TV show *Oh Boy!* His big break came when brother and sister artists Dusty and Tom Springfield (born Mary and Dion O'Brien) were seeking a replacement for old Etonian Tim Feild, the third member of their trio.

Feild had seen the light, had become Reshad Feild, and had gone off to follow an alternative path as a spiritualist teacher, mystic and author. The Springfields with Mike Hurst became the UK's number one group in 1962, as well as the first British group ever to enter the US Top 20. Their brief high-profile career ended in 1963, when Dusty went solo. Mike launched a new band, The Methods, with Jimmy Page (of future Led Zeppelin fame) and Albert Lee ('the guitar-players' guitar player', who has worked with everyone from Eric Clapton to former Stone Bill Wyman). Mike then began producing for

Andrew Oldham, who became The Rolling Stones' manager, and Mickey Most, whose stable included The Animals, Arrows, Herman's Hermits, Suzi Quatro, Donovan and the Jeff Beck Group. Although Bolan fans will often have read otherwise, it was Mike Hurst, none other, who produced Marc's first formal singles for Decca, and another Mike, Mike Leander, together with an American 'producer', Jim Economides, who got the credit for them. Well whaddya know?

'Mike Hurst was there before record producers got any kind of recognition,' explains Jeff Dexter.

'What they contributed didn't really "count", until about 1967 – unless you were a big public figure like Phil Spector. Plenty of people have said they produced Marc who in reality never got near him. This kind of thing happened all the time. It happens to this day. Mike was relaxed about it, he didn't go around moaning about getting credit where it's due. He didn't need to. He wasn't a fly-by-night pretender. He was a good guy on the inside with a job, making money.'

The studio arrangement in those days was not dissimilar to a medical patient registered with a particular consultant, who is then operated on by a surgeon from that consultant's team. It's still the consultant's name on the paperwork, even though he personally may not have performed the surgery.

'That's how it worked in the studios back then,' affirms Dexter. 'Producers' memories become distorted over the years, like everyone else's. Nothing sinister about it. They often "remember" producing records they didn't produce, and confuse an artist with someone else . . . because it's all so long ago, they recorded so many, and they've actually forgotten.'

Jim Economides was a Californian studio engineer who had worked for Capitol Records in Los Angeles, where his main claim to fame had been recording sessions for rockabilly artist Johnny Burnette in 1963.

'He arrived in this country in 1965,' recalls Mike Hurst, to whom I am introduced by David Stark, and who was very willing to talk despite the fact that he had never before been interviewed about Bolan.

'The Springfields had broken up, and I was learning how to produce records and generally wondering what to do next. One day I happened to read an article about this Economides chap in one of the early *Sunday Times* magazines. "... *and* he produced The Beach Boys," it said, which made me do a double-take and think, "utter rot!" I was obsessed with The Beach Boys. I was a total surfin' sound nut at that stage. I liked to think I knew everything about them. I knew it wasn't true that he had produced them, but still. I was intrigued by the idea of someone who had the gall to say such a thing. I tracked him down, called him up, asked for a meeting, and he employed me. He had these incredibly palatial offices at Albert Gate Court, overlooking Hyde Park. I fell for it all, hook and line. As it turns out, I was conned, like everybody else.

'Economides called everybody "Boob". You'd want to punch him in the mouth for it, but you knew you had to button your lip. The job he gave me was producing practically everything he came up with ... because he was not really a producer, but a recording engineer. What he had going for him was this great gift of the gab. Plus, he was American, which was everything.

'Jim's forte was going around doing deals, extracting substantial advances of several thousand pounds a time out of record companies like Decca, and then getting me to do all the work – for which he took all the credit.

'I don't know exactly how he found Marc,' says Mike, 'but he did – on the Denmark Street vine, probably – and promptly signed him. I was a bit distracted by the fact that Cat Stevens had walked into my life, with whom I would go on to work for several years. So there we were with those two, all in the same office. One day, Jim said to me, "this Cat Stevens is crap, he'll never happen. Get rid of him, we're going to go with this kid Marc Bolan".

'Off we went into Decca's West Hampstead studios, and set about recording his first singles. "The Wizard" (with "Beyond the Risin' Sun") was the first, which was terrific, wonderful. Marc's voice was perfectly of the moment . . . perhaps even a little ahead of it, which might explain why it didn't happen.'

Arguably the first English 'underground' record, 'The Wizard's' vocal had a modern, hip and trendy snap to it, with no hint of the strange, tortured warbling to come.

'The single was released in November 1965, to something of a fanfare by Decca,' recalls Mike, 'and of course failed to chart, unfortunately. The follow-up, licensed single, "The Third Degree", which came out in June 1966, was even better.'

'The Third Degree' gained airplay on offshore pirate stations, reaching 'boss sound 15' on American-backed Radio England.

'This record was definitely ahead of its time,' insists Mike. 'When you listen to it, you can hear everything that he would become. That, for me, was really the beginning of T. Rex.'

Mike says that he 'absolutely loved' recording with Marc.

'What was so great about it? Primarily, the sound. Very basic electric guitars. Guitar, bass and drums, that's what I really liked. But also because the boy was delightful. Let's not forget, he was still only 18 at this point.

'During the 1960s, through the haze of pop and everything else that was going on, the best of the young musicians then were so *keen*. When they were in the studios, they really wanted to nail it and make something happen. Marc had something extra, however, he was quite magical. He was like a kid in a sweet shop. You knew that this was his big chance, the thing he'd been waiting for, and he was determined to do it right and make the most of it. From what I've heard since, that in-built enthusiasm and commitment never left him.'

Mike remembers Marc as being the complete opposite of Cat Stevens, who was a more difficult artist to work with.

'Cat had issues: sometimes about money, certain people, about what he would do or would not do, or feeling compromised. He did settle in eventually, and things got much easier.'

Marc was so easy to work with, reports Mike, because he was clever enough to know that he could achieve what he wanted by getting people on his side.

'If they liked him, they'd do a good job for him. Simple, really, but not everyone realises it, do they? He was immensely likeable, I have to say. Music is a ridiculously hard business to make it in. It was even then. The industry taints and spoils so many of them. Only the toughest keep going. You have to try and forget about all the record company people and all the crap they feed you, and just be producer and artist, a bunch of musicians, working together to do the creative work. You're there to do something right, not stuff it up. Marc really got that. He worked hard.

'In those days, among musicians,' he explains, ' there was very much a sense of wanting to make a statement, wanting to make something memorable, wanting to make a difference. Making money was genuinely secondary, I believe, for most artists. The other thing was that pop "stardom", if you want to call it that, was so ephemeral, so here today and gone tomorrow. The Rolling Stones, for example, never thought they'd last beyond 1967, 1968. That was very much the feeling at the time, it was the whole Sixties approach. Get in, get on, have your moment, get out, do something else. Jagger and Richards had no idea they'd still be doing it fifty years later. I've never been a Stones fan, I have to say, but there is no way I could pour scorn on them – they are known in every nook and cranny of the globe. Doesn't matter that Jagger is now a wrinkled old prune who can't hit the notes the way he used to. What people still see is the Jagger he was back *then* – and that's the magic of it.

'In the same way,' he says, 'a lot of the world knows Marc Bolan: and this is magic too. If, all these years after your death, someone is still playing your records on the radio, and your kids hear them, and you are effectively living on through your music, that's fantastic. It's better than that, actually. It's everything.'

Given that by his own admission he loved Marc, that he remains so enthusiastic about his music, and that their producer-artist chemistry seemed so promising, why did Mike and Marc not continue to work together? What happened?

'Jim Economides doing a bunk is what happened,' sighs Mike.

'By the time Marc's second single with us had flopped, the debt collectors had caught up with Jim. He apparently owed a fortune back in the United States, and now he owed a fortune here in the UK. It all imploded overnight. I went to the office as usual one morning, and he'd packed up and gone back to Los Angeles without a word to anyone. The place was empty. He owed money to absolutely everyone, including me. He had also screwed Decca, who then dropped Marc, which was to be expected. Jim was no longer around, the deal had gone sour, they couldn't quite see the potential in the artist – all the usual. I never heard from Jim Economides again. A couple of years ago, I heard that he was dead.

'But I don't think the work that Marc and I did together was a waste of time,' Mike insists.

'Whenever I listen to Marc Bolan now, I still hear his tremendous energy, and I feel so privileged to have worked with him.

It's not just the "teen spirit" that Nirvana referred to. He had all that enthusiasm, that urgency, that desperation to deliver, and to do it right. In this business, which is so full of shit, it's only the music that counts. Marc knew that, better than anybody.'

The media still had to be courted. Marc had the measure of the make-you-break-you music press, right from the start.

'I knew this kid as Mark Feld, Toby Tyler and Marc Bolan,' remembers "Godfather of Rock Music PR" Keith Altham, who as the industry's most celebrated journalist wrote for every major title of the era, including *Fabulous*, the *NME*, *Melody Maker*, *Record Mirror* and *Sounds*, as well as a number of Fleet Street nationals, for whom he interviewed just about every major act under the sun: not least The Stones, The Beatles, The Beach Boys, Eric Clapton and The Byrds. He was with Pete Townshend when he conceived *Tommy* for The Who, and conducted Jimi Hendrix's last-ever interview at London's Cumberland Hotel, five days before he died. The poacher later turned gamekeeper, acting as press agent for a vast roster of artists: The Who, Police, Van Morrison, The Kinks, Ozzy Osbourne, Donovan and Marc Bolan included.

'Marc used to get with us in the Brewmaster pub on Cranbourn Street,' remembers Keith, when we hook up in Richmond Park, close to both his home and the Bolan tree. It makes a change from the Groucho Club.

'It was where all the old journos from *Sounds*, the *NME*, *Record Mirror* and *Melody Maker* hung out. In those days, we all talked to each other.

'He would come up there because he thought maybe he could get his name in the papers, if he was cute enough. He'd piss about, telling us he was going to be bigger than the Beatles and Elvis Presley, and we'd all indulge him, pat him on the head, go "yeah, all right Toby (or Mark or Marc or whatever his name was at the time), sit down and have another Coca Cola. When you're old enough, you can buy us all a drink."'

Had Keith heard any of his music at that point?

'No. He was always banging on about it, though. Always about to make a record, or was in the process of doing so. He'd done modelling, and was doing bits and pieces: Marc would be in anything to get himself written about.

'I remember him being in *Town* magazine, and doing something for Angus McGill.[1] He did an article in the *Evening Standard* about the fact that he had twenty five suits, which was a lot of nonsense, he didn't have anything like that many! But he was always smart and dapper, his mother kitted him out well.'

Keith met Marc's mum Phyllis on several occasions.

'She was real sweet,' he says.

'When Marc used to help out on her stall, he'd nip round the corner to the 2i's coffee bar on Old Compton Street, over the road from my old offices.'

What were Keith's first impressions of him?

'Hard to say! With Marc, you had to read between the lines a lot of the time,' he chuckles. 'He told stories. He'd exaggerate something to make it more attractive. I'm thinking of times like him carrying Eddie Cochran's guitar from a gig at the Hackney Empire. He was only a kid at the time . . . Maybe it was true, maybe it wasn't. You never knew, with Marc. Sometimes he'd just make stuff up for effect. Sometimes they were things he dreamt which he then embellished, just to tell a good yarn, and then he'd repeat them often enough to the point that they became "true", and part of his legend. Reminds me of that film *The Man Who Shot Liberty Valance*: "When the legend becomes fact, print the legend".[2]

'You never quite knew how to separate Marc's fact from his

fiction,' Keith goes on. 'He played to it. He loved it. He loved fantasies. Journalists were always going to love him, because he made their job easier. His fantastical tales were irresistible.

'He stood out from the crowd because he was young, hip, stylishly-dressed and cocksure. It made an impression on me: I wasn't hip or into clothes. I came from the generation when youngsters dressed like little adults. I'd be in a sports jacket with a carnation in the lapel.

'He was very pretty,' he concedes, 'and he definitely had star quality. You occasionally meet, in this business, very young people who'll say to you "I'm going to be a star" and it's not just "I *want* to be a star", it's "I'm absolutely going to *be* one". And they do it. And you think, "how do they *do* that?" I remember meeting Cilla Black, and she was the same kind of person.

'You'd laugh in her face, and she'd say "don't laugh, I'm serious". That kind of self-belief can eventually see them to the point when they do become stars. They've got to not just go around saying it, but genuinely believe it themselves.

'Marc did. Marc was one of those. "I am going to be bigger than The Beatles", he would tell you. No, he never quite was, but he got very close. Closer than anybody.'

On 19 November 1965, Marc was deployed as stand-in for an absent John Lee Hooker at a gig at Wembley's Empire Pool. This might have turned out to be Understudy Night, with Donovan also performing in place of The Kinks, if not for the welcome appearances of The Who and The Hollies. The event was a Glad Rag Ball for the London School of Economics (where Mick Jagger had studied until autumn 1963), with some 8,000 students in attendance. Not only did Marc have to perform for his first proper live audience, but also for the television cameras: the ball was being filmed for ITV. Neither he nor Donovan wowed the crowd. Marc's hubris began to wobble. Further appearances ensued, on shows such as *The Five O'Clock Fun Fair, ThankYour Lucky Stars* and *Ready Steady Go!* These were also lacklustre.

The ensuing months saw his most prolific output to date, with stories, poems, letters and songs pouring out of him in note-books and diaries, many of which survive to this day. While Bob Dylan remained the artist he sought to emulate most, there was another Dylan on his horizon by this time – Dylan Thomas.

The wild Welsh poet who was as famous for his drunken, adulterous and reckless ways as for his distinctive writing, had died in 1953, aged 39, when Mark was only 6 years old. The Grim Reaper tracked him down in New York, where Thomas was hugely famous thanks to his public readings of self-penned works, delivered in his richly resonant Celtic accent. His 'play for voices', *Under Milk Wood*,[3] was first broadcast in 1954, after Thomas's death, and was later adapted as a stage play. This was recorded with an all-Welsh cast starring Richard Burton. The production was then re-recorded by its original producer Douglas Clevedon, and broadcast on 11 October 1963, which was probably when Marc first became aware of it. The play's alliterative musicality impressed Marc deeply. He sank as if on pillows into such poems as 'In My Craft or Sullen Art', 'A Grief Ago' and 'If I Were Tickled by The Rub Of Love'.

Thomas's obsession with life's cycles, with death, procreation and the forces of nature, coughed up fierce poetry filled with pagan power and Biblical passion, the like of which Marc would soon be striving to write himself.

'I should say,' said Dylan Thomas, attempting to explain his art in an interview, 'that I wanted to write poetry in the begin-ning because I had fallen in love with words . . . the words alone. What words stood for was of a very secondary importance . . . I fell in love . . . and am still at the mercy of words.'

'Marc was exactly like that,' reveals Keith Altham. 'It was partially due to the fact that he gave up on his education quite young. He wasn't properly schooled, as one might say. He was virtually dyslexic. He was therefore more interested in the *sound* of words than in the meaning of them. His spelling was atrocious – he often wrote the "q" and the "u" round the wrong way. Consequently it helped him in some ways in the writing of songs, because the sound of words meant more to him than the definition. He would hear sound rather than significance, in literal terms. Hence, he got "Metal Guru", "Telegram Sam" – all those onomatopoeic phrases. "Tone Poems", he used to call them. He played with words, and he loved doing it.'

Dyslexics are often unusually creative with the words they are supposed to be 'blind' to; Marc was clearly no exception.

'Marc had this extraordinary love of words,' agrees Simon Napier-Bell, 'of the sound of them. He invented complete fantasies around the sounds of words.'

'There are certain words that have a kind of poetry in themselves, and he seemed to sense this,' remarked DJ John Peel to writer Rob Chapman. 'Even though they possessed a kind of silliness at times, I liked the effort that he went to to make it into a coherent whole. I used to get up and read the children's stories he wrote at the Albert Hall, and if you analyze them, they're complete bollocks, but at the same time they're not. I'm not going to say they're Joycean, but they still retain a certain charm . . . You encounter genuine naïve painters and you also meet people who affect naïvety. But I think Marc, as far as his lyrics went, was genuinely a naïve.'

Whence came the idea to plunder literature for poetic and songwriting inspiration?

'Fashion,' asserts Keith Altham.

He simply read fashionable literature. He probably had a sketchy idea that certain poets and writers existed, but it was a patchy knowledge. He didn't come from the kind of family that had such books at home. But he was very conscious of trends of what was cool and popular, what people were into at any given moment. He was inquisitive, and hungry for knowledge, and he'd always make it his business to find out'.

There were other influences, Keith points out.

'The Beat writers. Ginsberg. Kerouac – he'd pick up on the fact that someone was reading *On The Road*. He had Bowie for a mate, who was actually very literary, a bit of a culture vulture. Marc was impressed by all that, and would read whatever Bowie was into. David was only a few months older than him, they were born the same year, but he always appeared that bit older, more cultured and more sophisticated. Marc's habit was to seek certain "important" books out, get them and skim them – so that he didn't have a deep understanding, but a superficial knowledge – which was enough to make him appear clever and deep.'

Regarding himself now as a poet as well as a musician, but having not yet thought of a way of blending the two, Marc had literally to 'find his voice'. No one who knew him could have imagined at the time what a unique and unforgettable voice it would be.

As for Bolan and Bowie, was Keith ever together with the two of them?

'Yes, of course. There *was* a certain rivalry, although they were always *very* close. They had a special relationship which people have tried to dilute and pour scorn on over the years. They had what they had between them, they didn't have to prove it to anybody else – which is why, I think, David doesn't ever speak about it. There was a real love there, I believe. They were very similar, in so many ways. They could have been brothers.'

As for lovers . . . sharing Marc's sheets for a while during his sojourn with Mike Pruskin in their Manchester Street flat-share days was a young, Devon-born lass by the name of Theresa 'Terry' Whipman – his first serious girlfriend. For a while, Marc was devoted to Terry, who would often spend long nights capturing his musings and chantings and tryings-out of verses in notebooks. By 1966, he had clearly discovered J.R.R. Tolkien and C.S. Lewis (if he had not yet got around to reading them), and was now venturing into the realms of epic fantasy. It was around this time that he began to invent creatures – gnomes, dragons, angels, unicorns, trolls – in dark, quasi-Gothic homage to some of his 'favourite' writers.

Reality came knocking, as was its wont. On the run from their landlord, whom they could not afford to pay, Marc and Mike Pruskin parted company, and Marc meandered all the way home to Mum.

6

Nomis

It was a hell of a year: 1966 was the zenith of the vibrant Swinging Sixties, when all the music, youth culture and fashion trends radiating from Carnaby Street and the King's Road were at their peak. Hip London partied its eyes out; to paraphrase the hit Anthony Newley musical, no one could stop the world, let alone get off.[1]

Sociology feeds on hindsight – received wisdom being that this was a 'great time to be British'. But was it really? Oh sure, it was all going on: The Beatles, The Stones, The Who, The Kinks and The Small Faces dominated the pop charts, while psychedelic rockers Pink Floyd, Cream, Jimi Hendrix and their kin, beloved of pirate radio stations Caroline, London and England, were on a roll. *Ready Steady Go!* presenter Cathy McGowan was a Queen of the Mods in her tight mini-skirts, as was Mary Quant, who designed them. The first supermodel Jean Shrimpton continued her reign as The Face of The Sixties, while Twiggy bagged The Face of '66: a year crystallised in movies such as Antonioni's *Blow-Up* starring David Hemmings and Vanessa Redgrave, *Alfie*[2] with Michael Caine, and *Georgy Girl*[3] featuring Lynn Redgrave, James Mason and Charlotte Rampling. Nostalgia may have blinkered us to what was essentially a shallow period defined by the kind of hedonism which would spell downfall and disaster for many.

'The Sixties were a lie, a total lie,' declared the Kinks' Ray Davies in 1981, and he was there.

Perhaps the decade was saved by its soundtrack (much of which we cherish to this day). At least we had a home victory in the FIFA World Cup, when England beat West Germany at Wembley Stadium before a 98,000-strong throng. The score, for the record, was 4-2 in extra time. Football has been trying to come home ever since.

A reality check, meanwhile. War raged in Vietnam as Dr Martin Luther King gave his first speech in New York. Harold Wilson's Labour party claimed victory in the General Election. Buster Edwards was arrested in connection with the Great Train Robbery,[4] Moors murderers Ian Brady and Myra Hindley went on trial, and notorious gangster Ronnie Kray killed rival George Cornell in cold blood in an East End pub.

LSD was made illegal in the US, Walt Disney checked into the animation factory in the sky, and, in the year he met Yoko, John Lennon made his reckless declaration that The Beatles were 'more popular than Jesus' (he later apologised). The Fabs released their legendary album *Revolver*, gave their last-ever public performance (save the 'gig on the Apple roof') in San Francisco's Candlestick Park, and began recording sessions for *Sgt Pepper's Lonely Hearts Club Band*. The Beach Boys released their seminal album *Pet Sounds*. Bob Dylan did the same with *Blonde on Blonde*. It was all happening.

Imagine Marc in the middle of all this action. Gagging to get in on it, to be a part of everything that swung. While he had known for years what he wanted to do, there were still a couple of pennies left to drop. When they did, he awoke to the realisation that it wasn't as easy as wanting it, and that he was going to need a heavyweight to make things happen. Enter flamboyant pop manager and man-about-town, the twenty-something Simon Napier-Bell.

'Marc had somehow managed to get my home phone number, and called me one evening in September or October,' Napier-Bell tells me.

'I was already managing The Yardbirds, that's how he knew of me. I had a flat in Bressenden Place, between Victoria Station and Buckingham Palace: a modern block that is now a hotel. I was on the eleventh floor, and the windows in the living room looked out over the back gardens of the palace. Sometimes in the mornings you could see the Queen come out into the garden to feed the flamingos. No thought of security and assassination in those days. It was the same when she had garden parties, we could watch the goings-on from my sitting-room window – all the Royal family, the Prime Minister, the entire cabinet would be there.'

Never short of an outrageous anecdote or two, Simon lets slip his first encounter with David Bowie:

'Late Sixties model (when he was still a Jones, and fronted The Lower Third). I was never his manager, but a chap called Ralph Horton was.

'Ralph called me out of the blue one day and introduced himself. He asked if I would come to see him and have a chat about a project. His flat was a basement in Pimlico and the project was sitting in the corner: David Jones. Ralph asked if I would be prepared to help with David's management and, as an introductory offer, suggested I might like to have sex with him. I couldn't tell if this was a joke but I was rather put off.

'Consequently, I neither slept with Bowie nor managed him. In retrospect, I admit that both things might have been worth doing.'

Napier-Bell's flat was 'posh and expensive. I had an American

Ford Thunderbird – a big, flash, pale blue convertible. They cost twice as much as a Rolls Royce in those days, what with 100% import tax on American cars.

'I was also managing John's Children and a couple of others. I'd picked up some guy at the Apollo Club and during the course of a shag, I had obviously promised him something, because he turned up in the office the next day – small, blond and pretty – asking to see me. And then there was a girl I'd hired to sing on a TV commercial (I also had a company that made documentary films, and TV advertisements). I'd shagged her and had probably promised her something too. Anyway, I thought I'd put my two problem shags together and turn them into a pop group. I continued to have an affair with both of them. At the same time, I was having an affair with a 19-year-old Cambridge student who lived in Bridlington . . . and also with his sister, whom I'd met when I went to visit him in Yorkshire, and whom the parents (realising I was gay) had asked me to look after when she came to London to study. So all in all, I was doing a lot of shagging. But then, this was the Sixties.'

Irresistible company to this day, Napier-Bell was the Simon Cowell of his era, the pop magnate supreme.

'I didn't try too hard,' he says, 'I didn't have to. I always wore casual clothes. Kids bought their clothes in Carnaby Street; people with money who dressed casually bought them at John Michael, or maybe Cecil Gee. I never liked lace-up shoes – haven't worn a pair since I left school. Only slip-ons, usually light in colour. Trousers usually a bit tight round the crotch so it all stood out well. At home, I played Nina Simone, Ray Charles, Dylan's *Blonde on Blonde*, and lots of jazz. Friday night at 6pm was always *Ready Steady Go!* – "The Weekend Starts Here". Friends came round all the time – I *always* mix business with pleasure. I have to like the people I work with, and if I like someone, I try to find a way of working with them. So, work, restaurants, friends and sex all got muddled up. Diane and Nicky, John's Children, Marc Bolan, it was like that every day.

'I ate out every night – I have done all my life – occasionally alone with a book, which I like very much, but in those days more often with whoever I was intending to shag, or had just shagged, or who I was planning a career for.'

Marc turned up towards the end of Diane and Nicky and the beginning of John's Children.

'He was full of it, you could hear the swagger down the phone. He was going to be this massive star, he just needed a good manager to take care of everything. I tried to fob him off, telling him to send me a tape to my office in Dean Street – No. 72, Royalty House, a modern block of offices opposite Quo Vadis. But Marc was persistent, which I liked. He said he was just round the corner, and could he deliver it in person. He was on the doorstep with his guitar less than ten minutes later. There was no tape, he confessed disarmingly, but he offered to sing for me there and then. I was never keen on that kind of thing, but I couldn't say no. I could tell in an instant that he had the one vital ingredient needed to make it as a rock star. They call it 'star quality', as if it's some kind of magic that a chosen few are 'born' with, but it's much simpler than that. What Marc had came very naturally to him, and was just what he had been doing for years: the ability to perfect a unique image and lifestyle and to project his uniqueness around. He was his own blank canvas. He could have been an artist of any kind, I think – he certainly had the charisma – but what he had chosen to become was a rock star.'

Did Marc himself seem aware, at that point, of what he had? Did he understand that he was 'different', or 'special'?

'I don't think you have to understand yourself to be the material of your own art,' Simon says.

'I think, in most cases, artists work at their art as a means of finding out about themselves. So perhaps not understanding yourself and wanting to is an important part of being an artist.'

Dressed in 'street-urchin' clothes and with a guitar that dwarfed him, Marc sat cross-legged in Simon's biggest armchair, owned up to being an average guitarist but then reassured Simon that his songs would blow him away. The pixie wannabe rock star then sang for close to an hour, by the end of which Simon was on the phone, booking De Lane Lea recording studios in Holborn. It was already close to eight in the evening, but they went straight away.

What did it for Simon was Marc's unique voice, which he had never heard anything like before. Some have described it as a bleating lamb, while others hear more kid goat. A newborn baby choking, an Atlas moth flapping frantically in his throat, a juddering, wavering, orgasmic gurgle which had his one-man audience on the edge of his seat. Wherever this boy had got it from, he was enchanted. Simon wanted more.

'He'd already decided on the image of a Dickensian urchin – although a scrupulously clean one - and had already discovered his warbly voice (a combination of Bessie Smith vibrato on blues LPs played at 45rpm and Billy Eckstine 45s played at 78). He was ready-made, his image an extension of the songs. Marc was the whole package. I was enraptured with what I saw and heard. I thought the whole world would be too. But the whole world wasn't a sophisticated jazz-loving middle-class gay like me. It took many adjustments before the world was ready for Marc – most of them made after he left me.

'It was all there,' Simon says, 'the stuff of Arthurian legend. Fantasy, imagery, strong evocative lyrics which made no real sense, but which at the same time made every kind of sense to him. This is key: believing it yourself. It was all quite eerie and magical.'

After they'd demo'd more than a dozen songs – which took less than an hour, all the songs once through, one take – Simon took Marc to dinner at the Lotus House restaurant on Edgware Road.

'The beauty of the place was that it was open till 2am, and full of showbiz people – especially the ones who'd done a theatre or TV show and wanted to eat afterwards. It was very posh. I invaded it frequently with all of John's Children, who behaved abominably, and we ran up vast bills drinking Champagne and throwing fried rice around. There, Marc and I started getting to know each other. It was where he told me all about his theory of sleeping with people to extract the best of their brains. Which we went and did afterwards. It just seemed easy and natural. His manner had already showed me he had no problem with it, so there was no reason to ask – just get on with it. I'm not usually a great violent heavy shagger, I like love, romance and eroticism. Kissing above everything. Over dinner, he'd made a surprising comment about kissing being perhaps the best method of capturing someone's intellect, so that was a good place to start. Though I would have been shocked to have woken up to find my mind filled with hobbits and wizards, so I'm glad that his theory didn't work.'[5]

The Lotus House was run by a Chinese queen, Johnny Koon, son of Cheung Koon, who owned and ran Cathay off Piccadilly: until the mid-1950s, the only Chinese restaurant in London.

'The Lotus House was so popular that it was almost always full,' remembers Simon. 'Disappointed customers waiting to get in but unable to, often asked if they could take some food home instead. So it became Britain's first take-away Chinese. It was big and grand, like the Savoy Grill, with a pianist who always played "You Don't Have To Say You Love Me" when I walked in.'

Thus began their short-lived manager-artist relationship, and apparently much besides. Looking back, despite the detail which suggests that they knew each other inside out, Simon sometimes feels that they barely knew one other at all.

'I never visited Marc at home, never met any of his family, and never saw his prefab. Nor did I ever introduce him to my parents', he says. 'We obviously came from very different backgrounds. But there was no sense of shame about his past or his upbringing. Like almost everything in his life, Marc talked about the family prefab with wonderment, as if it had dropped here from heaven, or from another planet. He seemed blessed in his ability to find a way to enjoy every situation. He was a little gnome and the prefab was his woodland home: that sort of thing. He dropped me no confidences about his past.

'I had no feeling that there had been anything untoward. But if it had, I'm sure I wouldn't have been told. Marc would have made it into a wondrous story: perhaps arriving on earth after something cataclysmic had happened. Nor did I get that he wanted to leave his lowly social status behind. Rather, he saw it as part of what he was and wanted to be.'

Did Simon ever feel that Marc was hung up about being so small? His 'full adult height' is given as being between 4' 9" and 5' 7", although in reality the discrepancy could never have been so great. Danielz, who wears some of Marc's original stage clothes, says that Marc and he were exactly the same height: 5' 7". Tony Visconti corroborates.

'Not at all,' Simon insists. 'Anyone with any brains makes do with what they've got, or what they are – including small people. I've met a few little folk who fit the "Napoleon complex" theory, but I've known far more who were content to be themselves. Black, white, tall, short, fat, thin, gay, straight – all the well-adjusted, intelligent people I've ever met have learned to be happy with it. Marc was one of those. But then you are probably looking at it from the point of view of a woman observing heterosexual men. They do feel the need to impress women, and find it difficult from below a woman's chin. Short gays, on the other hand, find it an immediate advantage to be small and cute, and rarely object to it. Marc liked being fancied. Gay, straight, bisexual? He was none of those really – just available to anyone who was intelligent, worth knowing, who fancied him and found him cute . . . and clever. He needed to be treated at least as an equal, if not as a superior. He didn't care about being small. He didn't care what it was that made him attractive to other people, so long as he was. Hence: gay men. As for black girls (tired of macho black men, eager to play mother), he was the perfect plaything. I've found that a lot of gays discover black girls as a semi-bisexual alternative to gay life.'

A short while into their relationship, Simon recounts, Marc started turning up at his flat at around 7am:

'. . . perhaps just to see who I had in bed. Or perhaps to make me nervous of having anyone there. Marc said he would get up most mornings at 5am and that he liked to walk. So that meant when he came to see me he'd walked all the way from Wimbledon (about nine miles). He'd wake me up with the doorbell, then make us both a cup of tea and come and get into bed with me. There was lots of good talking – life, art, music, people – and a bit more shagging. Really, I was just a walking talking penis in those days. I knew he had a girlfriend, Terry, but she seemed beside the point when Marc was with me.

'What we really liked to do was talk and cuddle. If we had sex, it was never penetration, more an extension of kissing and cuddling. He told me he hadn't had a decent erection since the day he discovered masturbation at eleven. Because any time his willie even began to get hard, he couldn't resist doing it again, right there and then. So it never had a chance to fully refurbish itself. He reckoned seven or eight times a day.'

Did Simon ever get to know the real Mark Feld, does he believe?

'That's not something I'd ever think about with anybody,' Simon insists. 'I never think there's anyone else below the surface person we see. I reckon it's all there on top to be seen, and what isn't there doesn't exist. I don't believe in any of Freud's theories of the subconscious. If you delve below the surface of the human brain, you'll simply find animal brains, not a deeper layer of human brain.'

What does he think Marc would have done, had he not gone on to earn his living as a musician?

'I never gave it a thought,' he shrugs. 'I never think of things like that. I don't think about the endings of films or books before I get there. I never waste my time on fantasy.'

Of the many tracks demo'd in De Lane Lea that first night, it was 'Hippy Gumbo' which Simon and Marc agreed together should be recorded. By slowing the tempo, adding the strings and giving the song a more sensual thrum, they came up with what they thought was bound to be a hit. Simon pulled every string, got the record a minor deal on Parlophone through EMI (where he had The Yardbirds on Columbia), and the record was released. Despite a comfortable performance on *Ready Steady Go!* on 13 December, where he met Jimi Hendrix for the first time, 'Hippy Gumbo' came and went. Marc, undeterred, was determined to keep going for it. This had more than a little to do with his discovery of John Peel.

Originally plain John Ravenscroft, Peel would become the BBC's longest-serving presenter on Radio 1 from its inception in 1967 until his death in 2004. One of the first to broadcast progressive and psychedelic rock on UK radio, he was especially fond of giving airtime to young, unusual and unsigned acts.

'Marc started writing letters to John at Radio London out on the pirate ships, where he had a show called *The Perfumed Garden*,' explains Jeff Dexter, who was still estranged from Marc at the time.

'I knew this because I'd made John's acquaintance in London. He'd become friends with me and my little gang of stoners. He was one of us, part of the scene, and he was reflecting on the radio what we were listening to. This, for the time we're talking, was quite incredible.

'We'd never really had anyone playing totally alternative stuff on air, until John,' Jeff elaborates.

'We had been immersed in that kind of music from the end of 1965, all through 1966. But there was no sign of it at all out there in the "mainstream".

'What John was doing was a revelation. To have all that great music come on the radio, and in the laid-back style in which he presented it, instead of "And now here's another one, Pop Pickers!" and then playing yet another cheesy hit. That was sensational to us.

'I was DJ-ing in Tiles Club and in the ballrooms in those days, and we all thought that was how you had to act. That was the mould that you'd been set in. We even spoke in fake American accents, between "*reckuds*". We'd learned our craft from the DJs over there, and that was what they did. It was all about expression. There was a different kind of energy coming off the records filtering in from the States.

'We listened to American stuff so much as youngsters, and were so influenced by all things Yank, that it was only natural that we'd emulate their style. 1950s, early 1960s America was so cool, so trendy, so exciting and different, compared to the greyness and stiff-upper-lipped-ness of old Blighty.

'I did go there, yes, and tried living the life,' Jeff says. 'LA, New York. In some ways, for me, it happened great. But I encountered too many thick people! America was a very alien place back then, to a streetwise kid from London – as Marc was to find, a few years later. Even New York. You get seduced by all this energy, but in fact the energy coming off the Yanks was just purer bullshit than off the traders down the market on Berwick Street. If you're a bullshitter yourself, you can read it so easily.

'Anyway, there we were, listening to all this great stuff that John was playing for us. John was writing back to this kid Marc, and getting all his squiggly hand-written poems in return, and digging it. What happened next was inevitable, really, after one of my girlfriends started writing letters to John.'

7

Everything's Spinning

In April 1967, six years after the building of the Berlin Wall, London's premier instrument-smashing outfit The Who embarked on a tour of West Germany to promote their latest single, 'Pictures of Lily'. They would be joined en route by various home-grown bands, including Hanover rockers The Scorpions and a beat group called The Lords. They also took with them two English mod groups as support acts – The Action, and John's Children – and would live to rue the day their manager Kit Lambert did the deal.

The Action, from Kentish Town, were nice young men, delivering cool, soulful pop not quite thrilling enough to save them from the Parlophone chop that year – despite the fact that they enjoyed a massive cult following as the antidote to the 'bit too pop' Small Faces. John's Children, on the other hand, were upstarts, not to mention pretenders to The Who's own throne. These pre-punk louts from Leatherhead were more pop-art, mod-er, mad-er, and out of control on stage. They had the indomitable Simon Napier-Bell for a manager – who had co-written, with their bassist John Hewlett, their first single 'Smashed, Blocked/Strange Affair' – often credited with having been the first 'official' psychedelic record.[1]

'I discovered John's Children living close to the wind in St. Tropez,' explains Simon. 'You might say they were professional vagrants. I bailed them out, and discovered that they were a group. One of the conditions of my bailing anyone out is that they work for me for three years.'

They also had Napier-Bell's latest protégé, Marc Bolan, on guitar and vocals. Simon had just recorded Marc singing a strange self-penned song, 'Jasper C. Debussy', at Advision Studios in Gosfield Street, with Nicky Hopkins on piano and future Led Zeppelin star John Paul Jones on bass. He had also just hatched a new master plan: to gain Marc and his songwriting exposure on the John's Children bandwagon. Once the record-buying public had grown used to his alien voice, Simon theorised, he could then launch him with flourish and fanfare as a solo star.

'It was partly Kit Lambert's idea,' admits Simon. 'He decided he wanted to sign John's Children to his new label, Track, but he didn't much care for their fainting guitarist. He suggested that I replace him with Marc, whom he'd met at my flat.'

Simon took Marc out to dinner in order to try and talk him into it.

'We were discussing some of his heroes. Elvis. Chet Baker, of course. James Dean. Marc adored Dean's image, and the mythology that had grown out of his death. I seized my chance. "Joining the group will start you off on the path to eventual stardom," I assured him, "and you've got to start getting rich soon if you're going to be like James Dean and buy a Porsche."

'"Oh no," said Marc. "A Porsche wouldn't be right for me. I'm too small. I think a Mini is the right car for me. If I was going to die in a car crash, it ought to be a Mini. I think I'd like that. It'd be nice."'

★　★　★

'We had a good management deal with Simon Napier-Bell, a deal with Columbia in the UK, with White Whale in North America and another one in Germany, and we were starting to get some-where,' John's Children lead singer Andy Ellison reminisces.

Andy and I are introduced by Paris-based American film-maker Susie Kahlich. Several meetings in London ensue.

'Simon had done the German tour deal with Kit, and turned up at our club in Leatherhead one day that March, saying , "I want you to meet this guy Marc Bolan. See what you think about him joining the band."

'The idea was that Marc would replace Geoff McClelland, a really nice bloke who had founded the group in the first place, supplied the vans and the equipment and so on, but who was not much cop as a musician. Simon took me over to a bunch of prefabs past Wimbledon Stadium, dropped me there and drove off, telling me that he'd pick me up later.'

Andy arrived dressed head to toe in white with a gold medallion dangling from his neck, which was the band's 'look'.

'We had to dress like that all the time,' he groans, 'we lived in laundrettes when we were on the road.'

He climbed the front steps and knocked on the door. Marc opened it.

'"Hello, I'm just about to cook some mushrooms on toast," was the first thing he said to me. "Would you like some?"

'He was holding a copy of *The Tin Drum*[2] by Günter Grass, and going, "Oh man, you've really got to read this." He looked quite mod-y at that time, and was very polite, sweet and engaging. After we'd scoffed the nosh, he went and sat cross-legged on the sofa, all folky with his acoustic guitar, saying, "I'm gonna play you some tunes."

'All the time, I was thinking "this guy won't fit into the band at all." Marc was too gentle for our style. We were very wild, really naughty – deliberately contradicting our whiter-than-white angelic image with vile behaviour. We smashed up our equipment, had fights on stage, we used chains, blood capsules, feathers ripped out of pillows, I was stage-diving before anyone else had thought of doing it. Our act was always pandemonium.

'Simon had bought us twenty incredible Jordan amplifiers patented by NASA from the States. They were the best in the world at the time, and were being used by artists such as The Mamas & The Papas and The Turtles. They threw the sound out by about twenty more feet. They'd be all linked together when we played, a wall of sound across the back of the stage, with a volume that you imagined could kill someone. Marc was about to be introduced to all this the next day, and I sat there wondering what the hell this sweet little boy was going to make of it. When Simon came back to pick me up, I didn't say a word.'

The next day, Simon turned up for rehearsals at the band's club, the Bluesette in Leatherhead, with Marc in tow.

'We handed him a red Gibson SG, plugged him in, switched him on, and wham! Marc almost jumped out of his skin. Simon winked at us and said to Marc, "I'll pick you up later. I know your mum wants you home in time for tea."

Marc appeared to know only three or four guitar chords, Andy remembers.

'He wasn't very good, and kept going "Oh my God!" He couldn't believe how much power these things could release. When Simon collected him we did moan a bit, but he said, "You've got to have this guy." What Simon wanted, Simon got.'

A couple more rehearsals and things began to look up.

'He had this mild rockabilly style,' Andy recalls. 'It was quite nice. Our drummer Chris Townson had to tune his guitar for him every day, but he picked it up quickly. We felt really awful when we had to tell Geoff that he was out of the band, but he was good about it. He wished us luck. We thought we were going to need it. But Marc was a lovely guy. Harmless. Loved music. Loved laughing. His giggle was so infectious, he could have had a corpse in hysterics. He was very fond of teasing and joking and larking about, just like us. When Marc met us, he met his match. He was great to have around, we all got on with him.'

Marc intrigued Andy, who would have liked to spend more time with him alone; he wanted to find out how this little guy from a humble prefab in Wimbledon, who had quit school early and had never really had a proper job, had such a clipped accent, refined manners, an undeniable air of sophistication, and seemed so well-read.

'They were a real working-class family,' says Andy. 'Without wanting to sound snobbish, there was no way that they could have exposed him to all that. I was itching to know where it came from.'

He never did find out. But by the time they got out on the road together, Andy and Marc were good mates.

'He was always laughing, we could make him roar. It was a joy to hear,' smiles Andy. 'He did have his quiet moments, especially in the car, when he'd sit quietly scribbling away in one of his many notebooks. He never shared what he was writing, either. Whether it was about us, or made-up stories, or lyrics for new songs, I never knew.'

The first few gigs with Marc were terrible.

'He'd get so drunk – on red wine, a couple of bottles at a time. That was new to us. We were doing everything else – blues, uppers, and later, LSD – but we always did that stuff *after* the gigs, never before a performance. We didn't need to, we'd be high enough on adrenalin. Marc had to be shit-faced before he could go on. So you had this little pixie getting pissed every night, going out there, making a complete hash of it, showing us up, then crying all the way home in the van. We had to really tick him off and tell him to get a grip.'

It wasn't long, however, before the wild Bolan child began to emerge. Did Andy see John's Children as a stepping stone?

'He never really gave that impression at the time,' says Andy. 'Looking back, though, that's exactly what we were.'

'My first-ever interview with Marc in the *NME* was via Simon Napier-Bell, while Marc was briefly a member of John's Children,' says Keith Altham. 'I wound up interviewing Simon more than I did Marc. Their album *Orgasm* [appropriately, a faked live album with overdubbed screaming which had been "lifted" from the soundtrack of The Beatles' 1964 movie *A Hard Day's Night*] had been banned in the States. They'd just had a record in the charts – "Just What You Want, Just What You'll Get", and later brought out a song Marc had written, "Desdemona", and which was banned by the BBC for having the line "lift up your skirt and fly". "Quite right too!" said Simon, who was obviously delighted and gagging for more of the same: getting banned was priceless publicity. He said he had "something filthy" as a follow-up, exclaiming "that'll *really* give them something to talk about."'

'We are writing and arranging all our own material on stage,' Marc told Keith Altham for the *NME* in March 1967. 'Although I still hope to record independently as a solo artist, as far as this group is concerned, Andy is lead and sings on the disc.'

'I think it was all a bit of a culture shock for Marc to begin with,' admits Andy. 'He wasn't yet that full-of-it T. Rex figure that he eventually became. His experiences in John's Children gave him a huge amount of confidence. The tour in Germany turned out to be a really steep learning curve for us all.'

★ ★ ★

'I'd got rid of my T-bird and had bought a Bentley,' remembers Simon Napier-Bell. 'When John's Children went on tour in Germany as the support for The Who, I went with them, and drove them there in the Bentley.

'In those days you could take your car across the Channel by air from Kent's Lydd airport to Le Touquet in a big old World War II troop carrier. It took just fifteen minutes to get from England to France. We then drove round the whole tour in my car.'

To while away the time on the boring autobahn, the band and Simon took to playing games. At one point, their role-play had band member Chris Townson pretending to be Marc's new Jewish manager.

'Suddenly,' says Andy, 'There was Simon, chuckling over his shoulder from the steering wheel, going, "You know, the best move that you could make now, Marc, in terms of guaranteeing super-stardom, is to DIE! In a white Rolls Royce!" "No, man," Marc said quietly, and in all seriousness, "I told you, it's got to be in a Mini."'

John's children arrived in Nuremberg, Bavaria – infamous as the location of the Nazi Party's vast pre-war propaganda rallies, and of the post-war Holocaust Trials. By 1967, an estimated thirty thousand Jews were again living in West Germany, after an extensive programme of community rehabilitation. If Marc felt unsettled by the ghosts of atrocities past, he made no comment.

'We were playing in a massive hall where the Trials had taken place, it was quite eerie in a way, I would have thought even more so if you were Jewish,' Andy comments, 'but he didn't say anything.

'The Who had got there ahead of us, and had already set up. Our roadie arrived, and set our stuff up in front of theirs. Pete

Townshend was livid, he thought we were trying to use their gear. Keith Moon ran out and started kicking the crap out of Chris's drum kit and our amps, but they were too strong for him to do any damage to. There was a punch-up before the gig, as we all had to share a dressing room, so it was a really bad vibe before we started. Marc and Chris later made more mischief by pulling the same girl. They had to find a ladder to smuggle her into the hotel.

'We played Mannheim and Dusseldorf next. We'd go out around the bars after the show with John Entwistle and Keith Moon – the only members of The Who who liked us. I can remember Moon marching around a bar doing the Hitler salute one night, which was not a good idea. Pete did lighten up for an evening, and came out with us, but Roger never did. None of them liked our music much, but I can't say we cared. Just to be there was enough. The Who were our idols.'

'John's Children out-Who'd The Who, there was no contest,' remembers Keith Altham, still a rock journalist at the time. 'No wonder The Who threw them off the tour!

'I saw one date. It had the same routine. John's Children tore out into the audience and created absolute mayhem. There'd be feathers everywhere, and the security guys would be going bananas. I'd be in hysterics, tears rolling down my face. The whips and chains used to come out, the works.

'It was supposed to be outrageous and shocking, but it was the funniest thing I'd ever seen. It was Simon Napier-Pantomime! That man was so ahead of his time, and very amusing.

'Entwistle would be stomping around with a miffed air, getting all cross, going "who sanctioned this? It's a fuckin' disgrace!" but he and Moonie were the ones drinking with the guys after the gig. Yes, they were stealing their thunder, and Moon's outraged reaction to it all was only par for the course. They weren't upset really. It was Kit, Pete and Roger who never saw the funny side – Roger primarily because the feathers would stick in his throat, so he couldn't sing!'

As the tour progressed, things got increasingly out of hand.

'The problem was', says Andy, 'that we'd created havoc already, before The Who even came on. Marc really got into all this. He started lashing his guitar with chains with more gusto than the rest of us. By the time we got to Ludwigshafen, Simon had issued an ultimatum: tone it down and stay on the tour, or keep on as we were doing and we'd be off it.

'The band talked. "But that's what we *do*," we agreed. It was a no-brainer as far as we were concerned.

'There we were, on 12 April, in another massive stadium: the 12,000-seater Friedrich-Ebert Halle. And we were going to go for it. As we came on, I leapt into the audience and shattered the lights at the front of the stage while Marc started slashing his guitar, having a fight with John, and trying to smash my face in.

'That fragile little elf sitting cross-legged on the sofa in his mum's house, strumming his acoustic guitar that day, kept going through my mind. I could hardly contain myself. How quickly we'd corrupted him! The audience went berserk, storming the stage, chucking chairs and leaping about. Someone had Chris on the floor, jumping up and down on his chest, all that. Things had gone nuts in a matter of minutes. We had a riot on our hands. Simon was frantic that someone would get killed, in which case we'd be arrested and had up on murder charges.

'Somehow, he managed to get us out of there. As we were legging it across the car park towards his car, we saw the fire engines tearing towards the venue. We fell in the Bentley, and span round in time to see the water cannons being fired. Simon put his foot down and flew out of there like a banshee. The scene from the rear window was war.'

The trouble-makers made it to Munich, where they learned they were off the tour and had to leave Germany as soon as possible.

'No time like the present', declared Simon. It was back in the Bentley and over the border, another 270 miles on the clock.

'I headed for Luxembourg and just happened to arrive there the evening Ravi Shankar was playing a concert,' he says.

While they were driving around Luxembourg City trying to find a hotel for the night, the hapless bunch passed a hoarding announcing the concert that would 'change Marc's life'.

Born Robindro Shaunkor Chowdhury in 1920 in the United Provinces of the Indian Empire, Ravi Shankar, who had first visited Europe as a young dancer, was by 1967 a globally-celebrated sitar virtuoso and India's most esteemed musician. The eight-times Grammy award winner was booked to appear at the Monterey International Pop Festival in California that summer, the world's first official rockfest, alongside Jimi Hendrix, The Who, Janis Joplin and Otis Redding.[3]

'Let's all go and see Ravi,' decided Simon.

'We were up in the gods, looking down on this performance, at this guy sitting there cross-legged with his bongo player and a lot of headache-y incense wafting about,' Andy yawns. 'I can see Marc now, leaning forward, watching the performance intently. It was his turning point.'

'It's often said that once he saw Ravi Shankar, the rest of his pennies dropped and he changed his style from then on,' remarks Jeff Dexter. 'But they forget that he'd already seen "The Woolly Jumper" – Donovan – a couple of years before.'

Indeed, Donovan might have even harboured a grudge for having 'ripped off his vibe'. But then Donovan did return the compliment, with his 1973 album *Cosmic Wheels*.

Shankar's simple and dignified presentation could not have differed more from a typically riotous John's Children gig. A 'Ravi-lation'?

'Within a few months, he would have turned his music on its head and would be sitting like that himself, cross-legged on a stage,' Andy says. 'You could almost hear him thinking, "I'm getting out of this madness. I'm going to do something gentler. I'm getting myself a bongo-player, and going back to an acoustic."'

They had to get back to England first. The next day, Simon pointed the car at Calais, and with one or two hiccups involving drunken members of the band being ejected from the French dockside navvy bars – more blood, even more mayhem – they found themselves on a Dover-bound boat.

'The next thing I saw,' laughs Andy, 'was Marc Bolan standing on a table in the lounge, pissed out of his brains, reciting poetry from one of his notebooks to a nonplussed throng. It was fascinating to see'.

After that, he remembers, John's Children fell apart and faded away.

'We had no equipment for a start,' he points out. 'Simon said he'd go back to Germany and try to retrieve it, but we never did get it back. We sulked off to our club in Leatherhead, just the three of us. Marc wasn't there anymore. Simon told us eventually that he'd left the group. I don't think any of us was surprised.'

Little wonder that forty-five years have blurred the memory. It wasn't quite like that. 'Desdemona' was released in April, but earned its BBC ban and was therefore not a chart success. John Peel loved it, however, and promoted John's Children on his high-profile *Perfumed Garden* Radio London pirate show. The band played several further gigs in the UK with Marc, notably the

'14-Hour Technicolor Dream': an all-night fund-raising extravaganza at London's Alexandra Palace featuring musicians, poets and artists. Pink Floyd headlined. John and Yoko, the Pretty Things and the Soft Machine also starred. John's Children recorded further songs in the studio, and a radio session for the BBC.

The final nail in the coffin was the band's next single, 'Midsummer Night's Scene', scheduled for a June release. Unfortunately, this was ruined almost beyond recognition in the mix. Marc was so incensed when he heard the final cut that, as Marc himself would later put it, 'I walked out and never came back.'

History was being made on all fronts, that summer of '67. In August, Charlie Watkins of Watkins Electric Music launched the first WEM P.A. system with hi-fi quality at the National Jazz, Pop, Ballads & Blues Festival at Royal Windsor Racecourse. The sound was beset with problems – outdoor P.A.s being in their infancy, and the local council badgering the organisers to keep the noise down, causing speakers to blow.

'We had a basic starting power of 1,000 watts, power unheard of since Hitler's Nuremberg rallies,' laughs Charlie. Still, the occasion marked a watershed for live music, from which Peter Green's Fleetwood Mac, The Small Faces, The Move, Cream, Jeff Beck, Donovan and Denny Laine would benefit greatly on the day, and to which much is owed by live touring bands to this day.[4]

Watkins, who would soon become 'a close and cherished friend of June's and Marc's', says Jeff Dexter, saw active naval service, where he learned how to play accordion and was introduced to the guitar. A brief spell as a professional musician in London led to him opening a Tooting record store with his brother, which in turn led to a Balham music shop selling accordions and guitars.[5]

'My fascination with the guitar, its mechanics and now its

electronic reproduction paved the way to the first Watkins "Westminster" guitar amplifiers, and, in 1958, the "Copicat" Echo and "V"-fronted Dominator amps, which revolutionised music overnight,' says Charlie, now an accordion-playing nonagenarian.

'No printed circuit boards, just a few valves, a tape loop and a bit of imagination.'

Charlie's amp is still regarded as an important element in Sound of the Sixties chemistry – the other two being the Vox A.C. 30, and the Fender Strat. WEM P.A. made possible all the great early festivals, from the Isle of Wight to the Stones in the Park, and Charlie is revered to this day as the 'Father of British P.A.'

'The curtain lifted on a new world of music,' he says. 'Multi-thousand audiences were now practical, possible, desirable and certainly available. And they could at last hear! Now, all these brilliant young musicians could emerge and do their thing. Back-line gear could be mic'd up to help it all along. The singer could be heard for miles. The rest is their history.'

It was the Summer of Love, when 100,000 hippies gathered in San Francisco's Haight-Ashbury district and brought to a head the cultural and political changes that epitomised the era. Across America, Canada and much of Europe, a 'hippie revolution' ensued. Their bubbling melting pot of music, creative expression, sexual freedom and psychoactive drugs was offset by the 'Long Hot Summer' of widespread race riots and violence. The hippie movement had come of age. Marc's stars were aligning. All this, and *Sergeant Pepper* too.

'It is perhaps hard for younger generations to understand the phenomenal significance of *Sgt Pepper's Lonely Hearts Club Band* when it was released in June 1967,' comments Jonathan Morrish, former CBS and Sony Music executive, of the ground-breaking album which encompasses everything from music hall, Indian music, pop, classical and rock'n'roll, and which remains one of the world's best-selling records of all time. Jonathan and I have been friends and colleagues since the early 1980s.

'Whatever you think of it musically – and it *is* astonishing, although not the most popular Beatles album – it is arguably their most important. This was the first album they'd made since they stopped touring, which was a conscious decision. Throughout the Sixties, the theme had been to achieve a hit record so that you could charge more for concert tickets. Albums were simply a stringing-together of extra material including covers, generally put together cheaply and quickly! But The Beatles turned all that on its head – and from then on, it was them saying "we're going to spend all our time on the album and focus our attention on what you can do in the studio. That's the real art, the real craft. And we are real artists."

'Record companies at that time did not spend a huge amount of time or money on making albums,' adds Jonathan, who was Michael Jackson's confidant and publicist for 28 years, and who now acts as Director of PR & Communications at PPL, the company which protects music performance rights.

'Suddenly,' he explains, 'the album as a concept became more important than the single, more important than anything. This was not what any other artists were doing, and it changed everything. On the business side, the album as an art form began to make serious money for the record companies. An LP in those days was 32s/6d which would nowadays be about £40. The profit margin was phenomenal. Who needed a pop single anymore? That was sort of low art! We could suddenly buy an artist's whole vision and statement, and that's one of the things that makes *Sgt Pepper* such a landmark moment. 'Our' music

Mark Feld's
birth certificate.

REGISTRATION DISTRICT				Hackney					
1947 BIRTH in the Sub district of Hackney South East				in the Metropolitan Borough of Hackney					
Columns:- 1	2	3	4	5	6	7	8	9	10
No. When and where born	Name, if any	Sex	Name and surname of father	Name, surname and maiden surname of mother	Occupation of father	Signature, description and residence of informant	When registered	Signature of registrar	Name entered after registration
193 Thirtieth September 1947 Hackney Hospital	Mark	Boy	Simeon Feld	Phyllis Winifred Feld formerly Atkins	Cosmetic Salesman 123 Stoke Newington Common Stoke Newington	P.W. Feld mother 23 Stoke Newington Common N.16.	First October 1947	P. Weaver Deputy Registrar	

Brothers Mark and Harry Feld in the garden of their childhood home, c. 1949. 'Mark loved to lug that big old china dog around', remembers Harry. 'He dropped and smashed it shortly after this picture was taken. He was heartbroken.'

John's Children in the studio, 1967. Andy Ellison second from left, Marc on the right.

Smashed? Blocked? John's Children perform live on stage under the watchful gaze of their biker bodyguards. Andy Ellison at the mic, centre. Marc on the right, next to the dude in shades.

'All the world is made of faith, and trust ... and pixie dust.' (J. M. Barrie, *Peter Pan*).
From the 'Garden' shoot, Edenbridge, Kent, 1968.

Marc and June's wedding day, 30
January 1970. L-R: Sue Worth, Mickey
Finn, June, Marc, Jeff Dexter, Alice
Ormsby Gore.

Jeff Dexter and June Child at Furnace Wood,
Felbridge, East Grinstead, April 1969.

Oscar **D**eutsch **E**ntertains **O**ur **N**ation – and so does T. Rex. 1971 ad for T. Rex gigs in Birmingham and London.

T. Rex backstage at *Top of the Pops*, January 1972.

Mickey Finn (centre) poses with Marc's driver Alphi O'Leary (L) and a friend.

Marc, aged 24, in 1971–1972, taking time out in the Bahamas.

Recording at Château d'Hérouville, Auvers, near Paris. He liked the quality of sound in the open air.

Marc gets to grips with his Telecaster in Chinatown.

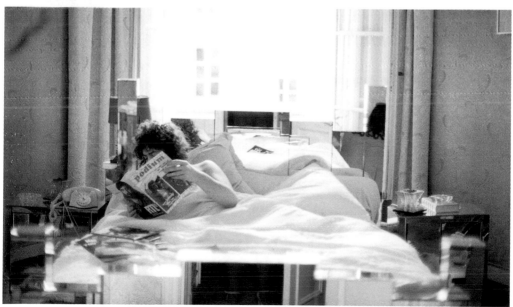

Just a rock'n'roll child . . .

Marc peruses his press cuttings at the T. Rex offices at 16 Doughty Street. 'He was obsessed with cutttings,' remembers Mick O'Halloran. 'He'd send us out for all the music papers, he never missed one.'

Tony Visconti with T. Rex at Rosenberg Studios, Copenhagen, March 1972. Sitting: Tony Visconti, Marc Bolan. Standing, L-R: Mickey Finn, Steve Currie, Danish recording engineer Freddy Hansson.

Marc and Ringo film scenes for *Born to Boogie*, which Ringo directed and in which both Starred, May 1972.

Elton, Marc and Ringo, stars of *Born to Boogie*, at the film's premiere, December 1972.

What a groover (honey), c. 1972.

On the Road (a la Kerouac): during T. Rex's 1972 UK tour. June Bolan seated behind Marc on the coach.

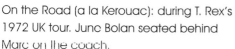

Marc asleep on a plane, captured by Tony Visconti, c. 1973.

Almost Famous? Marc with Cameron Crowe, during a session for American rock magazine *Creem*, July 1973. Crowe became an Oscar-winning film producer, director and screenwriter (*Jerry Maguire*, *Almost Famous*).

Who's the man in the mirror?
Late 1972/early 1973.

Advert for T. Rex's 1974
'Truck Off' tour, to promote
the *Zinc Alloy* album.

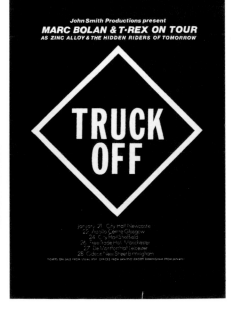

She's dirty sweet and she's his girl: Marc
and June at his parents' home, c. 1973.

suddenly became important, suddenly really mattered. It had beautiful packaging, a front cover you could pore over, and was pretty much the first album to have the song lyrics included, which we could peruse while we were listening.

'You couldn't pick out a particular track, either, and just play that. There were no grooves on the vinyl. So the commitment was to sit there for twenty minutes and listen to the whole thing. Like a classical recording, it was all in one piece. This raised the perception of pop and rock music as art.

'The Beatles were also addressing wider themes about life and the universe from a higher state of consciousness. They had been taking drugs for quite some time by then. It was no longer simply "boy meets girl, boy falls in love with girl, boy and girl live happily ever after or break each other's hearts". This was about taking their audience along with them on an epic journey – into their past, back to Liverpool, their whole philosophy and set of beliefs, around the landscape of their dreams and fears – in a way that had simply never been done before.'

Producer George Martin was undoubtedly essential to all this, says Jonathan, in that he was able to interpret their vision onto tape in a way that perhaps no other individual could have done.

'They could do whatever they wanted, of course, because they were making EMI so much money. This album transcends its own music, brilliant though it is, to stand alone as definitive proof of when and why the music industry changed. Its broad-canvas approach was ground-breaking, and inspired thousands of other artists to imitate them. Pop music was now important for its own sake, and not just as an also-ran to classical.'

Another turning point, as Jonathan explains, was that the work was all their own.

'Mitch Murray wrote "How Do You Do It", which The Beatles did record a version of, but then turned down.[6] They said, "We're writers. We write our *own* songs." They did do covers on the first few albums, sure. But their bold declaration was now, "We're musicians. We are self-contained. We write, we perform, we record, we do everything."

'They were not manufactured artists, the way so many if not most in the Sixties were. The likes of Marc Bolan and his producer-to-be Tony Visconti looked on, and took note. This was the way forward. Everything changed from then on.

'People often wonder about the notion that The Beatles created the modern music industry – but this was, without question, the moment it happened.'

To Marc, *Sgt Pepper* was nothing if not the purest distillation of his own ambition. Little did he know that within four years, it was he who would be the biggest thing since Beatlemania.

8

Solid Silver Geni

He could have gone either way. On the one hand heeding the sirens' call of the pop world, Marc was also deafened by the lure of the underground. Sell his soul for fortune and fame, or cling to creative integrity and salvage the cool that he'd surrendered to John's Children? He was by no means first nor last to wrangle with this dilemma. That he dithered at the fork, and even attempted to take both roads, is to his credit rather than to his detriment. Pop-Marc or Hippie-Marc, it barely mattered to him which, as long as he made it – or so many people thought.

The Marc Bolan band, aka Tyrannosaurus Rex – 'because we're gonna be KING!' – was a traditional four-piece put together via an ad in the *Melody Maker* in summer 1967, while Marc still cowered under the wing of Simon Napier-Bell. It resulted in a one-off gig, of which his manager washed his hands, at Covent Garden's Electric Garden (soon, in a nod to Tolkien, to be relaunched as the more famous Middle Earth.) Tyrannosaurus Rex featured tasty geezer Steve Porter on drums, who would stick around long enough to become that long-haired bongo-player with the Hobbit-y name: Steve Peregrin Took.[1]

Although times, dates and venues are disputed, the gig is

remembered clearly by Jeff Dexter, who attended, and by Simon Napier-Bell, who did not. It failed miserably, as Simon knew and had tried to warn Marc that it would, on the grounds that a bunch of novice musicians can't just get up there unrehearsed and blow the guts out of a place. 'Booed off and thrown out' was how Simon described his protégé's reception.

He was still recording Marc at this point, what would eventually become known as The Beginning of Doves sessions. One song in particular, 'The Lilac Hand of Menthol Dan', failed to secure a release, but remains memorable as the first example of Marc in full goat-throat. The track is a get-me-out-of-here blend of rock'n'roll, go-go and psychedelia, cut with the smash-up sound of someone swinging a kid in a plate shop. Marc's plaintive scatter-gun vocal assaults the listener at full retch. It's a must-hear.

Napier-Bell introduced Marc to David Platz at the Essex Music publishing company, who were involved with Who manager Kit Lambert's Track label – see how incestuous it all was? Marc and Steve Took were whisked into the studio to get cracking on demos. Back to the drawing board? A change of tack? Marc and Steve are said to have taken to busking in the Hyde Park underpasses with borrowed bongos and a beat-up acoustic, in order to eat while they considered their options. In the end, Marc was more or less relieved of the decision by DJ John Peel, who had championed Hippie-Marc's cause so zealously that his devoted listeners were gagging for more.

'He used to write me these fey letters, although not disagreeably so,' said John Peel. 'Given the level of pretension and bullshit that was around at that time, they seemed relatively modest.'

On 14 August, on his final Radio London *Perfumed Garden* show before he departed for the BBC and its new flagship pop station Radio 1 – launched by Tony Blackburn on 30 September,

Marc's 20th birthday (and where Tyrannosaurus Rex would record the first unsigned Peel session) – John span some acetates sent personally by Marc.

'What a voice that is,' Peel enthused. 'That's Marc Bolan, who I'm going to go and see as soon as the opportunity presents itself. I've got to meet him and find out where that strange voice comes from.'[2]

'John Peel came on shore leave in summer 1967,' remembers Jeff Dexter, who had by this time hung up his ballroom dancing shoes and reinvented himself as a major underground DJ, MC and scene-ster, with a finger in the pie of most A-list rock acts. 'We were pissing about one day when he said to me, "I met that kid who's been sending me all the poems and stuff. He wants to meet *you*, Jeff. You'll really like him."

'Marc hadn't said a word to him about the past, of course. So John and I go together from Chelsea to Hyde Park to meet this kid Marc Bolan. And when we get there, he's thumbing his nose at us, going "Na-na na-*naa*-na!" John just couldn't believe that Marc and I had been mates when we were nippers.'

Reunited, all altercation and animosity forgotten, Jeff and Marc were to remain bosom buddies and active colleagues for the rest of Marc's life.

What did Jeff think of Marc's radical departure from his early rock'n'roll aspirations?

'Well I didn't think it *was* that, really,' he counters. 'It was all just a variation on a theme. Rock'n'roll bands are like warriors in a way. All those medieval characters, the minstrels, the troubadours, the court jesters, their songs and their poetry – that was what Marc was fetching back to life. Those guys were the forerunners. Marc was just returning the whole thing to its roots, ready to go again in another new guise that would be right for the turn of the decade. The thing about Marc is that he was always that step ahead.'

The Marc Mark II, 1968–1970 Tyrannosaurus Rex model produced four gorgeous albums of almost mystical complexity, their titles indicative of the fantasies they explored: *My People Were Fair And Had Sky In Their Hair . . . But Now They're Content to Wear Stars On Their Brows; Prophets, Seers & Sages, The Angels Of The Ages; Unicorn* and *A Beard Of Stars*. This was Marc in all his whimsical and medieval glory, a reconstituted pagan warlock with coiled locks and velvet smocks. Inhabiting a realm of mythical creatures, he wove spells with odd and strangely-juxtaposed words, looking to legends and lullabies, nursery rhymes and hymns, chants, poems and fairy stories for inspiration.

Such a dramatic departure in music and style from his mod phase aroused predictable disruption and scorn among some critics, who should perhaps have known better. On what grounds denounce this creative departure as 'suspicious', 'fake' and 'calculated'? They had only to compare the image and recordings of the 1967 Beatles to see how they had looked and sounded in 1962 . . . just as, over the next two decades, rock writers would be able to contrast Freddie Mercury and Queen circa 1970 with the way they presented themselves visually and musically in 1986. Not to mention the master of self-reinvention, David Bowie, who would transform himself as if effortlessly from mime artist to psychedelic folkster to Ziggy Stardust to Thin White Duke to Berliner to Tin Man to neo-classicist. Nobody ever dared tell *him* that his dramatic images and radical departures in musical style were 'fake' and 'calculated'.

Some remain unconvinced by Hippie-Marc: notably Dr Robert, lead singer with new wave/dance sensations The Blow

Monkeys, globally-known since their late-Eighties hit 'Digging Your Scene'.

'Peter Jenner, who managed me for a while, also managed Marc during the Tyrannosaurus Rex phase', he reminds me. 'He thought that Marc was basically a fake hippie, with an eye on becoming a "pop star". John Peel later felt the same way – that Marc (had been) hiding his "harder edge" to get what he wanted out of the relationships (with supporters such as Peel). He was probably right. But Marc made some incredible and original music as Tyrannosaurus Rex. Who can judge the motivation? It's the work that matters, and the work is spectacular.'

'As for John,' Jeff Dexter argues, 'you might as well say that his decision to champion the cause of young, untried, unsigned acts was just as cold and calculating a move as Marc's "insincere" jumping on the underground bandwagon. Peel knew that nobody knocks you when you're supporting the underdog. When he decided to go that route, it was as much to his own advantage as it was to that of all the little bands he nurtured and launched.'

Criticism notwithstanding, was Marc not simply going with the flow John Peel had stirred for him, and creating new music with genuine intentions, rather than responding cynically and immersing himself in the so-called zeitgeist?

'"Tapping into the zeitgeist" is not a term we would ever have used at the time,' scoffs Dexter. 'It's a strange piece of language, that. While you're in it, whatever "it" is means nothing at all. People love to make it all complicated and sinister, and read things into scenarios that weren't really there. The reality was very simple. Marc had been getting great encouragement from *The Perfumed Garden*. People were sending him the most tender letters via John, writing him really beautiful things. These were music fans taking note of someone doing something completely different from everything else that was out there. Marc responding to that was only logical, and genuinely heartfelt. They gave, he gave in return. You create something, people like it, you've got a result.

'You give more. This is only human nature. Marc was sharp enough to realise that there was merit in making more of what the fans wanted. You'd be an idiot not to. Key to proceedings was the record he made with Joe Boyd.[3] That was the track that captured John Peel's heart.'

Boyd, an American record producer hugely instrumental in the careers of many artists including Fairport Convention, Syd Barrett's Pink Floyd and The Incredible String Band, had come to Europe to stage concerts for Stan Getz and Muddy Waters. He handled sound at the 1963 Newport Folk Festival on Rhode Island, at which Joan Baez and Bob Dylan starred, and first landed in the UK in 1964, returning a year later to open Elektra Records' London office. More significantly, he launched UFO Club, the capital's original psychedelic ballroom.

It was Boyd who produced the last Track Records demo sessions of Tyrannosaurus Rex late in 1967, including the song 'Château in Virginia Waters'. This later became an album track on *My People Were Fair* . . . The song is haunting, Shakespearian, with sublime melodies and magnificently obscure lyrics: 'Her pearly author's teeth tore the seasoned, cedar-coloured pheasant,' and so on. Peel became obsessed with it.

'My role in Marc's career was minor in the extreme,' Joe Boyd tells me, when we are introduced by Jeff Dexter. 'It was interesting – and probably says more about me than it does about Marc – that, after finishing "Château in Virginia Water" that night at Sound Techniques, I had little desire to work with him further. Not that he was unpleasant – I always got along well with him – but he was definitely from a different world. He claimed to be influenced by wanting to follow in the path of (Scottish psychedelic rockers) The Incredible String Band; everyone compared the early acoustic Tyrannosaurus Rex to the ISB, but I realized that, while the form might be similar, the essence couldn't be more different.

'That good old British class thing!' chuckles Joe. 'Marc was a working class kid craving stardom. Robin [Williamson] and Mike [Heron] were middle-class hippies seeking enlightenment, and were rather bewildered by my idea that they could be stars . . .

'John Peel also started writing pieces about Marc in his column in *International Times*,' says Jeff.

'Every little helps.'

International Times, also known as 'it' or 'IT', was a London underground newspaper founded in 1966, part-funded by Paul McCartney and issued fortnightly. It was launched at the Roundhouse at a gig featuring Pink Floyd, an occasion described as 'one of the two most revolutionary events in the history of alternative music and thinking.' Considered subversive by the establishment, its offices were raided often by police. It was first pulled in 1972, after the owners were convicted of publishing contact information for homosexuals – which was still against the law, despite the fact that homosexuality had been legalised in England in 1967. IT reappeared at various points over the years, and has recently been revived as a web journal.

Featuring columns from Allen Ginsberg and William Burroughs, its most prominent contributors in 1967 were the feminist writer and critic Germaine Greer, who became a friend of Marc and Jeff Dexter's, and John Peel – via whom Marc was discovered by the next greatest champion of his cause.

'He was utterly genuine, of course,' says 'Whispering' Bob Harris OBE, the acclaimed BBC Radio 2 and *Old Grey Whistle Test* presenter, who met Marc just as Tyrannosaurus Rex were starting to hatch. Our paths have crossed for years, as we have Bob's former producer Phil Swern in common.

'You couldn't make music like that and not be genuine about it – because it was such a risk,' he points out. 'It was unlike anything else out there. John Peel would have smelt it a mile off, had it been calculated and fake. What Marc was doing musically was astonishing. I got to know him well enough to know that it was real, and from the heart.

'Tony Elliot was the editor of *Unit* magazine at Keele University. We met when he came to London looking for a correspondent to file pieces to the magazine,' Bob recalls. 'He would later take a sabbatical to launch a one-off guide to the Underground. *Time Out* magazine, which we launched together the following year, grew out of that.

'He started commissioning me, and was keen for me to write more. When he asked me what other kinds of things I would like to write about, I told him I'd really like to meet John Peel: he was who I wanted to be, and doing what I'd always wanted to do.'

The interview took place at John's home in Fulham.

'As he was doing with everyone at the time, he had Marc with him,' Bob remembers, 'so I met them both for the first time on the same day. I was concentrating more on John Peel to be honest. So that day, I wasn't taking too much notice of Marc Bolan.'

Marc, nonplussed, sat cross-legged on the floor, minding his own business as he strummed away on his guitar.

'He had this fabulous smile,' says Bob. 'It took your breath away. Marc was very seductive. John gave me a copy of the album *Forever Changes* by American rock band Love, which had just come out. The whole experience that day was intoxicating, and I have never forgotten it.'

Bob met them a few more times together after that.

'Peel was something of an idol of mine, but Marc and I forged a genuine friendship,' he says. 'Although we were not necessarily each other's obvious companion, we did have a lot in common. He seemed to take me under his wing. Marc was about five years older than me.' [In fact Bob was the elder by seventeen months, but a good deal less mature and streetwise, so must have seemed the younger of the two.]

'I hadn't arrived on radio yet,' Bob continues, 'and there was no professional imperative. I couldn't do Marc any favours, so I knew he wasn't using me. I was a bit out of my depth at that point, to be honest. I'd only been in London for a couple of years. My dad was a policeman. I'd not yet been anywhere near the music business.'

Looking back, Bob believes that he became Marc's touchstone with reality.

'He was always his north London/hippie self with me, there was no pretence,' he asserts. 'But when it came to his art, he seemed to have a very clear idea of who and what he was. He was unashamed about that. And he was unique. He'd always say that he was a poet as well as a musician, and was constantly striving to create new images with words. They were phonetic sounds, he worked wonders with them. The early albums, even the album titles were very wordy and lyrical. Songs such as "By The Light of the Magical Moon" and "King of the Rumbling Spires" were inspired. Lyrics, sounds and rhythms were all his thing. It was different, and very refreshing.'

Harris still has the book of poetry which Marc published in 1969.

'The feeling, mood and atmosphere at that time was very conducive to what he was doing, and he threw himself into it wholeheartedly. But pretty soon, he found himself in a niche that was almost entirely his own. I don't think he ever stopped thinking of himself as a poet, as well as a musician. But he always, *always*, wanted to be a star.'

If the overview persists of that period in Marc's musical development of a pop artist in 'fake hippie' mode, using 'the scene' and its movers and shakers to further his own cause, it was his infamous falling-out with John Peel which sparked this misunderstanding.

'But that was after Marc was accused of having dumped him,' Jeff Dexter points out. 'Marc *didn't* dump John, actually. Fame got in the way of their relationship, that was all. It got silly and childish and hurtful, and we all felt really bad about it at the time. It needn't have happened.'

'John Peel championed Marc and Tyrannosaurus Rex until "Ride a White Swan",' says BBC Radio 2 producer and record collector Phil Swern, a close friend of Peel's – and with whom I go back further than my date of birth, it sometimes seems.

'Until they had a hit, that is. This was John's thing, he was always doing that with bands. Once they crossed over into the commercial mainstream, that tended to be it, for him. "They don't need my help anymore," he'd say, and he'd be onto the next thing. I always found that rather strange,' Phil goes on.

'I remember him doing more or less exactly the same thing to The Move, too. Loads of these acts were on *Top Gear* with him. A lot of DJs hang onto the artists they "discover", and ride on the coat-tails of their success. John was really anti all that, as much as to the idea that anyone would think he was even remotely like that. Not that he really cared what people thought of him – so it was all a conundrum.'

'Fame is a terrible monster,' Dexter shrugs. 'It consumes all your time. It takes away your individuality. It makes people think differently about you, as much as it makes you think differently about yourself. Both sides lose perspective. There's a perfectly simple explanation for what happened. John just couldn't get hold of Marc whenever he wanted to any more, once the bright lights kicked in. Marc got busy, and John got miffed.

'"Just go round there and knock on his door, that's what *we* have to do," we used to say to him. But John wouldn't. It's a peculiar kind of pride that some people have. Once the rocket goes up, your whole life changes. It's all-consuming. You're on call twenty five hours a day.'

But all that was to come.

Exit Simon Napier-Bell, who never got the point of the underground anyway, and who could not envisage a place for himself in it – still less as the manager of a hippy-dippy duo called Tyrannosaurus Rex. Theirs was a most amicable divorce.[4]

Enter John Peel at Middle Earth, all things *Lord of the Rings* being all the rage at the time, as well as the primary influence now over Marc Bolan's songwriting. Thanks to Peel's and Dexter's combined efforts, Tyrannosaurus Rex were virtually in residence on the club's weekend bill for the best part of a year. It was the kind of exposure and promotion mere money couldn't buy. Marc also began making regular appearances on Peel's new *Top Gear* radio show. Such was John's commitment to the cause that he began carting Marc and Steve and all their gear with him in his Mini to his DJ'ing gigs around the country.

It got better. Cue two of the most pivotal figures in Marc's existence. The first came with the key to unlock his creative brilliance. The second was to become much more than a wife.

Young American Tony Visconti had already achieved considerable musical success when he began writing and producing for the Richmond Organisation. Turning his back on his native New York and the quest for chart stardom with his wife and singing partner Siegrid, the painfully good-looking and multi-talented Brooklyn boy accepted an offer from British producer Denny Cordell – best known for The Moody Blues' 'Go Now', Procol Harum smash 'A Whiter Shade Of Pale', and his work with The Move,[5] to come to London as his assistant. This was at the height of the Summer of Love. Cordell had recently forged an unusual relationship with Essex Music in which they covered the cost of his studio time in return for copyright and publishing rights. That year, he had also gone into business with Essex Music supremo David Platz, launching a new independent production company called Straight Ahead, based at Essex's offices on Oxford Street. Further deals with EMI led to the resurrection of the Regal Zonophone label, which was to become significant in Marc's career.

Enchanted by the British music scene and determined to find himself 'the next Beatles', 23-year-old Visconti went talent-scouting one night and wandered into Middle Earth (although he remembers that it was UFO). It was there that he first saw Marc, cross-legged on the floor and singing gobbledegook. Intoxicated by the sight and sound of this charismatic elf, Visconti openly admits that he fell in love with him.

'[Marc was] . . . a very pretty man with dark curly hair, who was singing and strumming his guitar,' he writes in his excellent autobiography *Bowie, Bolan and the Brooklyn Boy*. He was wearing '. . . ragamuffin clothes: torn jeans, a torn silk shirt, with a handkerchief tied round one upper arm and a maroon waistcoat. The bongo player [Took] was dressed in a similar fashion, but he had long straight hair past his shoulders. I thought they were the "real deal", gypsy hippies that lived in a caravan somewhere in a wood on the edge of London.'

Tony goes on to describe the audience that night as having been in the grip of what appeared to be a religious experience.

'The singer sang with an intense vibrato in his voice – a warble . . . I had no idea what language they were singing in . . . I thought it could be French.'

The hairs on Tony's skin stood on end as he listened and watched, blown away by a completely new experience.

'It certainly wasn't rock'n'roll,' he says, 'and then again it wasn't folk; it was eccentric and new'.

Thus began the partnership which was to generate ten albums and embrace Marc's metamorphosis from underground folk child to the king of glam. They shared, as Tony acknowledges, some of the most wonderful experiences he has ever enjoyed in the recording studio. However, there were also lows that would take them right to the edge.

Visconti wasted no time in bringing Marc and Steve in to play to Cordell, his boss, who was suitably impressed, as was the coolest rock publicist in the business then, B.P. Fallon: 'a peculiar but not charmless little man', as rock journalist Nick Kent would remember him, 'who looked like a . . . leprechaun and spoke like an effete Irish Hobbit.' It was with Led Zeppelin that 'Beep' (as he is still known) would make his name. He just happened to be lurking on the premises that day, and Cordell coaxed him in for a listen.

Beep liked what he heard, and would eventually become T. Rex's P.R. Denny Cordell, meanwhile, made the astute observation that they should do a few demos before they signed the deal, as there was no way of telling, unless they did this, whether the Tyrannosaurus Rex magic would translate success-fully onto tape.

Soon afterwards, Visconti was introduced, in the same office, to the other musician who would change his life: Marc's chum

David Bowie. This could not have contrasted more dramatically with his first encounter with Bolan. Sparks flew, the chemistry between them on some astral plane. It was with David that Tony shared a deep rapport and exotic interests – foreign art films, Tibetan Buddhism – and with whom he would go on to co-create a classic catalogue of some of the greatest rock music ever recorded. Marc Bolan and Tyrannosaurus Rex would at first play second fiddle to Tony's adoration of Bowie. Although Visconti would describe Bolan as 'the most focused artist I've ever worked with', it was Bowie that his producer would always love.

Following lengthy rehearsals at his Lexham Gardens flat, Tony Visconti recorded the debut Tyrannosaurus Rex album *My People Were Fair . . .* at Advision Studios in just four days on a shoestring budget. The intricate sleeve artwork was by George Underwood, the school friend who had punched the pigment out of David Bowie's eye. The LP was released on Regal Zonophone through EMI that July. John Peel read a Bolan fairytale as the closing track. 'Frowning Atahuallpa (My Inca Love)' also featured one of the earliest Hare Krishna chants on a British pop record, two years ahead of George Harrison's 'My Sweet Lord'.[6]

As Tyrannosaurus Rex began studio sessions at Trident for their second album, Marc started writing a never-to-be realised epic, his own *Lord of the Rings*. August saw the release of their single 'One Inch Rock/Salamanda Palaganda', which would earn them a Number 28 placing, their sole Top 30 hit. The band played gigs in Belgium, appeared at the first Isle of Wight festival, and made a string of live appearances across Europe and around the UK.

The follow-up album *Prophets, Seers & Sages . . .* was made in eighteen days, was released only three months after the first, and failed to chart. This did not make them failures, however: their underground following was now impressive, and their fans couldn't get enough.

Both *My People* . . . and *Prophets* . . . were wonderful, melodic and exotic albums; toyshop jumbles of curios and little 'extras', such as Steve Took's 'Pixiphone'™ which he had purchased in Harrods' children's department on the cheap. Budgetary constraints inspired Bolan and Took to adapt their own voices as a whole range of inventive additional 'instruments' and quirky sounds. From screech to scat to chatter, from mumble to croon, one moment a brain-splitting convulsion, the next a humming-bird's wing, it was all there. These albums were frustratingly under-appreciated at the time.

'Marc was just grateful to get a chance to go into the studio at all,' recalled Visconti. 'In those days, the industry really disliked him. John Peel, Jeff Dexter and I were pretty much his only supporters.'

Now that he had met his enabler, Marc had only to encounter his muse. She wasn't far. He found the original love of his life the first time he visited Peter Jenner, Andrew King and the founding members of Pink Floyd, all partners in Blackhill Enterprises. These were serious players, too. Jenner had a first class honours degree in economics from Cambridge University, and was lecturing, aged 21, at the London School of Economics when he met students Syd Barrett, Roger Waters, Nick Mason and Richard Wright.[7] He quit to work with the band, and staged the first celebrated free concerts in London's Hyde Park.

Barrett, whose tortured genius inspired the band's surreal singles 'Arnold Layne' and 'See Emily Play', as well as their 1967 debut album *The Piper At The Gates Of Dawn*, was an exquisitely broody late-Sixties incarnation of the Shelley-Byron Romantic poet. Velvet-clad and long-haired, Syd was also a favourite muse of Mick Rock, the coolest photographer of the era, who would become famous as 'The Man Who Shot the Seventies'.

Syd went around looking tormented because he was. Those wide and terrified eyes were no act. An artist as well as a musician, his potential was incalculable, probably greater than Bowie's, but he took more drugs than his body or mind could stand. He lost the plot.

He splashed his mental anguish onto countless canvasses at his Cambridgeshire home, but never managed to paint away the psychosis. Much in his superlative songwriting pre-echoed Marc's own poetic meanderings: 'Like Lennon in his pomp,' said rock writer Rob Chapman, 'Barrett bent language out of shape until it made a new kind of sense.'

Tyrannosaurus Rex were suddenly well on their way, playing serious venues now: the South Bank's Purcell Room and even the Royal Albert Hall. Jenner and King became aware of them, spotted huge potential, and invited them in to discuss management. A short-lived deal was struck which saw Marc and Steve playing a string of UK dates including the Royal Festival Hall, where they were supported by David Bowie, as well as opening for Pink Floyd at Jenner's free Hyde Park gig.

It was in the Blackhill Enterprises offices that Marc met and fell head over heels for Floyd employee June Child. June, born in August 1943, was four years older than Marc.

'She was "the older woman",' says Jeff Dexter, 'a fact which always bothered Marc's parents, Phyllis and Sid. June made a lot of effort with them, and they got on ok – but they were suspicious of her. In those days, the man was always "supposed" to be older than the woman.'

Although she was at times inclined to give the impression of 'coming from money', and counted a number of aristocrats as friends, she and her sister Fiona hailed from an ordinary Fulham family. With a father who worked for the books, journals and stationery retailer W.H. Smith, there was no extra for school fees. June was educated modestly at Holland Park Comprehensive. Before Blackhill, she'd worked for a company which imported fabrics, and then for a photographer. It was when she and her boyfriend, jewellery-maker Mick Milligan, found themselves sharing a Edbrooke Road, West London flat with Floyd man Peter Jenner that June, between jobs, began fielding phone calls and helping out with band business. As Pink Floyd's fame and fortune increased, the flatmates grew out of their bohemian lifestyle.

June began working full-time at the office, acting as receptionist and secretary, driving their van to gigs – Jeff Dexter reports that she was a brilliant driver – and eventually handling the finances.

June projected a sweet but practical personality, and charmed most with whom she came into contact. She was striking rather than beautiful, with long blonde hair and shark-blue eyes. To Marc, it has been written, she was 'the most gorgeous bird he'd ever seen'. Her style was sexy, her manner frank and self-assured. She was also, according to those who met both, a dead ringer for Terry Whipman.

Crucially, as well as having dated Eric Clapton, and having remained on good terms with him, June had been Syd Barrett's girlfriend. Was this the deal-maker? Marc must have salivated on hearing it. His vampiric inclinations stirred. Who knew what kind of inspiration he could suck out of Barrett via his ex!

'Syd was very special in an extraordinary way,' June once said in an interview about her former partner. 'He wrote wonderful songs, the lyrics were incredible. He was very much the creator of (Pink Floyd) in those days. When he would sit at home and write a song, he'd think of what the drummer ought to play, how the bass line should be. He played good rhythm as well as lead, and he'd know what he wanted to hear.

'He was also like a model. Everything he wore fitted him perfectly. And he had this quality that was like a candle about to be snuffed out. He took lots of LSD. Some people can cope with it in their lives, but if you take three or four trips every day . . .'

June went through many of Syd's acid breakdowns with him, as she revealed before her death in August 1994. After their relationship had ended, he would still turn up at her home at all hours, covered in mud following a rampage in Holland Park, or soaked to the bone after a stretch of sleeping on the streets. Pink Floyd played more than eighty shows between May and September 1967, many of which were two-gigs-a-night engagements. Relentless touring eventually took its toll.

'Once Syd lost his grip,' she said, 'I feel they were really wicked to him. Perhaps had they been kinder, in those early days of his breakdown . . . he may not have been hit so hard.'

The minor complication for Marc and June's 'love at first sight' was that he was still 'officially' dating Miss Whipman. It was time at last for poor, long-suffering Terry to bite the dust. Not that Marc himself had much say in the matter.

'June went to Terry's flat with £500 in cash [around £6,500 today. One wonders how she raised such a sum]', says Caron Willans. She and Danielz had tea with Terry in April 1997, after Terry saw Danielz on television, got in touch, and came to their home.

'She offered it to Terry if she'd stop seeing Marc! In the end, Terry refused the money but was fed up with it all. Marc didn't want to lose June because of her connections with Pink Floyd, so Terry decided never to see Marc again. She was very upset,' Caron reports.

'She did follow his career. She met him again by chance in mid-1973, when Marc was still with June, but had just started seeing Gloria. They spent the afternoon and evening together, and even went to the cinema. Marc was in disguise for the outing, with his hair tucked into a hat.'

Terry told Caron and Danielz that she didn't like the way Marc had 'turned out'.

'He wasn't a vegetarian anymore. He seemed to love his fame and wealth, and was very materialistic by then,' says Caron.

Terry never saw him again.

When she was told by a friend that Marc had died, Terry was deeply upset. The friend suggested that she sell her letters and poems from Marc, and the story of their love affair. Terry was horrified by the suggestion. Years later, however, she did offload some possessions to Christie's, as she and her mother were struggling to get by. Last heard of, she was living a simple lifestyle in a south east London council house.

'She described herself as a white witch,' says Caron. 'To us, she looked like June. She was clearly a hippie, with hippie ideals. She didn't like material things, and wasn't interested in money. Terry told us that 'Hot Love' was about her. She said she had to fight to get her name on the first Tyrannosaurus Rex album (which was all she wanted, not money), as she was still seeing Marc then – but that June tried to talk Marc out of putting it on.'

'We'd known each other only a short while when I asked her home to tea late one afternoon at my parents' prefab in Wimbledon', Marc would say of June, in an interview. 'The sun was bright and hot. We sat with our tea on the lawn. After we had held hands, there was silence for a while. Then I said, "June – I think I love you." She replied quietly, "I feel the same way about you, Marc."

'June was the best thing that had ever happened to Marc

– until then, at least,' insists Jeff Dexter, who clearly worships the memory of her, but does not wish to undermine the importance of Gloria.

'She believed in him from the first moment, and she loved him to death. She'd learned her ropes, she knew the business inside out. She'd seen Syd and others fall victim to the madness. She was never going to let that happen to Marc.'

Genuinely in love? Manipulative minx with her own best interests at heart? Or a combination of the two? You decide. Whatever, it was June who owned Marc from then on. At least, she thought that she did.

With their respective squeezes out of the way, they became an item – camping out in June's van on Wimbledon Common while they looked for a place to live.

9

Dazzle Dawn Man

Real life rolled on. Against a backdrop of Vietnam, American civil rights activism, the assassination of Martin Luther King in Memphis, Northern Irish revolt, French and Italian socialist uprisings, the Israeli-Palestinian conflict, the Cold War, and fierce radical feminists versus the patriarchy, baby boomers raged against everything they could lay their hands on throughout 1968. Cultural perspective and public opinion were whacked for six by such seismic events, and songwriters were overwhelmed with subject matter. Whether paid-up peacenik or a rebel of the cause, there was a soundtrack for everyone. But still the mainstream ignored Tyrannosaurus Rex. Marc had no interest in reflecting or reacting to the gloom consuming the planet. He was the antidote to it. His music was escapism. Bolan never wanted a revolution, he wasn't looking to change the world. He was never moved to write songs about politics, unlike many – not least Lennon and McCartney, who started their own record label, Apple, that year, and whose song 'Revolution' was directly inspired by the protests.[1, 2] Relatively few appreciated Marc's kookiness, or got the point of his extended-play *Midsummer's Night Scene*.

'I first became aware of him thanks to John Peel playing

Tyrannosaurus Rex, who were quickly adopted by a few of my fifth form school mates as their precious cult band,' remembers David Stark, publisher of Songlink International.

'It was oh-so-trendy for them to walk the corridors and changing rooms of our public school in Elstree clutching their cherished copies of *My People Were Fair* . . . , but to be honest, I didn't really get it all. I was much more into The Beatles, The Who, Jimi Hendrix, The Kinks, The Move and all the chart bands of the day.[3]

'However, I did quite like their single "Debora". I ended up seeing Bolan perform with Steve Took shortly after the single was released, at the very first Hyde Park free concert on 29 June 1968. They played second on the bill to Pink Floyd, the other acts being Roy Harper and Jethro Tull. I can't say I have any great memories of that performance, but I certainly embraced this new experience of hearing live rock music for free in the centre of London.'

He didn't have the time of day for most of Bolan's folk stuff, admits David.

'I equated it with another cult of the times, *Lord of the Rings*, which those same pals were reading avidly, presumably while listening to their Tyrannosaurus Rex albums.'

When June and Marc found their first home – a tiny attic in a house on Blenheim Crescent, Ladbroke Grove with a shared toilet, no hot running water and with only 'Poon' (the Pan statue which Riggs O'Hara had given Marc) to brighten the place up – life began to fall into place. Their set routine included two baths a week: one at Marc's parents', the other at Tony Visconti's. To Tony's flat, Marc would cart his carrier bag of LPs. Countless happy hours were spent devouring The Beatles and The Beach Boys.

'There were a few nights when David [Bowie] came over and we jammed,' recalled Tony Visconti in his autobiography.

'Marc and David on guitars and me on bass. It never ever occurred to me to run the tape recorder, this was such early days and quite honestly I didn't have that much tape; it wasn't like it was big-time. Also, if I had bought tape, it would have blown the food budget, and we wouldn't have eaten.'

Neither Marc nor David was into 'hashish', Visconti recalled. Nor did Marc take psychedelic drugs, Tony insisted, so he wasn't 'hearing' colours or 'seeing' sounds the way so many were at the time. What they couldn't afford, they wisely never craved? Jeff Dexter begs to differ.

'Marc did join in the chain when everyone was smoking a joint, but he never inhaled,' he says. 'He didn't like smoking at all, not even cigarettes. It made him feel ill. When we used to try and smoke as kids – because you had to, because we wanted to look naughty and big, it's what boys did – he'd get really dizzy. It made me feel sick too!

'It was never that Marc disapproved of drugs, he just couldn't really do them. There was always plenty of dope about, everyone was doing it everywhere, but it wasn't his thing.'

This went against the grain of the times, Jeff explains, because rolling a joint was 'a really big deal'.

'It was like a sacrament to us. You did that, or you smoked the peace pipe together, the way the American Indians did. This was all part of our ritual, which was an issue for Marc. It was something he could never properly take part in.'

As for acid, Marc never did it, Jeff insists.

'I'd put money on it. Apart from the one occasion, when he got spiked at the Hanover Square launch party of British *Rolling Stone* magazine – he tripped so badly that June was terrified he was going to die – Marc never took LSD. He may have pretended he had, again to look big. But I knew Marc like the back of my hand, and there's no way he did it voluntarily. He was too afraid of the demons inside himself. The madness. He was terrified that LSD would awaken all that.'

'Marc had never had acid in his life, and with a mind like his, like Syd, it was the worst thing . . . that you could possibly take,' June told writer Jonathon Green for his memoir of the Sixties, *Days in the Life.*

'As for him disapproving of me and others taking drugs,' adds Jeff, 'that never happened. He accepted drug-taking as part of the culture. The only thing he couldn't stand was people getting so completely out of their heads that they lost the plot. That was why he had it up to here with Steve Took.'

Tragically ironic, then, that before too long, Marc would be doing just as many drugs himself, but of a different kind. Jeff Dexter cannot explain the change of heart. It is perhaps worth noting that June ran with a much more sophisticated crowd than Marc had hitherto been used to – many of whom, Eric Clapton not least, were experimenting with the hardest drugs available . . . mainly, perhaps, because they could afford to buy them. What is not in doubt is that Marc would have been exposed to high-level drug-use on countless occasions. He was young, he was impressionable, and he wanted to impress. You do the math.

Their social life in those days consisted mainly of going to friends' places, drinking cheap wine and playing music, because they didn't have the money to do much else. There were a few picnic trips to Stonehenge and Glastonbury Tor with John Peel and his girlfriend Sheila, and, significantly, a burgeoning friendship with Bob Harris, with whom Marc would trawl the record shops in search of oddities and rarities.

'One thing led to another,' recalls Bob. 'Marc and June and

my wife Sue and I started hanging out together – mostly in our flats.'

According to *Honey* magazine at the time, late Sixties Notting Hill consisted of 'scruffy streets filled with big houses filled with bedsits filled with either enormous black families or else pale young people ... who burn joss sticks and spend their lives trying to get it together.

'This is where the underground is, with all its religions, philosophies, prejudices, freedoms, newspapers, organisations and music. And this is where Marc Bolan lives ... up through a house where bits of prams and peeling paintwork set the tone of the place, in a flat which is all plain colours with music drifting out of the bedroom and a nice bunch of flowers on the scrubbed wood table, and the smell of incense hanging in the air around the colour television set.'

The 'Bolan Child' (as both fans and journalists began calling Marc after finding out where he lived and noticing that the street doorbell label stated 'BOLAN, CHILD' - the surnames of the flat's two tenants) 'sits at the table ... in velvet trousers and a little jumper which ties up in the front, and in shoes with straps on them' – the brightly-coloured leather Anello & Davide tap-dancing shoes which would become one of his staples at the height of his fame.

'Marc and I loved to have Record Hops,'[4] says Bob Harris. 'We'd just get out loads of singles, and play tracks we loved on the record player. Marc had a phenomenal knowledge of rock'n'roll, the music of the Fifties and Sixties.

'He could have been a DJ himself. He had a great collection of singles, it was really something. If all this sounds idyllic, it really was. June used to cook, and the place would be filled with delicious aromas of food. The joss sticks would be burning, June and

Sue would be chatting, and Marc and I would be on the floor with records all over the place. To us, it was heaven.'

'Marc was ever-present around Notting Hill in those days. Everywhere you went, you tripped over him,' remembers Judy Dyble, the first female voice of folk rock group Fairport Convention, who lived in the area during her late teens.

'Notting Hill then was an odd place. The Ladbroke Grove end was full of houses divided into flats and squats, and you didn't want to go there late at night. Then you had the area consisting of Elgin Crescent, All Saints Road, Blenheim Crescent, Arundel Gardens – a mixture of half-hippie and half upwardly-mobile people. The locals all went to the market during the week to get their vegetables, and on Saturdays we all crowded with the incomers into Portobello for the "tat". Yes, we had "vintage" even in those days, but to us it was stuff from the 1920s and 1930s. Nowadays, people are buying as late 1960s, early 1970s clothes which I wouldn't have been seen dead in at the time!

'Today's view of life then is all a bit rose-tinted,' says Judy, of the area world-renowned as London's answer to New York's Greenwich Village or San Francisco's Haight-Ashbury – a 'glamorous enclave' of artists, musicians, fashion designers, drug-dealers, cool drop-outs and misfits, as well as the stomping ground of future music magnates such as Richard Branson (Virgin) and Chris Blackwell (Island Records).

'Life in that neighbourhood was actually very hard,' she remembers. 'There were a lot of distressed people living there, many of them victims of the drug culture.

'We all had a go at marijuana, but I stopped there, I was too scared to try anything else. LSD, "acid", had screwed a lot of people up. Cocaine and heroin would become much more prevalent during the Seventies, when alcohol also made a big comeback.

'Notting Hill is remembered as a "village", but I can tell you it wasn't at all a country-style village, the kind where everyone knows everyone and where you all say hello,' Judy reveals. 'It was a place where you learned how not to look people in the eye as you walked along the street. The hippy-dippy airy-fairy folk and the alternative anarchic lot were not a happy mix.

'Everyone went around saying "I won't live long," or "I'll be dead by the time I'm 30, 40" – it wasn't *just* Marc! The feeling was that it didn't much matter what the world was turning into, because we wouldn't be around to see it. It was all about the here and now. No one could envisage being old. We lived for the day.'

Many remember the smells of the late Sixties, as much as the sounds: sweaty armpit disguised with pungent patchouli oil; damp duffle-coat; the sour-milk stench of sodden sheepskin; the nauseous, all-pervasive waft of weed.

When Judy started singing with Fairport Convention, the band played frequently at Middle Earth.

'Marc was on the same kind of circuit as us, but we didn't get to know each other intimately. In a band, in those days, you'd get up at 2pm, whizz up a just-built motorway in a clapped-out van to do a university gig somewhere, and go home via a few drinks at the Speakeasy or somewhere. We'd bump into each other at 3am and say hi.'

What did she think of Tyrannosaurus Rex?

'I didn't quite see the attraction,' she admits. 'I didn't hear what his hordes of fans appeared to be hearing. I couldn't get over the vibrato effect of his voice.'

Judy's husband, the DJ and scene-ster Simon Stable played bongos on Ten Years After and Bridget St John albums (under his real name Count Simon de la Bedoyère) and had a popular record shop on Portobello Road called 'Simon's Stable', where he'd bring in the imports.

'Independent record shops were very important in those days,' Judy points out, 'because DJs went out with the bands, played records at the start and during the interval to keep the crowds amused, and they were constantly looking for new stuff to play. Musicians and DJs were always in the shop. It was a real hub, and all very exciting and upbeat. Marc was an enthusiastic member of that scene, as was his future publicist, B.P. Fallon. 'Beep' would bring Marc round to ours, Simon was also writing bits for the *NME*, and snippets about him would start to appear in the papers. Marc was quite an operator, he invariably had a plan – and so much energy.'

June was always a favourite of Judy's.

'She would often be with Marc and Beep when they came to our flat. A couple of times we went round to their place to listen to stuff. She had her head screwed on. She kept Marc focused and out of trouble, but she wasn't a control freak. She clearly loved him and she was very nice.'

Perhaps too nice.

Marc and June soon graduated to the more spacious flat below the attic in Blenheim Crescent, where they had much more room to entertain.

They left Blackhill Enterprises that autumn, apparently under a cloud: something to do with them having been found in Andrew King's bed while he and his bride were on their honeymoon. Undaunted, the pair struck a new management deal with the Bryan Morrison Agency, based at 16 Bruton Place in London's West End, where the band's first fan club would also be launched in the New Year. Next door was the Revolution Club, where Judy Dyble worked as membership secretary.[5] Before Christmas

1968, Tony, Marc and Steve convened at Trident Studios in St Anne's Court, Soho, to record some early sessions for the single 'Pewtor Suitor', as well as some album tracks intended for the third Tyrannosaurus Rex album, *Unicorn*.

In January 1969, Tyrannosaurus Rex debuted their *For The Lion and the Unicorn in the Oak Forests Of Faun* show, at Queen Elizabeth Hall on London's South Bank – supported by sitar player Vytas Serelis, and by David Bowie, who had been studying with Lindsay Kemp and was now a mime artist. When the show reached the Fairfield Halls in Croydon, south London, it was attended by Marc's brother, Harry Feld – who also nipped across the road to the Greyhound pub, that same night, to watch Status Quo.

Marc had never lost his enthusiasm for poets and poetry. He had even started to quote his own during Tyrannosaurus Rex gigs, and made a point of attending live readings given by writers he admired – including Brian Patten, one of the famous Liverpool Poets who, along with Adrian Henri and Roger McGough, dominated the Sixties scene.[6] Brian lived next door to Judy Dyble when she was flat-sharing in Notting Hill Gate and about to begin recording with Jackie McAuley as the duo Trader Horne.[7]

'My room had a spiral staircase leading down to one of those wonderful communal gardens you get in Notting Hill,' recalls Judy. 'Next door in the basement lived Brian Patten. He was sweet, looked like an elf, and always spoke in poetry, naturally, like breathing. He took my breath away. I used to look after his typewriter whenever he had to go away.'

Brian gave Judy a poem which she set to music years later, 'Enchanted Garden', probably inspired by memories of the little backyard they shared.

★ ★ ★

Given the nature of the Notting Hill scene at that time, it was inevitable that Bolan's and Patten's paths would cross.

'I met Marc at one of the Roundhouse events in 1967 or 1968,' Brian confirms. 'It was not long after *Little Johnny's Confessions*, my first book of poems, was published. There was no deep conversation – you couldn't hold a conversation in the place back then. Those events were rather chaotic, held in semi-darkness; most of the audience wandered around pretty stoned. After that, I'd bump into him in the pubs on Portobello Road. I'd started giving poetry readings quite widely by 1966, and maybe he came to a couple of those early readings. Sometime after my second or third collection of poems [*Notes To The Hurrying Man*, 1969/*The Irrelevant Song*, 1971] were published, I got a postcard from him, saying how much he liked the poems. It is lovely to think of him reading them.'

Almost certainly seduced by elfin Brian's success and profile – although Patten maintains with great modesty that he could never lay claim to having influenced Marc's writing – as well as recognising similarities in their looks, Marc's enthusiasm for poetry-writing naturally soared. His own fanciful collection *The Warlock of Love*, published by Bryan Morrison's Lupus Publishing Company in March 1969 and containing lines like 'His cloak of caution, threadbare and patterned, fell/To the moorland mire like a lamented autumn leaf/He dribbled his thoughts like a mastiff . . .' was a muddled journey from Narnia to Camelot to Middle-earth and back again, yet was surprisingly well-received – probably, as John Peel remembered wryly, 'because we were all a bit beholden to the rule of *The Emperor's New Clothes*.'

In other words, if discerning critics who also happen to be friends refrain from telling an artist the truth about inferior work, but instead pour praise all over him, what reason is there for him to fear that it's 'a pile of shite'? Whatever: despite the fact that 'The Warlock of Love' is essentially a poetic trifle and 'Tolkien-lite', it is a highly sought-after collectible today.

The greatest irony might have been that, despite his self-declared 'passion' for Tolkien, Marc had never read *The Hobbit* or *Lord of The Rings* in his life. Such works were far longer, denser and more intellectually demanding than his thresholds of patience could ever tolerate. Once June arrived on the scene, however, it was a different story. Having read and got the measure of Marc's poems, she was able to interpret his needs. This made her all the more indispensable. Lying in bed night after night, she would read Tolkien to him. Marc would absorb, in broad brush-strokes, as much as he required to be able to write 'in a similar vein' himself.

Internationally acclaimed Canadian mythology and ecology writer and poet David Day, best-known for his literary criticism of the works of J.R.R. Tolkien including *The Tolkien Bestiary* (1978) and *Tolkien: The Illustrated Encyclopaedia* (1992), has long followed Marc's evident obsession with the writer.

'Marc Boland [sic] and I were born the same year, just two weeks apart,' the author tells me. 'I remember vividly that he died in a car crash only a fortnight after I moved to live in London in 1977. Strangely enough at exactly the same time, on my 30th birthday, I began work on my first book on J.R.R. Tolkien. I guess working with a guy who changed his name to (Steve) Peregrin Took, it would be impossible for him not to have Tolkien as an influence![8]

'I don't think Bolan would have arrived at Tolkien, had it not been for Donovan's forays into Celtic Rock,' he states, controversially. 'Not that I think that Donovan arrived where *he* did through Tolkien, but through his interest in original Celtic myth, folklore and song, i.e., some of the same sources as Tolkien had for *his* writing.

'In terms of bringing the subject matter of Celtic mysticism into the British music scene,' Day explains, 'Donovan was a major force: as evidenced by his brilliant "Season of the Witch".'[9] Despite Bolan's tribute to Dylan, I suspect that Donovan was secretly far more influential. Stylistically, of course, the glam rock scene which Bolan would move on to was the antithesis of Donovan's soft-sell, tree-hugger-hippie style. Bolan's highly-charged electric T. Rex music was entirely different from what he'd been doing in Tyrannosaurus Rex, but he was good at picking up what we nowadays call "buzz words" that were around in popular culture. Often they were random and out of context, but somehow Bolan made them work for him.'

According to Day, Tolkien, who died in Bournemouth, England, on 2 September 1973, aged 81, loathed modern music and would not have appreciated Bolan.

'Except for the subject matter of Celtic mysticism, Bolan and Tolkien had nothing in common musically,' Day insists. 'By "modern", I mean written after the 19th century – and even then, J.R.R. had no time for Beethoven! In poetry, he didn't care for much of anything after Chaucer – so there was little they could have touched base on there.'

Soon the dinosaur would be whimpering its swansong . . . while in the wings, a gilded bird of prey . . .

Eagle in a Sunbeam

On the brink of stardom, but with little sign yet of the flunkies, fawners and flatterers who would soon invade his world, Marc confounded his critics, for the moment at least, by keeping his head on. A major contributing factor here was his close relationship with his mother, Phyllis, and to a lesser extent with his father, Sid – both of whom worshipped their son and encouraged him to come home whenever he wished.

'He talked about anything and everything with my mum,' says brother Harry. 'All the stuff he was keeping from those closest to him, it would all come pouring out with her. There were no barriers, no taboo subjects. He was never embarrassed and was always open; he could talk about anything with Mum.

'He also dropped the showbiz accent when he was at home with us. Our accent was always Cockney. Behind closed doors, with his family, Marc's was too. He'd pop round on his bike sometimes. And if no one was coming for lunch or anything, he might just lie down and sleep all day long. He said he never really slept properly anywhere the way he did under Mum and Dad's roof. He'd tell Mum that he "wasn't in, not for anybody." So even if David Bowie came round to see him, Mum would just tell him "he's not here"!'

Of June, Tony Visconti, David Bowie and Jeff Dexter, only Dexter would remain at Marc's side until the end. But he was not alone. There was one other devoted companion who stuck by Marc through thick and thin, but whose worth is all too often overlooked.

Mick O'Halloran, like Dexter, was from the wrong side of the tracks made good. A south London boy with family connections to the underworld who might well have taken the 'easy' route and rascalled away his life, Mick chose a clean living, married young, started a family – his son is called Little Mark, whom June taught to play chess – and found employment as a roadie.

'Mick is the most gentle man around, a total teddy bear,' is Dexter's description. 'Marc *loved* Mickey. In fact, he worshipped him.'

Mick worked for The Rolling Stones and Pink Floyd before joining the team of The Love Affair – a London-based R&B, soul and pop group formed in 1966, whose first single 'She Smiled Sweetly' was penned by Keith Richard and Mick Jagger. Mick had also toured with The Small Faces, and with Roy Orbison. He met Marc through Charlie Watkins at WEM.

Mick and I are introduced to each other by both Jeff Dexter and Danielz. Having suffered a stroke which has left him infirm, he was most reluctant to see me. He has often been misquoted over the years, and he finds the interview experience stressful in the extreme. He and his wife have since invited me to stay on the Isle of Wight, where they now live.

'When Charlie first heard Tyrannosaurus Rex,' explains Jeff Dexter, 'he thought they were so good, he just gave them a P.A. free until they could pay for it. If ever Marc or June needed more, it was always there for them, and never mind the money. He really believed in them, and went everywhere with Tyrannosaurus Rex and early T. Rex. Charlie and Mick

O'Halloran were like brothers. Every new gadget that came up, the first three off the production line would go to Mick, to Marc, and to me.'

'I was always down at Charlie Watkins's in Kennington, picking up equipment,' recalls Mick. 'One of the staff there was a woman called Pinkie. She knew I was out working nearly every night, but that I was married with a young child and that it wasn't ideal. Pinkie asked me one day if I was thinking of changing jobs. "I know a couple who come in here quite a lot", she said. "They're looking for a new roadie, and they only work once a week – universities and underground clubs, at week ends. They don't use big equipment, and they're really easy-going," she added.

'She meant Marc and June. Marc was already quite famous on the underground scene, but his was not the kind of music I liked to listen to. My taste in those days was soul – Marvin Gaye and Smokey Robinson.

'Pinkie spoke to June the next time she came in, and arranged for me to go up and meet them at their top flat in a big house in Portobello. This was late 1968. I went along for the interview and rang the bell. Someone shouted out of the window, "Are you Mickey?" I said I was. Down came the big bunch of keys, and I was told to let myself in.

'As I was half-way up the stairs,' Mick remembers, 'there was Marc, coming down the stairs to greet me. He was so small and polite, like a little elf. Beautiful. Really clear skin, not a blemish on it. His hair was lovely. He was wearing dungarees, and a bright yellow jumper – and I mean *bright yellow*. I'd never seen anyone like him in my life. I was really nervous of him at first,' he confesses, 'but I needn't have been.'

As for the flat, Mickey says it seemed 'like a dolls' house'.

'You wouldn't believe how small their place was. They only

had two rooms. There was an archway with a little space beyond it, no more than a cupboard really, without a door. He'd go in there, sit on a cushion and play his music.

'June offered me a drink, and we had a chat. We clicked immediately. "We'll start you on £25 a week, would that be all right?"' she said.

'It was fantastic. That was the same money as I was getting working for The Love Affair, but that was every night and this was only once a week – never dreaming that the band would explode so soon, the way it did.

'"We'll give you a fortnight's trial," June said.

'"Tell you what: I'll give *you* a fortnight's trial!" I joked back. Marc liked that, it made him laugh. He was very, very humble at that time, and he did as he was told. As I went to leave, he said, "I'm really looking forward to working with you." I could tell that he meant it.'

From that day forward, Mick was hooked.

'They were a super couple, him and June. I was very big at that time. [Since his illness, Mick's a shadow of his former self.] June used to call me Leadweight O'Halloran, while Marc would call me Mickey or Micko. I called him Son – because I felt very protective towards him. I was only a few years older, but at times I did feel like a father to him. He certainly treated me that way, whenever he needed to.

'I loved working for him,' sighs Mick. 'I never stopped loving it. Not even when it all got crazy, and Marc lost the plot.'

As Tyrannosaurus Rex's reputation grew, they began to play regular gigs on Sunday afternoons at the Roundhouse.

'There would be Floyd, Elton John, The Who . . . it was a great venue,' Mick remembers. 'Marc would pitch up, sit cross-legged and do his thing, and the fans would go wild for him. He'd get standing ovations, the works. He loved it, we all did. We had a lovely relationship with all the people we worked with.'

Was there a favourite?

'Tony Visconti', Mick responds, without hesitation. 'I liked him very much, he was a good bloke. We'd have our ups and downs, naturally – usually when he tried to advise me on certain things, but I never took much notice. I used to feel he was imped-ing on my situation – ok, bossing me about – say when I was setting up equipment or something. I remember having an idea once to go back to Charlie, get two amps, and make a stereo one. We'd bodge them up with separate leads. We were experiment-ing. On the early recordings, you can hear the guitar going from left to right. The only other people doing similar things at the time were Pink Floyd.'

With new managers David Enthoven and John Gaydon of E.G. Records now (briefly) in charge – the artist management and independent label who cared for the career of King Crimson, and who would become famous for their associa-tion with Roxy Music – Tyrannosaurus Rex's future was beginning to look bright.

Marc's partnership with Steve Took was by now on wafer-thin ice, on account of the latter having immersed himself in the acid-driven end of Ladbroke Grove. With Took demanding more money, greater influence and that his own compositions be recorded (but with Marc disinclined to share vinyl space), the writing was on the wall.

Shortly after Visconti commenced work on the *Unicorn* album, which would include one of Marc's Woodland Stories read by John Peel, came a significant turning point: Marc's purchase of his own electric guitar. His legendary white Fender Stratocaster – complete with a multi-coloured teardrop symbol created specially for him by Tony's girlfriend Liz, which she had made using an enamelling kit purchased at Hamley's toy shop – was perhaps an inevitable move. Not only had his spell in John's Children whetted his appetite, but he'd had the luxury of being able to play around with electric instruments whenever he wanted to, in his producer's flat. There was also the influence of guitar heroes such as Hendrix, Townshend, Beck, and Clapton – June had already introduced Marc to Eric – and the direction in which rock music generally was moving.

It was during *Unicorn* that Visconti first met and worked with exuberant African-American actress and singer Marsha Hunt, who was appearing in the London stage production of the Broadway musical *Hair*: a racially-integrated 'tribal love-rock' piece which celebrated the counter culture, the sexual revolution and the peace movement. With nudity, obscenity and blatant depiction of drug use, the 'shocking', 'risqué' show also starred Elaine Paige, Floella Benjamin, Paul Nicholas (with whom Marsha was enjoying a 'glorious fling'), Oliver Tobias, Richard O'Brien and Tim Curry.[1] It spawned such hits as 'The Age of Aquarius' and 'Let The Sun Shine In', and was described at the time as 'the strongest anti-war statement ever written'.

Marsha had fronted various minor groups, and had sung backing vocals for Alexis Korner. She was also a stable mate of Jimi Hendrix.

'Jimi and I shared something,' she was fond of saying. 'Black Americans who came to London, were transformed and repackaged for the US. Although I never became successful there, and he did.'

She was signed to Track Records, began recording with Tony Visconti, and caused a major sensation when she performed her minor hit single (a cover of Dr John's 'Walk On Gilded Splinters') on *Top of The Pops*. Not because she silenced any lambs with her talent, but because one of her breasts flopped out of her top on television. Visconti thinks that the BBC may have banned the original rock chick (a description which irritated the pants off her). Given that they had a producer in common, the likelihood of Marc's and Marsha's stars colliding could be only a matter of time.

'It wasn't the idea of Marc having sex with another woman that would upset June,' says Jeff Dexter.

'It was betrayal and secrecy that did that. They *were* each other, you see, Marc and June. They were as one. She was fine with whatever he got up to – just as long as he always told her about it.'

Marsha had been seeking material for her long-drawn-out, perennially-forthcoming album – which she could only record late at night, after she came off stage. Tony pitched up one evening with two early Marc/Tyrannosaurus Rex compositions, for which Marsha expressed instant enthusiasm: 'Hot Rod Mama' (she sang 'Poppa') and 'Stacey Grove'.

Marsha would also cut 'Hippy Gumbo'. Marc, when he heard that such a high-profile rock chick was recording his songs, insisted on coming to the studio to meet her. It was inevitable that he would offer to sing backing vocals, although not clear why he contributed lines from the nursery rhyme 'Hickory Dickory Dock'. The heat was on. Marc and Marsha left the studio together in the early hours. Everyone knew what for.

When Marsha penned her autobiography, published in 1986 almost a decade after Marc's death, she revisited her 'affair' with him. Her prose gives the impression of an interlude of great innocence and purity which would forever lift her heart, or similar. The pages are purple.

'His cascade of dark curly locks commanded notice, and he was wearing girls' shoes that looked like tap-dancing shoes . . . his dark tee shirt . . . was also a girl's. He didn't look outrageous, just terribly pretty,' Marsha wrote.

'I blushed and he smiled, but not at me – although I felt I had his undivided attention while he greeted everybody else. Sometimes it's immediately obvious when two people are going to be together. It was that way with Marc and me before we spoke. We both had that feeling.'

An attraction of opposites, appears to have been the size of it. Marsha alludes to herself as having personified the things that Marc scorned. He was 'reclusive, macrobiotic, and professed aversion to success. He had no money, and acted as though he was opposed to it, on social grounds. Maybe his choosing to be with me was an indication that he was changing.'

Their relationship, it is suggested, was not driven by sex.

'It was a delicate sigh, a whispering that belonged to a moment in time when love could be taking an acid trip together or extending a flower plucked from someone else's garden to a stranger passing in the street . . . none of his friends were meant to have him for long,' she concludes.

'It was my great fortune to have had him to myself for a time while he was such an outlandish thing of beauty, who satisfied my need for a stroke of innocence.'[2]

'Relationship my arse,' retorts Jeff Dexter. 'More like a few shags!'

It occurs to me now that perhaps Marsha feared that it might be interpreted as sordid. She was well-known at the time and would soon have a baby by Mick Jagger – although it is said that

Jagger was more her groupie than she his![3] She was always quite something.

How ironic that Marsha was the one fling of Marc's during their time together that June had a problem with.

'Because Marc was very secretive about it,' Jeff explains. 'He wasn't up-front with her. June was fine with whoever Marc was seeing, as long as she knew about it. Why would he keep a couple of nights with someone like Marsha a secret from her? As June saw it, that meant that it had to be more of a threat.'

There is more to it. I wait.

'I *loved* June,' Jeff admits, eventually. He pauses.

I pose the question – tentatively, not wishing to offend, nor to drag up painful memories.

'Was I *in* love with her – as in, the one for me?

'No. It was much *more* than that. There was a direct link between us that was spiritual, as well as sexual. It was deeply human. Marc knew that we slept together.'

Jeff was in a relationship with Caroline Coon at the time.[4]

'I had my own flat in Hampstead, and we were a loose partnership from the summer of '67, together on and off for four or five years. The relationship dated from the night she got me out of jail after a drugs bust at a big house in Chelsea – for smoking marijuana. The nightclubs I worked in, particularly Tiles, were raided every six weeks or so. Kids – they still called them mods then – were carted off en masse in Black Marias for possession of Purple Hearts. Busloads of police would come in, divide the club down the middle, men one side, women the other. Kids were manhandled and abused. I told Caroline about it. She immediately came to see what was going on and what she could do about it. She was hugely instrumental in getting things changed.

'We were all great friends, always hugging and kissing,' he says. 'If Marc had to go off and do something, he'd say, "Don't leave June alone, be with her." This was free love. No jealousy. There were a few house rules. No penetration.'

Is that what made the difference?

'I suppose it did,' he muses, 'in a particular way. Without coitus, you haven't committed the whole thing, have you?'

'Committed' being the operative word, perchance?

Marsha was also a great friend of Caroline's.

'She and Marsha embraced each other. They had their thing together,' says Jeff.

'A lot of our relationship was to do with body juices and hair,' said Caroline Coon in an interview.

'June came round to Caroline's on the night in question,' says Dexter. 'I was sleeping on the couch in the other room, outside the main double bedroom. June told me everything. We had breakfast the next morning, and we talked and talked. Caroline didn't say a word.'

It still seems odd to me that June would be suspicious of Marsha, with so much free love going on. She and Marc were on a wavelength, and had pledged loyalty to one another. What on earth could she have been so worried about?

'Secrets,' Jeff repeats. 'Just secrets. Free Love was one thing. But hidden agendas were another. The free love thing wasn't, "Ok, let's all go and shag each other." It wasn't a case of us all being kinky together, although I often shared a bed with Marc at that time. We'd hug, nothing else. We loved each other. We cared for each other. It was tender. Our free love wasn't *three* love! It was nothing like a ménàge-à-trois.'

If anything, it all sounds quite innocent, I say.

'But that's exactly what we wanted!' smiles Jeff. 'We wanted that innocence back in our lives. The world had gone mad. What we had between us was tender love and care. It made things better. There wasn't enough of it in the world. The idea of the Summer of Love and of "free love" was to put the world to rights. I suppose some people couldn't handle it, and other people could. As long as you were doing it with TLC and not just out to put notches on your gun . . .

'Anyway, June had her antennae up. She was incredibly astute. I was with Caroline, Caroline was with Marsha, Marsha was with Marc . . . but June and I were with Marc. There was harmony in the arrangement until Marsha. She was a complication too far.'

What did June do, when she found out about her?

'June did what only June would do. She got dressed and said she was going to go looking for them. She was going to drive around London until she found them. That was typical of her – fiery and head-strong. She was magnificent. And find them she did: in a cab at King's Cross, heading somewhere. June pulled the car up alongside the cab, and stared at them both. Words were exchanged. Marc got out of the cab, got into the car with June, and they drove off home.'

Jeff appears exhausted by the revelations. But he's on a roll now. He trawls through his office, digging out diaries he hasn't peered into for many years. Although he seems, at times, upset and disequilibrated, he insists that he wants to continue.

'At that time,' he repeats, 'things were different. I adored both Marc and June. And they loved me too. What we kept between us was loving and personal. [Photographer] Pete Sanders was around all the time, for example, and he never had a clue about it. We didn't rub other people's noses in it. We were discreet.'

I feel compelled to pry further. Why has he chosen to share these things now, having kept silent all these years?

'Because I was asked,' he says quietly, getting up to make more tea, and turning his back to me.

'No one has ever asked me such personal questions before. It has only ever been superficial stuff about Marc and T. Rex and the music. You asked me some things that made me think deeply about who and what we were.

'Things have changed in my life,' he tells me candidly. His eyes are glistening. 'You say to yourself, "Oh, fuck it, I can say what I like now. I can express anything I want to." We won't be here that long. Since eleven of my friends died in one year, I have changed. I've got nothing to lose or gain by any of this.

'You've got to remember,' he adds, at last, 'that sex was a different currency from what it is now. There was plenty to go round. I know it's hard for people today to understand. AIDS reversed public attitude to sexual behaviour in the Eighties, and many people today seem more prim and judgemental as a result. I don't know whether that's a good thing or not. All I know is that sex, back then, was just another aspect of being human which we all shared. We were in it together. Ours was a genuine manifestation of love: "make love, not war", remember? I don't care if people nowadays think it sounds corny. To us, it was beautiful.'

When Bolan dispensed with Took, he was making an unambiguous statement. Tyrannosaurus Rex *was* Bolan. Despite his assertions that, 'I just grew apart from Steve Peregrin Took. He was into a drug-orientated and socio-political revolution, of which I did not feel a part . . . My life is music,' there was more to it than that. The subliminal message was that Marc would hire and fire his sidekicks as he pleased. Regardless of any individual musician he chose to include or eliminate, the personality, ethos and sound of his 'band' would remain 'his'.

In this, as in so many aspects of his career, Marc was ahead of his time. Until then, a 'band' usually consisted of its basic hard-core line-up – the 'Ringo-George-John-Paul'-type formula, however many of them there were – with auxiliary 'session' musicians brought in *ad hoc* for touring and/or studio work. To Marc, the Tyrannosaurus Rex 'band' was primarily a concept, the vehicle via which he channelled his work. Today we might talk in terms of 'Brand Bolan' or 'Team T. Rex', but there was no such marketing-speak back then. Bands had yet to become *brands*. Now that we consume music digitally, now that traditional record labels have largely lost their relevance, and that big-name consumer brands invest millions in the opportunity to be associated with the latest acts, the picture has changed dramatically. Today's sponsorship and promotional tools – merchandising, live appearances, websites, mobile phone ringtones, major advertising and licensing deals, professional fan clubs linking members to direct ticket-sales outlets, and so on – generate income which greatly exceeds that of recorded music royalties. Our 21st century music marketplace, in which an artist's brand is more valuable than their recorded output, was an unthinkable notion during Marc's lifetime. What he might have made of all this, heaven knows.

Unicorn, Tyrannosaurus Rex's third album, was released in May 1969 and only just missed the Top Ten, which was encouraging.

'For me, this is the quintessential Tyrannosaurus Rex album,' said Tony Visconti. 'Both the Beach Boys and Phil Spector influenced our thinking. Everything is bigger on this album, which includes the first use of proper drums, albeit a child's Chad

Valley kit bought at Woolworth's, detuned and played by [the subsequently departed] Took.'

July saw Apollo 11 deposit the first humans, Neil Armstrong and Buzz Aldrin, on the moon. The second release of David Bowie's 'Space Oddity', about the launch of a fictional astronaut, featured Rick Wakeman on Mellotron, future T. Rex member Herbie Flowers on bass, and someone other than Visconti at the controls. Tony had denounced the song as a 'cheap shot to capitalise on the moon landing', and handed the reins to Gus Dudgeon (although he did relent in time to produce David's next album for Mercury). The single could not have been better-timed. With the BBC playing it constantly during their coverage of the lunar happening, Bowie was at last in line for a hit.

In August, Marc and Steve undertook a six-week debut American club and festival tour.

'We realized it was just no good anymore when we tried to rehearse two days before going to America, and nothing happened,' said Marc. 'We went to America at that time in the worst possible frame of mind, having decided to split. I got to New York and got beaten up in the Village on three successive occasions [probably because of the way he looked], and retired to my hotel room.'

The disaffected bongo man, who was contractually obliged to turn up, did the tour under sufferance, loathed it, and spent the month and a half off his face. The shows made negligible impact, not least because America was in the throes of political upheaval and was anything but free, that summer. Besides, there was infinitely superior musical entertainment on offer. The legendary Woodstock Festival in upstate New York featured Ravi Shankar, Joan Baez, Janis Joplin, The Who and Jefferson

Airplane, but was boycotted by Bob Dylan, who made his way to the UK to star at the Isle of Wight Festival instead. Headlines that month were also dominated by the horrific Manson family 'Helter Skelter' murders.

At least, in San Francisco, Marc made the acquaintance of Turtles Mark Volman and Howard Kaylan, folk rockers turned popsters ('Happy Together') who as backing vocalists 'Flo & Eddie' for Frank Zappa's The Mothers of Invention would figure so prominently in Marc's future success.

The California leg of the trip was made memorable by an otherwise forgettable house party. It was the night that Marc met singer Gloria Jones.

Setting Bowie aside professionally for the moment, Visconti turned his attention to Tyrannosaurus Rex's fourth album, *A Beard of Stars*.

Marc's dishy new percussionist Mickey Finn, whom he had found in 'Seed', Gregory Sams's macrobiotic restaurant on Bishop's Bridge road near Blenheim Crescent, was now firmly ensconced.

'They did meet before Seed, actually,' reveals Jeff Dexter. 'Marc and Mickey were first introduced to each other by Pete Sanders and me. But Mickey was sworn to secrecy. Steve Took was out, but they couldn't just dump him. He was on the records and all the pictures, and was supposedly half of T. Rex. But he'd fucked up, and made it impossible for himself to stay. Things had to be resolved properly. So an ad was placed in the *Melody Maker* – and around the same time, "just by chance", Marc and Mickey "happened to meet" at Gregory's Seed restaurant. They were reintroduced, "afresh", by Nigel Waymouth – the famous psychedelic artist, style guru and owner of chic boutique Granny Takes A Trip, but perhaps best-known, at that time, as part of the group Hapshash and the Coloured Coat.'

'Dishy' was the operative word: Finn's looks attracted the girls, which meant swelling numbers of fans for Tyrannosaurus Rex. This album was created on a wave of positivity, thanks largely to Finn's cool mindset and laid-back attitude. The sessions are remembered as highly creative and experimental.

'A combination of Marc's growing proficiency on rock guitar and my engineering chops getting better helped the duo sound more aggressive,' Tony wrote. 'Something was definitely happening. We knew we were getting closer to what we wanted.'

It was also, sadly, when their relationship began to change. The more Tony became aware of Marc's growing arrogance and selfishness, the less comfortable he felt with him in the studio.

Marc's ego, admitted Tony, reluctantly, was dragon-sized. Tony soon learned to bite his tongue (never ideal in a producer), as well as to couch any criticism in diplomatic terms. He'd tread on eggshells to avoid diminishing Marc in front of Steve Took, then Mickey Finn,[5] and in the presence of any recording engineers or other studio staff. It was a Kissinger-like performance, almost worthy of a Nobel prize.

Thus, Marc's guitar would not be out of tune, but a string might have 'slipped a bit'. Tony also began to notice Marc's increasing tendency to manipulate conversations into being about him; and when he gave interviews, Tony was disheartened to note, Marc would hog the credit and would rarely name-check his producer, despite the fact that he'd lavish him with praise behind closed doors. Tony's perception was that Marc was turning Tyrannosaurus Rex into some parallel universe of his own creation, in which omniscient all-rounder Bolan reigned supreme.

'The three months between Woodstock and Altamont were when the general mood began to change,' reflects Bob Harris. 'We also had all those rock deaths between 1969 and 1971: Brian

Jones [3 July 1969]; Alan 'Blind Owl' Wilson [of Canned Heat, 3 September 1970]; Jimi Hendrix [18 September 1970]; Janis Joplin [4 October 1970]; Jim Morrison [3 July 1971]. We lost so many people, and we lost sight of what we were doing. There was a vague sense that we were beginning to fritter it all away. We probably knew this, but it happened anyway.'[6]

Altamont, 6 December 1969, was more seething broth of intoxication and violence than peaceful rock festival. Four months after Woodstock, The Rolling Stones staged this notorious free concert in California, featuring Santana, Jefferson Airplane, Crosby, Stills, Nash & Young and others, before an audience of 300,000 people high on alcohol, amphetamines and LSD. It went terribly wrong. Dominated by blind-drunk, brutal Hell's Angels, the event is remembered not for music but for a murder, a drowning, two fatal car accidents, four births, widespread injury, theft and incalculable damage. Some of it is preserved for posterity, if you can call it that, in the Rolling Stones' 1970 documentary *Gimme Shelter*. The 'make love not war' chant was suddenly all hummed out.

A death knell for the hippie movement tolled.

Some people still clung to the bohemian ideal, not least David Bowie and his future wife Angela Barnett – who set up their own 'hippie commune' in a turreted, stained-glassed Gothic mansion in Beckenham, Kent. The first friends they invited to share it were Visconti and his current partner, Liz. Living under the same roof as David while continuing to produce Marc made for compromising times.

Tony also took to playing bass in his housemate's live band, which led to a couple of Roundhouse gigs in February 1970. Deciding on a whim to go the whole hog and doll themselves up, David and Tony plundered the sewing boxes and make-up bags of their girlfriends. A cartoon-character line-up was assembled. With Visconti as super-hero, a pirate, a gangster, and Bowie himself as Rainbow Man, what else could they wind up as but Hype?[7]

As Visconti pointed out, rockers in those days were hirsute and shaggy-haired. They reeked of sweat, beer and cigarettes. They sported utility shirts and denim, and were unfamiliar with the interior of laundries. By comparison, this bunch was beautiful, fragrant, and exquisitely androgynous.

'For me,' teases Tony Visconti, 'this will always be the very first night of glam rock.'

But wasn't Marc supposed to be the original glam rocker?

'It's hard to say,' said Morrissey in Visconti's book. The latter would go on to produce the former.

'If you [compare him with] very early Alice Cooper albums or very early Iggy Pop photographs, Marc does seem to have been the first one who actually broke through into the mainstream. Wearing women's shoes and stuff . . . even though the Stones dragged up and so forth, and flirted with interesting Satanic themes.

'Bolan seemed to be the first one who appealed to *children*, and to young people. He definitely had an ambi-sexual image, if not an auto-sexual image. To me, that was truly fascinating.'[8]

Though the pictures from the Roundhouse gig that night show a denim-clad Marc looking on in mild amazement as Hype bunged it their all, he would later deny having even been there.

During January 1970, Visconti had recorded Bowie's single 'The Prettiest Star', which David is said to have written as part of his proposal to Angie - along with an 'immigrant song' he had penned earlier, called 'London Bye Ta Ta'.[9] At Tony's suggestion, Marc pitched up at Trident Studios on David's

23rd birthday to play lead guitar on 'Star', while the producer himself contributed bass.

'The overlap between Bowie and Bolan was quite extraordinary, when you look back,' Bob Harris remarks. 'Both recorded at Trident, they were working with the same producer, they sat in on each other's sessions. They were massively interested in each other, regardless of what might have been said and written since.

'I remember clearly the sessions for "The Prettiest Star",' Bob says. 'Marc's guitar solo on that is really lovely. It captures the mood just right.'

'I saw a great opportunity to unite them for "The Prettiest Star", because I knew Marc fancied himself as a lead guitarist,' explained Tony.

Although the session went well, with great chemistry between Marc and David (as Tony had anticipated), it was marred by uncharacteristically rude behaviour on the part of June.

'Marc is too good for you,' she snapped at Bowie, 'to be playing on this record'.

The single flopped. After the success of 'Space Oddity', this came as a huge blow to its composer. David would have to wait the best part of three years for his next UK hit – while waving off his bopping-elf chum on the multi-coloured scream-ride of fame.

Bowie would never return the favour. Not once did he play any instrument on any recording of Marc's. For all the rumours about him having blown sax sequences on various T. Rex cuts, Tony remains adamant that this never happened. There does exist a bootleg cassette of the duo writing a song together in a New York hotel room, which the producer has confirmed to be the real McCoy.

'Towards the end, their friendship was better, and they spent quite a lot of time socialising in NYC around the time that cassette was made,' Tony says.

But 'Marc's death stopped the possibility of them recording together.'

They were married only weeks apart: June and Marc on 30 January 1970, at Kensington Register Office, with only Jeff Dexter, June's friend Alice Ormsby Gore, Mickey Finn, his girl-friend Sue, and photographer and best man Pete Sanders in attendance.

After the ceremony, the small, moth-eaten-looking bunch repaired to San Lorenzo restaurant in Beauchamp Place, Knightsbridge.

David's and Angie's nuptials were an even lower-key affair, at Bromley Register Office on 19 March, with only David's mother for company – and even she wasn't invited, she just turned up. Nor was there any fancy meal to celebrate. That neither Marc nor David attended each other's wedding was never seen as significant. They did things differently back then.

Besides, Marc and Tony were locked in the studio together. Tearing himself between the two, Tony commenced sessions with David at Advision Studios for what would become the album *The Man Who Sold The World*. He also moved out of over-crowded Haddon Hall, its number swelled by a cluster of arachnids-in-waiting. Perhaps he thought he had better brace himself. It was all about to become a hair-raising ride.

A Beard of Stars, their most pop-sounding album to date, did well for Tyrannosaurus Rex.

'That's such an album,' says Steve Harley, the Cockney Rebel frontman who would become Marc's close friend. 'That's Marc's "Revolver".[10]

'I was a big fan of Tyrannosaurus Rex,' Steve reveals, informing me that he'd told his wife Dorothy on his way out to come and meet me that 'this is the last time I'm ever going to be interviewed about Marc Bolan.' He means it, too.

Steve's the only friend I could ask to sing at my funeral; the only one with the balls to respond, 'Have you got a date for that?' Besides, he wrote the song I want sung on the day I check out: 'Make Me Smile (Come Up and See Me)' says it all.[11]

'I saw them live three or four times,' he reminisces. 'I remember seeing them at the Greyhound in Croydon, that big room above the pub. They all played there: Argent, Jethro Tull, Black Sabbath, Black Widow. We used to sit cross-legged on the floor, like Marc . . . even for Black Sabbath. We'd sit there rolling spliffs. Those were the days of the Afghan coat. We sewed suede triangles into the hems of our jeans. I was only a weekend hippy, being too young to be the real thing. That vexed me, as I'd been too young to be a mod as well. Marc pipped me at so many posts!'

A Beard of Stars lingered long enough on the charts to make an impact – which was more than could be said for 'Oh Baby' and 'Universal Love' by Dib Cochran & The Earwigs, a spoof band that was actually Visconti on lead vocals and bass, Marc on lead guitar and backing vocals, and Rick Wakeman on piano. Conceived by Marc as an experiment, to see if he had what it took to create a hit single, he hadn't dared lend his name and voice to the project in case it flopped. Good call.

So which came first: the name change or the musical *volte-face*? No one remembers. Manager David Enthoven demands credit for having coined the moniker 'T. Rex' – 'because I couldn't spell 'Tyrannosaurus'! By about September 1970, Tony Visconti recalls, he had started writing 'T. Rex' on schedules, calendars and labels, simply because the word 'Tyrannosaurus' took up too much space. When he first noticed this, Marc feigned annoyance, but was secretly pleased: the fact that Tony and others were already abbreviating his band name gave him the perfect excuse to tighten it and give it punch.

It was Marc himself, his producer confirms, who took the decision to change the name officially. Gig poster-designers, journalists and DJs alike were also relieved at the dino-dropping by the time Bolan released his break-through track – a charming ditty with a simple four-stanza lyric which he had written at the kitchen table, with June hovering.

'Whether it was the record, the name change, a combination of those two or something else altogether, it changed our lives forever,' writes Tony Visconti, whose production was inspired: just enough strings, no drums, a tambourine keeping time and light hand-claps were all it took. Plucky guitar-playing (on Marc's beloved Gibson Les Paul,[12] with a hint of echo) and a clear, simple vocal backed by ethereal falsetto were allowed to dominate. The single was released on 9 October 1970 on Fly Records, a new label set up by Essex Music's David Platz with Chris Stamp and Kit Lambert of Track Records, and began its slow rise to the almost-top.

There were other contributing factors; not least, the happy accident of an independent record plugger getting involved. This was not common practice at the time, and was a first for T. Rex. That radio DJs fell for 'Ride a White Swan' had not a little to do with the fact that their sassy plugger, Anya Wilson, was the most drop-dead gorgeous promotions woman in town.

'I was the house plugger [promotional agent who represents an artist's record to radio] for Gem, a company owned by former accountant and lawyer Laurence Myers and Tony Defries [who managed David Bowie]. The company worked with producers and writers, including Lionel Bart, Tony Macaulay and Tony Visconti,' Anya tells me.

'You established contacts at the BBC – which at the time was the only thing that mattered – and you dealt with producers. You'd go to weekly meetings to talk them into playing your records. It was all extremely competitive.

'I was honest. When they asked me if a record had the legs for a hit, I'd say what I really thought. Producers respected my opinion. As one of the first female pluggers, I'd helped break "Love Grows (Where My Rosemary Goes)" for Edison Lighthouse, which was written by Tony Macaulay [composer, songwriter, nine times Ivor Novello Award-winner], and who was my ex-boyfriend.

'Tony Visconti and I had become good friends through our connection with Gem. We'd have coffee and lunch regularly. I remember saying to him one day, "I wish I had something I could really get my teeth into". Tony smiled. "I've got something," he said. He took me off to play me "Ride a White Swan".

'It was "one of those",' Anya remembers. 'I fell in love with it instantly. I adored the poetry. I loved that here was someone who dared to write lyrics like these. This song was way better than anything else I had going at the time. Tony explained that the single had been out for a while, but the Essex music plugger wasn't getting very far with it. He wasn't seasoned, and he wasn't closing. Although John Peel and the alternative shows were in on it, it didn't translate to the commercial programmes. The conversion from Tyrannosaurus Rex to T. Rex was an uphill struggle. Tony was devastated, because he really believed in the song. I agreed to have a go with it.

'"Oh man, they'll buy you a car if you break it!" Tony exclaimed.

'I didn't get a car, but I *did* get a new coat: suede, with yellow-ish fur edges, which I was allowed to choose myself . . . *and* a hat to go with it!'

Anya took on the record for love, not money. She went straight to Ted Beston. As producer of Jimmy Savile's hugely popular and highly-rated weekend show, Beston's support was key.

'Ted looked at me quizzically. "You *never* come to me and say something could be huge," he said.

'"No – but I'm saying it now," I told him. He played "Swan" for three weeks running on Jimmy's show. Then Emperor Rosko started playing it. Then Tony Blackburn cottoned on to it, and everyone else jumped on board after that,' Anya says.

The last thing she ever felt was that the song's success had anything to do with her personal beauty. 'I'm incredibly flattered if Tony thinks that!' she laughs.

'It didn't cross my mind. Being a female in a man's world was difficult. I tried not to let that kind of thing get in the way. Having said that, no one could ignore the fact that Marc Bolan was a truly beautiful man. He was flawless. I nearly fell over the first time I met him, which was at the BBC Radio One Club. For some reason I thought he'd be tall, like me. I wore big platform heels, and was about 5'10". Marc was tiny, and very fragile, with a really special charisma. My role immediately got very protec-tive. I felt more like his bodyguard than his plugger!'

Thanks to the success of 'Ride a White Swan', Anya was able to start her own business. 'June Bolan came to me and said, "Why are you still working out of Laurence's office? Why not start your own company? Work from your house, all you need is a phone. I'll guarantee you all of T. Rex's work."'

She launched the Acme Plug Co., and went on to represent T. Rex, Paul McCartney, David Bowie and others, riding the wave until EMI called all promotions activity in-house, and Bowie moved to the US. With former client Long John Baldry's encouragement, Anya moved to Canada, worked with Johnny Cash, and became hugely influential in the country music scene.

Canadian Tolkien expert David Day remains enchanted by 'Ride a White Swan', more than four decades after its release. But far from simple, he hears a song brimming with magic and loaded with complexity, owed entirely to the meanings of its words.

'One could easily argue that T. Rex's most famous song is drawn *entirely* from the writing of J.R.R. Tolkien,' he says. 'Although the bird in the title is a swan, the bird in the first stanza is an eagle. It is not until the second stanza that the swan appears. However, both of these birds have special significance in Tolkien; and they are the only ones of such gigantic size that are capable of carrying anyone into the air, so they might 'ride it on out like if you were a bird.'

Indeed, in Tolkien's Middle-earth there are several incidents in which he has a hero ride on the back of 'an eagle in a sunbeam'. Gandalf the Wizard is the most frequent eagle-rider, who seems to have taken Bolan's advice to 'wear a tall hat like a druid in the old days'.[13]

Bolan's lines in the second paragraph 'Ride a white swan like the people of the Beltane/Wear your hair long . . .' is, says Day, a reference to the long-haired Elves who were Tolkien's re-creation of mythical Elves of the Druidic Celts of the British Isles.

'That is: "the people of the Beltane". One of the emblems of Tolkien's Elves was the white swan. And it was in the magical Elven ships – built in the shape of swans with white-winged sails – that the heroes of the Ring Quest were carried into an immortal realm of the Undying Lands. So, one might argue that Tolkien's heroes literally "ride a white swan (ship)" to the heaven of "the people of the Beltane."'

Furthermore, explains Day, the third paragraph beginning 'Catch a bright star and place it on your fore-head/say a few spells and baby there you go' is an allusion to a Tolkien Elvish legend that explains the arrival of the Morning Star at dawn.

'The Morning Star is, in fact, the planet Venus, which appears in the sky just before the rising of the sun. It is always the brightest "star" in the sky, so "Catch a bright star and place it on your fore-head" appears to be a direct reference to Tolkien's legend of Earendil the Mariner. The Morning Star is the star-bright jewel (known as the Silmaril) that Earendil wears on his fore-head as he rides through the sky each morning in the prow of his flying swan ship.'

The black cat, Day points out, 'is the only image in the song that does not emanate directly from Tolkien. However, it does connect somewhat with Bolan's interest in the "people of the Beltane" and the Wicca revival of the Sixties and Seventies. The festival of Beltane is actually the pagan British celebration of May Day (the beginning of summer), as opposed to that other great pagan British celebration Halloween (the beginning of winter) – in which, of course, the black cat figures prominently.'

Was 'Ride a White Swan' a deliberate move to 'get a hit', as Visconti and various critics down the years have suggested? Who cares. The song hailed as 'the birth of glam rock' remains as unique and unforgettable today as when it was released. Straddling both his Tyrannosaurus Rex and T. Rex incarnations, it might well be the song that defines Marc best. It may have taken its time, but the single took T. Rex all the way to Number Two – where it peaked, eleven weeks after its appearance, on 23 January 1971. The star was born.[14]

Cosmic Rock

Despite its significance as a new beginning for its composer, 'Ride a White Swan' was also a swansong of sorts. Hans Christian Andersen could have written his most famous fairy story with Marc in mind, had their lifespans synchronised. Not that Bolan was an ugly duckling 'with feathers all stubby and brown' – far from it.[1] But the true meaning behind the tale of a displaced creature that sheds its kooky image to hold his head 'noble and high' and become 'the best in town' would not have been lost on him. The Danish author's swan was a metaphor for inner beauty, and for true talent finally revealing itself. When the symbolic little creature took flight, it transformed into something rare and extraordinary. Likewise, Marc left the enchanted forests and faerie glens for the big bad freeway. He withdrew, gently, from Tolkien, talismans and ancient legend to get down among the grease monkeys and the rock chicks. A faster, naughtier, more materialistic world beckoned, as did sex and cars: two of the three indulgences that preoccupy 'real men'.[2]

While allusions to gentler fantasy realms inhabited by nymphs and necromancers would continue to haunt his songwriting, Marc was now primarily fascinated by dirty sweet girls who were built like cars, wore hub cap haloes and had the universe reclining in their hair. Perhaps his 'genius', if we dare refer to it as that, was a basic instinct for tempering raunch with innocence. He managed this with such subtlety, flare and artistry that even his most blatant erotic references and orgasmic gutterals did not offend. Marc's superiority complex was in full flight.

After 25 years of the post-war boom, British families in the early Seventies began to prosper. People had jobs, free health, and money. City slums were cleared and replaced with new housing. Was there such a thing as a 'working class' anymore? Social distinctions, like the slums, were being erased. With Britain's entry into Europe in 1971 marking a major turning point in our political history, opportunity knocked. The vast majority of Britons who had never left the country were suddenly Carrying On Abroad. Our parents were drinking wine at home, giving 'dinner parties', serving 'foreign' foods in the kitchen. The new decade's ideals might have been, in part, a gut reaction against boring, had-its-day hippie-dom and wilting Flower Power.

Making an impression and showing off were what counted now. Bolan, personifying the spirit of the age, was cock of the walk.

'Timing is everything, and Marc's was always perfect,' enthuses Simon Napier-Bell. 'Life was all extremely brash and colourful at that time. Glam rock for the fans, cocaine for the stars. The gayness of the Sixties rock and pop managers had filtered down to the performing artists. Gay or not, they now took on a lot of the glamour and colour of the managers that their predecessors had had during the Sixties. Bowie, Bolan and all those glam groups – Slade, Sweet and so on – had straight managers, but camp was still in the air, and they grabbed it. The first few years of the Seventies had all the optimism of the Sixties, plus more . . . because this was a new decade, damn it, and we

were going to move on even further – in outrage, and acceptance, liberality and freedom. There was no stopping us.'

'We were all so idealistic at the end of the Sixties,' agrees Bob
Harris. 'We were pushing out the boundaries. But we were trying
too many new things at once, and so we weren't focused enough.
We wound up losing our direction in the Seventies, because life
became way too self-indulgent. We opened up a massive opportunity, but then smoked ourselves out of the idealism. It all
evaporated. I still regard the Seventies as a massive opportunity
that we wasted. By the time we'd begun to wake up, the Eighties
were already upon us, and everything was changing yet again. I
think that's part of the reason why we all still feel so nostalgic
about that decade: because it's unfinished business.'

It's incredible how much of the music made in the Seventies
is still so relevant now, Bob muses.

'Not just here, but all over the world. Elton John, Cat Stevens,
Led Zeppelin, David Bowie, Marc Bolan: all that amazing music
soaked into our DNA. You can't imagine that the records in the
singles charts today will have that kind of longevity. Play the
music, trigger the happy memories. We do see past decades
through rose-tinted glasses, it's true. There was actually a lot of
negativity throughout the 1970s. We forget the three-day working week, the miners' strike, the IRA, and that it was all pretty
bleak at times.'

Times were a'changing on all fronts. Germaine Greer, outspo-
ken Australian feminist and *International Times* and *Oz* magazine
contributor, was now a household name, thanks to her best-
selling 1970 work *The Female Eunuch*. Championing the cause of
women's liberation beyond 'mere' equality with men, Greer
became a high-profile figure on the London scene, and an
unlikely friend of Marc, Jeff and June. Jeff recounts outrageous

nights in restaurants, when Germaine could always be relied upon to let down her hair and get up to mischief while Marc would be beside himself with mirth.

'You don't want to know!' winks Dexter.

All systems go. With T. Rex's eponymous debut album climbing the charts, the band were out on the road to promote the new product. Visconti was now in such demand that he could not commit to playing bass for T. Rex at more than the occasional gig. So Steve Currie was hired. Marc being a vegetarian at that point, while Steve was a red-blooded meat eater, Bolan promptly nick-named his new bassist 'Beef Currie'.

They also needed a drummer, and Bill Fifield was just the job – soon restyled Bill 'Legend', which has long been thought to have been a nod to the band he'd recently drummed for, as well as because Marc thought it sounded 'more T. Rex'.

'Not quite true,' laughs Bill, the last surviving member of the original T. Rex line-up.[3] 'I *was* in a band called Legend, who were quite big on the Southend scene where I was living at the time. Our songwriter and guitarist Mickey Jupp had founded the band in 1968, and went on to work with Dr Feelgood, Procul Harum and a string of other musicians. Legend recorded several albums – one of which, the "Red Boot" album (although I think all the LPs were called "Legend") was produced by Tony Visconti, and which is where I knew him from. We'd always done well on the pub circuit, and Mickey was something of a legend himself. The fans used to write to me care of our office, but they didn't know my surname. So they'd write "Bill (Of 'Legend')" on the letter. When the office sent a cheque to my home, they'd put that on the envelope too – as a bit of a send-up, really, but it stuck.

'So it wasn't Marc Bolan, nor Tony Visconti, who re-named me "Legend". I can see how such misunderstandings happen: something gets said in an interview, it appears in print, and suddenly, *boom*, it's the truth. That wasn't, though. The reality is always mundane!'

When Bill was approached to join the band, he had never heard of Tyrannosaurus Rex.

'After they brought me in, I had to go out and buy all the old albums, and figure out how to play the songs. But Marc's music had changed by that time, we weren't performing much of the old stuff. Most of it now was full-blown rock'n'roll.'

How did the band members' relationship with Marc develop?

'At first we were all mates,' he says. 'I never used to say much, I kept my thoughts to myself. Well, it was Marc's band. I knew what my role was, and what everyone else's was. I never thought he valued what he had around him, to be honest. We were all on his side, but I didn't have the impression that he always believed that. One of Marc's worst faults was that he never wanted to delegate, and could hardly ever bring himself to do so.

'The best thing about being in his band,' Bill goes on, 'is that it gave me a chance to travel. I'd been, and am, a commercial artist. I never earned a living with T. Rex. It was only pocket money, what he paid us. My wages went back home – and I wound up owing money to people after every tour.'

'Marc really DID have a mean side,' confirms his friend Bob Harris. 'With money, in particular. The band were never paid all that much. They didn't get a fair crack at the whip, you'd have to say. But they were living a dream anyway.'

'Don't misunderstand me,' says Bill, 'we had a great time. It was fantastic for me to get out there – I was a few years older, I had a couple of kids already, my feet were on the ground. I'd cut my teeth on all the early rock'n'roll – Eddie Cochran, Gene Vincent, Buddy Holly – and I'd done a lot of recording, with artists like Billy Fury, and even Freddie Starr! I loved Stax and

Soul, and played along to Booker T albums. That was the solid feel that I brought to T. Rex.'

How was his relationship with the main man?

'I never got to know Marc quite as well as I would have liked to,' Bill confesses. 'Not in all the years. The potential was there, because we all went everywhere together. But T. Rex was always very much "us and them".

'"The band" was Marc, actually. The star, *his* partner, *his* producer, or manager, and the rest of us. The hired hands. That's all we were, Mickey, Steve and me. We never deluded ourselves. What would have been the point? We were under no illusions; we were just glorified session men. It never occurred to us to consider ourselves as "rock stars". You have to understand that T. Rex wasn't the usual band line-up arrangement. There was no democracy going on. Put it this way, in a crisis, nothing was ever put to the vote!'

Did he ever get Marc alone, and have his undivided attention?

'Not really. There'd be moments when we sat next to each other – on a plane or in a car, say, although usually in those situations he'd be with June, then Gloria, or Tony his manager. I was close to Tony Visconti, and Steve Currie. We did used to sit around and talk about it all. Well, you do.'

The worst thing about Marc, as far as Bill was concerned, was his lack of patience.

'Wherever we went or whatever it was for, Marc just couldn't wait. He was just like a kid in that respect – and as a father of seven, I know all about that! On the other hand, he was extremely good in the studio. Very concise. He'd get in there and he'd get on with it. We would never take all day just doing a backing track. We never had demos, we came up with it all there and then – which I think added to the spontaneity of T. Rex singles. It was all very creative, and I was excited by that.

'I don't mind saying that I contributed a lot in those situations. Many of the ideas that you hear were mine. But not just mine: everyone's. We all got stuck in, and came up with hook lines, melodies, all kinds of stuff. Marc did listen, and he did accept our contributions and kept things in. I think that's the kind of thing that made the music memorable. That, and the fact that Marc's songs were short and sweet. They were quite reminiscent of The Shirelles, the Everlys, Elvis. People couldn't get tired of the songs, because they weren't that long!'

The flashes of the 'real' Marc that Bill experienced were few and far between – which made them all the more precious to him.

'I remember once,' he says, 'when we were away somewhere, Marc calling me into his hotel room. He was going over one of his songs, and wanted to work through it with me acoustically.

'"What do you *really* reckon to this?," he asked me. I could tell that he genuinely wanted my opinion. There was nothing arrogant about him in those moments. That was the real Marc you were getting. He could melt your heart. The inner Marc could be very caring, incredibly tender. But I could see clearly how impossible it would have been for him to be that Marc all the time. He had a job to do, and at least half of that job required him to act like a star.

'I was just his drummer at the end of the day,' shrugs Bill. 'Marc had made it, and he was riding high. He was the boss. Had I ever tried to talk to him about the things that really matter, he wouldn't have listened to me. He might do now,' he adds wistfully.

'I would have loved to speak to him more about the meaning of life. I'm not saying that he might not be dead had we done so, not at all! But he might have approached his life a little differently. He might have respected himself a bit more.'

★ ★ ★

Bill lives in the California sunshine with his second wife, to whom he has been married since 2010. Their laid-back lifestyle is shaped largely by his Christian faith. He still plays live – a blend of 'Worship Rock', a few T. Rex hits and his favourite rock'n'roll tunes, a mix which he says is well-received. He still works as a commercial artist, well into his late sixties. He doesn't dwell too much on the biggest band that he was ever part of, and rarely thinks about those crazy days.

'It was all a very long time ago,' he says, and it *was* only three and a half years. Though I must confess, at times it felt like longer. We certainly crammed a lot in.'

Torn between two superstars in the making, Tony's time to choose had come. Bowie or Bolan, which was it to be? He would focus on the latter for now, to David's bitter disappointment. He would not be gone long.

T. Rex, Marc's and Tony's most successful album to date, soared effortlessly into the Top Twenty of the UK album charts early in 1971. Their second single, 'Hot Love', danced straight to Number One in February – where it stayed for six weeks, shifting an unprecedented weight of vinyl.

The band continued to tour, to ever-swelling audiences. One thing they had not anticipated was the speed with which the profile of their fan-base changed. As the duffle-coats began shuffling off in search of alternative hooks to hang on, squalls of young teenagers filled their place.

'I couldn't believe it the first time I went out on stage and saw all those new, young, little white faces,' Marc told Keith Altham. 'No one is going to convince me that their enthusiasm is a bad thing for T. Rex. If there is going to be any kind of revolution in pop, it must come from the young people; and if you ignore them, you are cutting yourself off from the life-supply of the rock music force.

'I've been doing interviews with all the teenybop magazines', he went on, '. . . they know what it's about, and even if they don't, they feel the thing intuitively. There is so much vitality and life to be drawn from youth.'

Altham was quite taken-aback by these remarks.

'It's a long time since I have heard such good sense,' he said at the time. 'It was something of a revelation to listen to this apparently placid, cherubic-looking figure in his blue romper suit, red and yellow hooped jersey, adorned with a "Derek is Eric" button, spill over with enthusiasm for his new scene.'[4]

Marc responded by slashing tickets to pocket-money prices, for which they adored him even more.

'We worked hard,' says Mick O'Halloran. 'Marc would be getting £1,200, £1,500 a night – which was a huge amount back then. He was aware that he was attracting a lot of younger teens –14, 15-year-olds – and he could well remember what it was like to be skint at that age. So he said he was going to keep the ticket prices down. He didn't want to rip them off. This was just a genuinely sweet thing about him, it was nothing contrived.

'Because of this, we found ourselves forever battling with promoters. We did the Fiesta Club in Sheffield once. When we got there, we discovered that the tickets had been marked up at 12s/6d.

'"Is it sold out?" said Marc. "Call the manager over."

'"You're charging 12s/6d!" he said to him.

'"Yes, that's the contract," the guy said.

'"I'm not going to play if you charge them that much," Marc told him, "I only charge half a crown [2s/6d] for a ticket. Give them all a refund immediately!" The manager refused.

'Marc was adamant that he wasn't going to do it, and he told the guy in no uncertain terms. In the end, management relented, refunded the fans on the door, and we did a great show. We even went back there several times after that. I didn't like doing those sorts of clubs, and neither did Marc. But sometimes you had to. That's just the way it was.'

Following the success of 'Ride a White Swan' and 'Hot Love', Marc and June left their Blenheim Crescent flat for a relatively luxurious apartment in Little Venice. Their rented property at 31 Clarendon Gardens was large, airy, and in a better part of town. Marc could now have his own music room, where he kept his guitars, his home recording equipment, and a huge, ever-growing record collection. June styled the place with a hippie feel, trawling the shops and stalls of Portobello Road for rugs, tapestries, velvet drapes and Art Nouveau mirrors. They also had a garage – which, towards autumn 1971, housed a stylish early-1960s AC sports car and a second-hand Bentley, with a Rolls Royce grille and frontage, for which Marc had paid about £2,000.

Energy was what it was all about, Marc told his future publicist Keith Altham, who at the time was still a journalist at *Record Mirror*.

'I've suddenly tuned into that mental channel which makes a record a hit, and I feel at present as though I could go on writing Number Ones forever,' he enthused. 'Let's face it: the majority of pop hits that make it are a permutation on the 12-bar blues, and I've found one that works. Once you've found that, the secret ingredient is "energy", some personal sense of urgency that you communicate through the music.'

Given that Marc was now projecting the image of the hot-shot rock star, he was surprisingly frank about his innermost insecurities – doubtless due to Altham's considerable skill as an interviewer, coupled with the fact that the pair had already known each other personally for several years.

Marc had nothing to hide from Keith, who had watched the younger man's progress from the outset with a paternal fondness unusual in his cut-throat ilk.

'I've never felt so insecure or such pain as I do now with my music', Marc confessed to him. 'Because I am so exposed – it's straight projection and giving of my real self, but that's really all I care about. The people I have always admired, like Hendrix or Clapton, have that ability to give something so soulful and personal that it gives their music an extra dimension.

'Don't misunderstand me,' Marc stressed, 'I'm not saying that I'm Hendrix or Clapton. I recently made a light-hearted remark about being the next Led Zeppelin, because we had switched from a basically acoustic sound to electric – and some people actually took it seriously. What I am saying is that I am getting through an identity now – and even some respect for myself as a musician.'

It's all it takes. Or so Marc thought. They all do this. Maintaining self-respect in the turbulent world of rock'n'roll stardom is the thing that very few of them ever appear to bargain for. Like it or not, it is the price.

12

Girls Melt

The madness continued to mount, as T. Rex soon found themselves on their debut American tour.

'Last time we lost money, but not this time,' Marc told Keith Altham for *Record Mirror*. 'We've got a different attitude, and the will to succeed. America is really important to me, because without making a go of things there, you cannot hope to gain the kind of financial freedom I'm looking for. I want to have a 16-track in my home and make my own movies, that kind of thing,' he said.

'When we come back we go straight into an English tour in May, which I'm really looking forward to – we're just taking DJs like Bob Harris and Jeff Dexter with us to play nice sounds to the audience, before we go on and do an hour and a half.'

In New York, Marc found himself rekindling an old friendship.

'I'd got out of fashion retail and gone to the U.S. in 1970, to rediscover myself,' remembers society photographer Richard Young. 'Like everyone else, I was desperate to work in the music business. I thought I'd try my hand at being a recording engineer, and I stayed in the States for four years. I worked in Electric Ladyland studios, which Jimi Hendrix had built, but sadly barely got to see before he died. They even put me up for a while in Jimi's duplex, and I was only the teaboy. I'd run errands, get supplies in, sweep the floors, lock up at night. I thought I'd made it. I hadn't kept in touch with anyone in London. I was far too busy making new friends in New York.'

In April 1971, Richard heard that his old school chum, now a newly-famous rock star with hits to his name, was about to play the hallowed rock venue Fillmore East in the East Village. It was not a sensational gig, by all accounts, not least because the band didn't yet have enough material to play.

'They were playing a few nights there,' Richard says 'I went down to the stage door on one of them, where I wrote a little note and sent it round to him. When I got inside and we came face to face, we fell on each other like long lost brothers.

'It was incredible to see him again. I never did make it as a recording engineer. I came back to London, got into photography, and the rest is history.'

Tony Visconti happened to be in New York at the same time as T. Rex, but independently, on a rare visit home to see his parents. Marc having expressed a desire to record while he was in America, Tony took time out of his holiday and pulled the band into a studio – the now-defunct Media Sound on 57th Street, made famous by Simon & Garfunkel when they recorded 'The Boxer' there. It was during preliminary recordings of the tracks 'Jeepster' and 'Monolith', further offerings towards what would become T. Rex's *Electric Warrior* LP, that Tony introduced Marc to an artist friend, Barbara Nessim.

At 32, Barbara was eight years Marc's senior. Another 'brief affair' is said to have ensued, after Marc allegedly attended a party at Nessim's East 15th Street brownstone apartment. A few days after they spent the night together there, Barbara was apparently present at a T. Rex gig at the Fillmore East. Although the still-respected artist has opened up recently about the time that she and Marc spent together, Jeff Dexter is dismissive.

'Just another bird', he shrugs. 'They came and they went, these women. They were flings. Don't be fooled by little notes and squiggly drawings, we all got those. Marc liked his birds, just as June liked her blokes. They were so alike, in that respect. They took it where they could get it. Good luck to them. It was only ever June for Marc, and Marc for June.'

Tony and T. Rex left New York for California, to rehearse at Howard 'Eddie' Kaylan's fabulous Laurel Canyon home.

Laurel Canyon was to 1970s' California what the Jazz Age had been to Paris in the 1920s; what the Brill Building was to Forties-to-Sixties New York.[1]

Just as the Brill was the most important generator of popular songs in the post-war western world, churning out everything from big band standards to Sixties mainstream pop, the Canyon was a leafy cathedral of Seventies folk-rock-country fusion, and lately the focus of America's music scene. Songwriting talent had migrated west, quitting Manhattan's polluted concrete canyons on a quest for inspiration within the cool, eucalyptus-scented serenity of the Hollywood Hills. It was here, safely north of Sunset Boulevard, that the Golden Age of California Dreamin' began.[2]

They refer to Laurel Canyon these days as '*the* legendary rock'n'roll neighbourhood'. Rock microcosm it surely was, but no one contrived it that way. Laurel evolved organically out of the dregs of hippie idealism. While the long-haired, the mini-skirted and the biker-booted flocked to the urban Strip for groovin' to far-out vibes, the bucolic depths of the Canyon was where the magic happened.

For The Byrds – America's Beatles – Jimmy Webb, The Mamas & The Papas, Frank Zappa, The Eagles, Joni Mitchell and Carole King (one of the few Brill survivors whose songwriting made a triumphant Sixties-to-Seventies transition), Laurel was a hedonistic, narcotic-fuelled fold, populated by acid freaks, cocaine cowboys, eccentrics, cultists and groupies; a parallel universe where the ideals would eventually fall spectacularly apart. For now, it was heaven, and Marc could hardly get enough of the place. Seeing himself as nothing if not the ultimate California groover (honey), he leapt at the chance to record at the fastest studios in the West.

The now-defunct Wally Heider Studios were a sweat of a ride out of Howard's gaff in the Canyon but a magnet to a newly-famous rock'n'roll dude who craved US recognition. The independent recording facility Studio 3 in Hollywood was one of the most successful in the world. Together with its San Francisco sister studio, it played host to a wild roster of West Coast-style artists, including Jefferson Airplane, The Grateful Dead, Harry Nilsson, The Steve Miller Band, Santana, Creedence Clearwater Revival, and Crosby, Stills, Nash & Young. Although the San Francisco branch's history boasts that T. Rex recorded *Electric Warrior* there, Tony Visconti confirms that it was definitely LA.

'The drive seemed long because we were Londoners,' he says, 'and to get to any place in or near LA seemed to require a long car journey (we were used to the Underground, buses and taxis). I have encountered this situation before, studios with branches in several places just lump all the famous names together.'

Marc was still carrying around his beloved school-style notebooks, into which he continued to pour poem after story after lyric at such a breath-taking rate that there must have been more than enough for five albums at any one time. At Wally

Heider's, Tony recorded the band in sessions for *Electric Warrior*, and laid down backing vocals by Flo & Eddie for 'Get It On'.

Yet another gig at a legendary American rock venue, the Whisky A Go-Go on Sunset Boulevard, fell flat and attracted criticism, primarily because Marc was running before he could walk. He would insist on fleshing out performances with tedious guitar solos. Despite Bob Harris's assertions that 'he was a much, much better guitarist than he was ever given credit for', Marc's musicianship, as Tony advised him diplomatically, wasn't quite up to the virtuoso solo interlude yet. Marc shrugged him off, he would do as he pleased. He swanned off back to New York, for the recording of 'Jeepster', and perhaps to daub a couple more canvasses with Barbara. Those were the days.

Be careful what you wish for, might have been Visconti's mantra from then on. The American who had journeyed to London on a mission to find 'the next Beatles' was now saddled with a dream come true. Having had a hand in creating the monster, Tony's job was now to tame it – while feeding it and continuing to prod it just enough to make it breathe fire all over the charts.

There would be casualties.

With Marc in full glitter-rock mode since June's friend, publicist Chelita Secunda, applied sparkle teardrops to his face for a March appearance on *Top of the Pops*, a craze was launched. There appeared to be no stopping him. Although Chelita has been described as 'Marc's drug dealer', and although she did later become one, Jeff Dexter says that Marc's own dealer was someone else.

July 1971 saw the release of 'Get It On': the band's greatest hit. This was the single that spelled the end of Marc's friendship with John Peel. The DJ hated it, and said so – both on air and in his music column.

'Once Marc read John's review of "Get It On", he excommunicated him,' says Bob Harris. 'John didn't like the way Marc's music was getting so electric. But I always knew that it would go that way. Marc worshipped Phil Spector and his style of production, we used to talk about it endlessly on our record nights in. T. Rex was Spector as interpreted by Marc. To John, it was anathema.

'Since I'd arrived at Radio 1 in 1970, of course, Marc had been in the habit of giving me personal copies of absolutely everything T. Rex were putting out. Tony Blackburn on The Breakfast Show hated that I was getting "Swan" and all Marc's releases before Blackburn got them because he was the presenter of the station's flagship show, and he was "supposed" to get the new releases before anyone else!'

Peel's pith notwithstanding, 'Get It On' languished for four weeks at the top of the charts, and shifted about a million copies in the UK alone. In the US, where it was released as 'Bang A Gong (Get It On)' – to sidestep confusion with a band called Chase, who had a track out by the same name (as well as to avoid offence, 'get it on' being slang for sex), it peaked at Number Ten on the Billboard Pop Singles chart in January 1972: T. Rex's only big American hit. Visconti reckoned he knew the moment Marc first strummed it that it was a smash.

'I can buy that,' says Steve Harley. 'Tony would also have played it back after he'd mixed it and gone "Jeez. I'm sitting on a gold-mine here." He would have known that and recognised that. It's not arrogance or over-confidence, that's his job. It's just a quiet kind of confidence that a phenomenally talented producer like him has. With experience, you learn to make quick comparisons. He would have said to himself, "What else sounds like this? Nothing. And what we've done here that's original: is it also *good*? OH yeah. You can dance to it. What about those bits that are completely nothing to do with the rest of the song? Well, they're there because we're quirky. We're not scared to try a bit of mad imagination." Tony would have thought all that, and more. He wasn't afraid of Marc's talent, which is absolutely key – because Marc was in a niche almost entirely his own.'

Was the 'egg being broken into a teacup' which fans down the years have 'heard' on the track an example of 'mad imagination'? When I raise this with him, Visconti is amazed, having never previously heard it referred to.

'Tell me where it is in minutes and seconds,' he says, when I try to explain the sound.

The more I listened to it, the more I began to hear a glottalised click, actually two of them, of the type common in Sandawe (Tanzania Rift Valley) and Khoekhoe (South Africa/Botswana/Namibia) native tongues. It had long struck me how clever Marc was at making 'instrumental' noises with his mouth and nose: tongue-slaps, lip-smacks, inhalations, grunts, groans, spurts and deep-throated nasalisations which could be extremely suggestive. His latent interest in hippie ethnicity, foreign languages and the cultures of antiquity may have had something to do with it, I thought; for Marc was nothing if not an artist straddling worlds, paying homage to 'pasts' ancient and recent, while taking his stand against the burgeoning global monoculture threatening to erase individuality . . . ish.

'You have a very vivid imagination,' Tony joked. 'I think it's Marc saying "OW!" in a high voice with a very glottal front, which equalization and sonic compression would emphasise. I'll check it again in my studio later,' he said.

He did so. It was just as he thought.

'The sound you hear is Marc, as I've described it – not an egg!'

★ ★ ★

'Get It On' remains the subject of lively debate, not least because of a hot dispute over who played piano on it. Former 'Yes' star, keyboard wizard and Grumpy Old Man Rick Wakeman, remembers in minute detail how he came to be hired for the session. Unfortunately, so does Cardiff-born session pianist and former Amen Corner-man Derek John 'Blue' Weaver – perhaps best-known for having toured with the Bee Gees (he's a Saturday Night Weaver) and who replaced Rick in The Strawbs.

'I was living in Ilford at the time,' Rick tells me, 'where my rent was nine quid a week. I was reliant on anything I could do to earn the nine quid. I'd done a lot of sessions for Tony Visconti by then, and we got on very well. That week I'd been up in London, lugging around the demo studios looking for work. I got hold of Tony to see if he could use me, but he said there was nothing going. I went to find Marc, whom I'd known since Tyrannosaurus Rex days and was great mates with.

'We went off down the Wimpy Bar on the corner, just up from the 68 Oxford Street offices, bought a Coke, and had two straws. He asked me what I was doing, and I told him, "I'm in shit. I've got to get back to Ilford, but I can't pay the rent. She'll be there, my landlady. She always is when the rent is due."

'I'd given up, we'd said goodbye back upstairs, and I was about to go off and get on the train when Tony Visconti found me and said, "I've got a session for you. A midnight session." It was a full session, too, for which you'd get nine quid, as opposed to a demo, which paid two quid for three hours.

'Well, this was Christmas. "What's it for?" I asked Tony.

'"For Marc," he grinned. "We're going to record a new single tonight."

'I went along to Trident, where I knew all the guys. Got settled in. Tony said, "I'll run it through, let's have a listen."

'Once I'd heard it, I said, "but this is a glam guitar track. There's no space for a piano."

'Marc piped up at that point. He said, "All I want you to do is stick your thumb on, and every time I nod at you, do a *glissando* down the keys."

'"You could have done that," I said to him.

'Marc grinned at me.

'"You want your rent, don't you?" he said. "You wouldn't have taken it if I'd just given you the money."'

I track down Blue Weaver on the road between Bremen and Malaga. His recollection goes like this:

'I remember the session quite well – or as well as anything from those days,' he tells me. 'I went along with Tony and only Marc was there, no group at this time. Tracks had already been cut, and I'm not sure what was on tape. I did get the feeling though, I may have heard some piano at one time coming from the control room. Both Marc and Tony had an idea of what they wanted, it is not just *glissandos*. They asked me to play a very simple boogie part, which I did along with Marc's guitar, vocal, bass and drums. The piano track is so simple, far different from anything I believe Rick would have done, and my style exactly – the type of thing I did with Amen Corner. They then asked me to put some *glisses* on also, and knew exactly where they wanted them.

'I also recorded some just on their own, one of which was used later on "Telegram Sam". I've spoken to Tony many times over the years. Last time was at the MPG [Music Producers Guild] Awards in 2011, where, unprompted when I produced my small video camera, he says this': (Blue then gives me the video link, on which Visconti does appear to call him 'keyboard player on 'Bang A Gong (Get It On)' and 'Telegram Sam'.

When I put this to Tony Visconti, he was perplexed.

'I was side-swiped by Blue's claim a few years ago,' he

admitted. 'I am 99.9% certain it was Rick on "Get It On", and Blue played on a very similar-sounding song, at least riff-wise, "Telegram Sam".'

But on 'Sam', there is no piano . . .

'Blue did play on T. Rex records,' concedes Tony. 'The problem is with Marc, he was very mean with credits. But so were The Beatles. Keith Moon and Eric Clapton played on their records, and were never credited.

'It's worth mentioning,' he says, 'that both [Rick and Blue] played at early stages of the overdub sessions. It is usual practice to keep the lead vocals very quiet, or completely off, so that they can just concentrate on the rhythm section. Afterwards they might sometimes be unsure of what song they'd played on. It just becomes beats and chord changes in their memory. In those days, session musicians played three sessions a day, for three different artists.'

But what about the 'video evidence'?

'You know, nowadays you can't say anything in front of a camera phone and not see it on the internet,' Tony complains. 'I was up for an award that night from the MPG, which I got, but I was very nervous . . . so my official statement is, my memory tells me it was Rick, but Blue has presented a very persuasive argument that it was him.'

Memory is an organic thing, Tony reasons.

'I don't listen very much to my old productions, so it has been very difficult to reconcile the Blue/Rick controversy. I haven't listened to "Telegram Sam" for years. I agree that there is no piano on it. Yet it sounds like Blue playing on the sessions that made up most of *Tanx*, and there is piano on other tracks. I did know Blue from an earlier period, yet I have no recollection of him playing on "Get It On". We had so many musicians walking in and out the door during the overdubs for *Electric Warrior* during a very intense effort to put out an album that would catch the same sales as "Hot Love". As I have already told you, the lack of credits is due to Marc not wanting to credit musicians. If anyone was very clear who played what and when, it was him.

'I moved on to produce hundreds of albums in my career,' he adds, 'and I can easily say I can't remember the names of more than half of the musicians I've worked with. Rick and Blue . . . have played on thousands of recordings, so I wouldn't trust their memory either.'

All too soon, it began to dawn on those closest that the rock star lifestyle was taking its toll. Too much cocaine and Champagne: the usual?

'It's what happens to people when they get that kind of adoration,' says Jeff Dexter. 'They can lose their vision. That's what Marc started doing. But sometimes when he was drunk, he could be the funniest c--- alive.'

'People turn to downs or drugs and stuff like that just to get away from all the shit for a while,' commented the Grateful Dead's Jerry Garcia, before his own death in 1995. 'Jimi Hendrix lived with it. I never saw him without half a dozen weird people hanging around him – vampires and shit.'

'It was possibly an even wider issue than drink and drugs,' says Bob Harris. 'This was more about Marc becoming very aware of what he was. It takes a huge degree of self-absorption to be a rock star. You are surrounded by all kinds of people telling you how great you are, and wanting a piece of you. You keep reading stuff about yourself, you see your own image everywhere you go. It's almost impossible to stop something like that going to your head. I got, completely, what Marc and others like him went through.

'During the mid-1970s, when I was presenting *Whistle Test*, I was dealing with plenty of demons of my own. It takes enormous strength to resist the many temptations. That was not a stable time in my life at all – and that was just me and my relatively modest career. Imagine the level of superstardom that Marc was experiencing at that point, and what it must have been doing to his head.'

Electric Warrior was released to great acclaim on 24 September 1971. It reached Number 32 on the US Billboard 200, and reigned at Number One on the UK albums chart – the biggest-selling LP of 1971.

It featured two of T. Rex's best-loved songs – 'Get It On' and 'Jeepster'. It would also be voted Number 160 in *Rolling Stone* magazine's list of 'The 500 Greatest Albums of All Time', and as such, ought to have consolidated the band's popularity in America during their lifetime.

Why didn't it?

'I always felt that we were simply not marketed properly here,' reveals T. Rex drummer Bill Legend. 'I mean, I was never very interested in the business side, it was all about music for me. But I would say that attitude has a lot to do with your success – in any territory. You can't just come over here strutting your stuff, cursing and swearing. They didn't like that in America in the Seventies. They don't like it now. You have got to be respectful. You are visitors, they don't have to put up with you. Especially not in the rock'n'roll capital of the world.

'To be perfectly honest, America didn't like Marc's arrogance,' Bill says. 'He wanted to be up there right away with The Beatles and the Elton Johns and the other big-name artists he hung out with. In some ways, he should have been – he was very clever, extremely creative, and he certainly had enough musical talent. He never understood that you have to earn your stripes, and that it has to happen naturally. You can't blast into a scenario and throw your weight around. You have to ease in gently, take your time, let them get them used to you. They like humility and courtesy in these parts.

"Let it happen," I'd say to him. "Do your stuff." He'd never listen. His style was to ram it down people's throats. Americans don't like that.'

'America just didn't happen,' shrugs Simon Napier-Bell. 'He tried like mad. Toured and spent money. Dreamed. But as always with Marc, there was more dreaming than actual reality. I'm not sure the US would ever take to someone like him. He was too ephemeral. Perhaps the American industry felt, even if he happened, it would be too much of a passing fad to risk the full investment. They just dabbled with him. He was too fey for them.

'But he certainly tried. I was in New York one time when he was staying in the City Lodge, right downtown, on Broadway. For fun he went out to the balcony of his room with some friends and threw a few thousand dollars worth of $100 bills over, to float down onto the street . . . and watched the reaction of the people below. Nothing to do with making it in America or not, it's just a good story, and something he did more than once.

'Listening to his music 30 years later on the soundtrack of *Billy Elliot*,[3] you can hear it would have been strong enough and distinctive enough for America to take to,' counters Simon.

'The trouble is, it was pop, not rock. And pop depends as much on the image of the person as on the music. Marc's elfin image and flippant chat when he was being interviewed just wasn't the American style.' In America, 'cross-dressing' was considered as threatening and out-of-bounds as The Velvet Underground's songs about sado-masochism and leather.

'But his *music* was,' says Simon. 'Just listen to how Prince resurrects those late-night storming choruses with the daft super-high unison falsetto (like forest Banshees – more Marc than Visconti) – on "Raspberry Beret", for instance.'

Publicist Keith Altham offers this: 'Glam rock as a whole didn't take off in the States, where it's a much harder rock culture,' he reminds us. 'They saw glam as a gay thing, as much as anything else. Outside the more sophisticated areas of New York and LA, they weren't ready for it.

'But at that point, if you went south or north, you were in trouble if you were wearing make-up and had a bit of glitter on you. Wearing lipstick was almost a lynching offence in Texas. A few years later the New York Dolls came on the scene, and things loosened up a bit; but America wasn't ready for the sexual revolution when Marc came along and waggled it all in their faces. He was ahead of his time. He had it tough over there.'

Keith cites a number of English bands that failed to crack America while enjoying massive success in other parts of the world – notably the UK, Europe, Australasia and Japan.

'Slade was another one,' he points out.

'They too toured the US like mad, but never got the break-through. There was something "too English" about them. Americans at that stage thought that all English people were gay, I think.

'There is a foppery which is associated with some of our rock bands which just wouldn't cross over.

'It was "musical", which doesn't translate into "vaudeville". They didn't get it. It would be "these guys are just dressed up in silly fancy dress. They are not to be taken seriously."

'It's teenybop stuff, isn't it? Teenybop in America lasted about two, three years, and then it was trashed.'

Why?

'Broadly-speaking, the student campus was responsible for that. They adopted rock music to replace jazz, which is what early rock was: Cream were playing jazz, for my money. Rock took itself much more seriously. Pop didn't get much of a look-in, really. Not too many pop artists came out of the States. There were a few: The Osmonds, The Monkees – Davy Jones being the one Englishman in the line-up, but it was a completely American concept. A TV show. The idea was, here are the American Beatles. It worked, didn't it, but Marc could never compete with all that.'

But we did occasionally get bands out there, especially during and just after The Beatles: The Dave Clark Five, Gerry and the Pacemakers, Freddie and The Dreamers, Merseybeat in partic- ular enjoying a wave of popularity.

'It was all considered cute and cuddly,' observes Keith.

'And then came The Rolling Stones.'

Given that Jagger, especially, was such a style plagiarist, wasn't this a bit coals to Newcastle?

'I think it was par for the course,' he shrugs. 'They were all magpies. Jagger stole from James Brown and Tina Turner, and Marc stole from Jagger. Marc was also picking up stuff from Chuck Berry, Little Richard, Elvis, and adapting it to his own performance. Everybody borrowed from everybody else. You could do that to draw attention to yourself, but you still had to have talent to take it forward. Nothing was really "new" or 'unique', anyway. Jimi Hendrix was the greatest thief of them all. He pinched entire sequences of guitar-playing, that whole psych- edelic scene. In turn, Marc was incredibly thrown by Jimi Hendrix, the first time he saw him. Because he fancied himself as a bit of a guitarist, Marc. Pretty average when I saw him in the early days with Took, but he did get much better.'

'I always thought T. Rex was a bit too clever for the US,'

remarks independent producer James Saez of the Audio Labs, Los Angeles. Having worked with a stellar cast of stars, from Bruce Springsteen, Madonna and Bonnie Raitt to Prince, Jimmy Page and Ringo Starr, his views are widely respected.

'T. Rex always had that very angelic soft English vocal, with Marc's Rangemaster fuzz distortion guitar sound,' James says. 'Marc was a very English frontman. I think that had a huge effect on them not crossing over as much here. America wants every- thing a bit big and rude, which suits our cowboy culture. Marc didn't really have the bravado of Robert Plant, Freddie Mercury or Roger Daltrey. Nor did he really have the drama of Mick Jagger or David Bowie. Their music was a bit more personal; and I think that tender vibe really lends itself to film, as well as making a perfect soundtrack for the growing years of artists like Morrissey and Boy George. I don't think they sounded like anyone else either, and the songs were recorded a bit more like pop songs rather than straight rock'n'roll. So they don't sound as date-stamped as many other things do.'

'There was a more basic reason why David Bowie blossomed and flourished in the US while Marc didn't,' Anya Wilson believes.

'Marc's songwriting was incredible, and the musicians he chose were solid. But whenever I went to a live T. Rex show, the sound was absolutely terrible. It was awful. The sound compa- nies they were choosing were all wrong. It was always distortedly high. It was never clear. This magical music needed to be heard clearly. People wanted to listen to his words. That's my theory as to why he never went the distance in America.'

After a series of promotional dates in the Netherlands and West Germany, and with new manager Tony Secunda at the helm, T. Rex launched the *Electric Warriors* British tour.[4] Secunda, the former husband of glitter queen publicist Chelita, was a menacing risk-taker with a brazen business approach, not to mention an instinct for publicity stunts. He did nothing by halves. With Procol Harum, The Moody Blues and The Move under his belt, and with Motorhead, Steeleye Span, Marianne Faithfull and The Pretenders yet to come, he was more than qualified to wield a few hatchets and contracts on behalf of T. Rex. Secunda was infamous in the industry for having brainwaved a promotional postcard for The Move's single 'Flowers In the Rain', depicting the Right Honourable Harold Wilson, Prime Minister, naked in his bath. The record which launched BBC Radio 1 hardly needed the boost. The card's innuendo-laden caption took the biscuit. Wilson sued, won, and redirected all royalties to charity – in perpetuity.

It was Secunda who helped Marc launch his own record label, the T. Rex Wax Co. through EMI, which led to a vast increase in Marc's own fortunes; not to mention a rise in the exchange of suitcases of cash.

'I went out as compère on that first massive "T. Rextasy tour", remembers DJ Bob Harris. 'I suppose I was more than the compère, in a way. I was the support act. I'd do my bit, and then I'd introduce him. We did so many dates together – maybe 45, that first tour.

'"Hot Love" was Number One, and Marc Bolan was THE biggest thing in this country since The Beatles, I kid you not. Marc was IT for that year and a half – spring 1971 into 1973. His hot spot was as hot as anyone's ever had in this country. Some people find that hard to believe today, but it really was the case.

'On *Top of The Pops*, which was massively popular back then, being pretty much the only mainstream pop and rock show on offer, and the best exposure that an artist could have, he really got the moves down. He owned the studio, he wiped the floor with the rest of them, and they screamed for him even more. As a pop superstar, Marc was a natural. Everywhere you went, he hogged the headlines.'

The scenes of 'fan-demonium' reported all over the media were every bit as wild as experienced by The Beatles in their heyday, Bob insists, with girls even wielding scissors to cut off locks of Marc's hair.

'It was dangerous, and we were scared at times,' he admits. 'But Marc was ecstatic, he lapped it all up. This was exactly what he'd always dreamed of. At that point, superstardom was still a huge novelty, it was all still enormous fun. I always travelled in the same car as Marc when we went to the gigs. You can imagine him, at the peak of everything, happy and excited in his Bentley. He was flying high, with one foot on the ground. He was still very much one of us. And he never passed up an opportunity to make a little mischief. He'd say, "let's come up with different ways to introduce the band." The girls couldn't hear what we were saying anyway, they were screaming their insides out. So I'd be going: "The Total Wrecks!" or "The Space Cadets", Ladies and Gentlemen!' It always gave us a laugh.

'I can remember going to the *NME* Poll-Winners bash with him too,' says Bob. 'The Stones were there, The Kinks, all the big-name acts. It was pandemonium in the auditorium that night, too. People were going crazy, losing their heads. All they wanted was Marc – who was in heaven, you'd have to say. "He'd achieved what he had always wanted. He was a star."'

Come 1972, for Bob Harris, it was a very different story.

'Like a lot of people in Marc's life, I was suddenly moved on from,' he admits. 'These things happen. There was no single reason, no specific, memorable event. It wasn't a John Peel moment, Marc just didn't need me anymore. But it in no way neutralises our fond memories of Marc and June. How lovely and how innocent those times were, for me. I do sometimes wish I could go back there.'

For Tony Visconti, the considerable amount of drink and drugs that Marc, the formerly fierce anti-narcotic non-drug-taker, was now ingesting – while denying to himself and others that he had become dependent – must have seemed the beginning of the end.

Had Marc sensed the cult of Bowie creeping up on him? If he had, he kept *schtum*. When David introduced androgynous alter ego Ziggy Stardust and the Spiders From Mars at the Toby Jug pub in Tolworth in February 1972, Marc was not in attendance. Perhaps he was already fearful that his old rival was now set to overtake him in terms of sales and status.

'That's not true,' argues fan Caron Willans.

'At least, not at that point. Bowie's chart positions in the early Seventies were nowhere near as high as Marc's. Bowie's only Number One single in the Seventies was in 1975, with the re-issue of 'Space Oddity'. Bowie had six top 10 hits, and one Number One single. Marc had seven Top Ten hits, and four Number One singles. Album-wise, Marc had one more Number One album than Bowie. Their other albums reached similar positions, though Marc was slightly ahead. Marc was clearly the more successful chart-wise. It was only when Marc went into decline in the mid-Seventies, before his comeback, that Bowie overtook him. Bowie's "cult superstar status" took a lot longer to happen than some people think.'

A two-week promo tour of the States to promote *Electric Warrior* saw the band play to 5,000 fans at the Hollywood Palladium. In the audience was Mick Jagger, who came to see Marc after the show, and advised him to perform longer sets. The tour culminated in the gig they had all been waiting for, when T. Rex headlined at New York's Carnegie Hall, fulfilling Marc's lifelong dream. Reviews were mixed, and the show was described as having 'failed to live up to the hype'.

It has even been said that Marc blamed his new manager Tony Secunda for 'a disaster of a tour', and that he sacked him unceremoniously at the end of it. Jeff Dexter remembers otherwise.

'I was at the Carnegie Hall gig in February 1972,' he says. 'After that first proper T. Rex US tour, Secunda was certainly on the road with us later on. There are lovely, happy shots of us all together, long after the Carnegie Hall. I know that's the way it has been written up, that the two of them fell out after a "disastrous" gig in New York and that Marc got rid of him, but it's definitely not what happened.

'If you look at the pictures of us afterwards, it doesn't look anything like it was a disaster. It was quite a night, actually. I was managing the band America at the time.[5] I brought them to the gig, as we got a night off. But it *was* over-the-top and over-loud. It was lost. When you get to Carnegie Hall, you've made it. But Marc blew it – by being over-loud, and drunk.'

After the eventual, inevitable split from scallywag Secunda, T. Rex moved into their own Warrior Music Projects Ltd offices in Doughty Street, run by June with the help of Chelita. 'Telegram Sam' appeared – their first single of the year, released on 21 January 1972, and Number One by 5 February – as if to mark another breaking dawn. The song was said to have been written for music biz accountant Sam Alder, who cabled Marc when 'Get It On' went to Number One. Tony Secunda bobbed around for years saying that he was the Main Man referred to, while others interpreted it as a reference to David Bowie.[6] Edward Lear met Lewis Carroll in characters like Jungle faced Jake, Golden Nose Slim and Purple Pie Pete – and an 'alright' 'Bobby' was reckoned to be Bob Dylan.

'Telegram Sam' is arguably the quintessential T. Rex record. Marc and Tony had now reached a peak of perfect harmony, if only musically. What was captured of the stone by his philosopher was alchemical; base elements were transmuted into discs of gold. The song was the ultimate aural extension of Marc, too: somewhat showy and sumptuous, granted, but also simply and recognisably him.

London was all swung-out in 1972, in part as a by-product of concerted efforts to control the drug culture. Most venues now closed too early for those seeking to see in the dawn. The social habits of the hip and trendy required something of a rethink. The 'underground' may have dissipated, but under ground was where late-night clubbing and drinking were heading.

'The only places that stayed open after midnight seemed to be hosting a perpetual gloomy wake for the Sixties,' recalled rock journalist Nick Kent, in his Seventies memoir *Apathy For The Devil*.

He also remembers a curious apparition ducking and diving around London at the time: Iggy Pop, of American punk forerunners The Stooges. The band had relocated to the UK at either just the wrong time, or at exactly the right time, given that Punk hadn't happened yet – but was about to. Their frontman was in the habit of turning up solo to other people's gigs. Blending unobtrusively into the audience, he would hang around and check out the 'competition'.

'He spoke highly of a T. Rex concert he'd witnessed at Wembley – the same show that was filmed by Ringo Starr for the

Born To Boogie film. Iggy was quite a fan of Bolan's back in the day,' wrote Kent.

'He'd even managed to get hold of a pre-release white-label acetate of *The Slider* album, and played it a lot at The Stooges' London headquarters. He seemed to hold Bolan in higher esteem than his new pal Bowie – at least on a musical level.'

13
Sting Like a Bee

'I didn't follow Marc's career particularly,' confesses his original producer Mike Hurst. 'I was doing Cat Stevens, The Move, and the Spencer Davis Group. You live in a studio, you don't get out much, you lose your handle on the world.

'But when he became a star, I was *thrilled*,' Mike says. 'I thought, *yeah*. That's what he wanted to do, and he's done it! We met up a few times at *Top of The Pops*, and it was always very pleasant. He was doing all the make-up, the glitter stuff, as was Bowie. They were extraordinary times.

'People said that Marc Bolan was "just a pop artist". But what a stupid thing to say. What *is* pop? It's *popular* music. That means, an awful lot of people like it. If you're popular, then good for you, what could be wrong with that? I produced Showaddywaddy for years, who were tremendously successful. Not to everyone's taste but they had eighteen Top 20 hits.[1] Even if you didn't like it, you couldn't say they were no good. If you called them idiots, you were saying that the general public were idiots too!'

In March 1972, the band decamped to Paris to commence work on the next T. Rex album, *The Slider*. It was an early Elton John LP that gave the 18th century Château d'Hérouville its nick-name, *Honky Château*; Elton himself raved to Marc about the facilities there. Situated in the Oise Valley village of Auvers, where Dutch impressionist Vincent van Gogh took his life in July 1890 at the age of 37,[2] the castle had once been the home of Polish pianist and composer Frederic Chopin, as well as the setting for his covert romance with Amantine Dupin.[3] So much tragedy, history and intrigue was music to Marc's classically-inclined ears.

The Château, approached through imposing, cast-iron gates and via a long sweep of drive, had solid stone walls which were several feet thick in places. Despite its air of elegance and tranquillity, it was quite a fortress – which suited security-conscious rock superstars fine. It had originally been adapted as a residential recording studio in the mid-Sixties by French composer Michel Magne. By the 1970s it was a rock'n'roll haven, not just for those on tax-limitation missions, but thanks to its then state-of-the-art 16-track studio. Instruments and vocals could be recorded inside the studio or out in the open air – which Marc loved, said Jeff Dexter, because of the exquisite sound that could be achieved. It was not in any flight path, and its rambling grounds were vast.

With two wings, some thirty bedrooms, a swimming pool, explorable out-houses, its own wine (complete with a very saucy bottle label), a haunted chamber and hot-and-cold stunning French girls – not to mention hearty home-cooked cuisine served on refectory tables in front of roaring log fires – the majestic Château and its Strawberry Studios were more than conducive to creativity. It played host to the cream of the bands of the day, among them Pink Floyd and Cat Stevens. The Bee Gees, Iggy Pop and Fleetwood Mac would all follow the *Yellow Brick Road* down there (that Elton album was recorded in d'Hérouville too). Marc recommended the Château to David Bowie, who would record *Pin Ups* there the following year – and also *Low*, in 1977, the year Marc died.

'I remember that trip like it was yesterday,' says former head roadie Mick O'Halloran. 'It was the only time Marc and I ever had a row. If ever anything blew up, I usually kept my head down, defended them quietly, made excuses for them, smoothed things over. I never wanted to get Marc and June a bad name. But sometimes things go too far.

'We were all in the Château, sitting round the table exhausted, when Marc came in and started demanding certain things. Well, I snapped. We'd travelled from America, and I'd driven the gear in the van all the way down from London to France – without a break. Marc wanted to rehearse there and then, the very afternoon we arrived; but he never told me until that moment. So it wasn't scheduled, and I wasn't prepared.

'"I wanna do it *now*, man!" he kept insisting.

'"We're not booked into the studio until tomorrow",' I reminded him. He wasn't listening.

'"I want the equipment up in the studio *now*!" he yelled. He wasn't joking. Well, this was the straw that broke the camel's back. Imagine the two, three flights of little old farm stairs in this place. Terrible to get up and down, for one great big bloke with a couple of tons of heavy gear. I was wiped out after all the travelling. I couldn't believe he was asking me to do this.

'All they'd done, him and June, was get on the plane, get off the plane, get in the limo, get driven. They had probably been asleep most of the way. We'd flown, loaded off, loaded on, and driven long-distance, all the way from London. I was driving a transit van, too, which you couldn't call comfortable.

'Marc started telling me, "I want it *done*, O'Halloran, and I want it done *now*!"

'That was it. I banged the table. I really lost it. It was the first time I'd ever done that, since I started working for Marc and June. The band all stopped what they were doing and looked at me. Steve Currie was amazed, I can see his face now.

'I always kept myself to myself, I never drank, I'd never done dope. Why? I'd seen the fall-out, and it wasn't sweet. I just wanted to do my work, get my wages, and go home to my wife and child. I suppose I snapped. I found myself weighing it all up in a split second. The wages I was getting, the amount of travelling I was doing: was it all worth it? I saw red. I started shouting at Marc. He didn't know what hit him.

'"You're getting too big-headed now," I yelled at him. "I can't stand this anymore. There's the keys to the van, I'm going back, you drive it home yourself." Marc seemed a bit scared. I didn't swear, on my life, and I didn't hit him. But I could have, and that scared *me*. I felt sorry afterwards, that I'd said such things. But it was out there, I couldn't take it back.

'"Come on, man, don't be like that," Marc said. I'd stopped him in his tracks, and now he was trying to be reasonable. He put his hand on my arm, and walked me outside. We sat down by the pool and talked.

'"Is it the money?" he asked me.

'"No," I said. "It's not the money, Marc. It's *you*. You are treating people so badly, without a thought for their feelings. Look where it's heading. It's no good."'

Why had Marc got that way, does Mick think? It takes him a while to answer, he is clearly choked by the recollection.

'Simple, really. The drink. The dope. Everything happening

too fast for him. He was out of control. It hurt me to see him like that. I'd seen it all before,' Mick adds, sadly.

'As you go up in the estimation of your many fans, you come down in the estimation of the people closest to you. Because it's gone to your head. Marc was upset, out there by the pool with me. He was talking quietly, like a little boy.

'"I'll give you a rise. From today," he said to me. That was his way of pleading with me to stay on.

'"All right then," I said to him. But I had his attention now, and I wasn't going to let it go.

'"It's the way you treat people in front of people," I said again. "It's not nice. It's not *you*, Marc. You've got to stop it."

'"Yes," he agreed, shaking his head, "I will."

'He never held a grudge against me for saying the things I said,' Mick tells me. 'I think in some ways he was grateful that I'd said it. But he didn't change,' he admits, shaking his head. 'As a matter of fact, it got worse. He started getting into the heavier stuff, drug-wise. He was losing himself to it – and he couldn't admit that to himself. I told him again, on several occasions. He just ignored me. Eventually, I felt I had to take him aside again. He was the kid and I was the dad. I felt responsible.

'"You'll go down and down, Marc," I warned him, "until they don't want you anymore."

'"It's none of your business, O'Halloran," he would say.

'"Well I can't stand it much longer," I would tell him, "and who's gonna tell you then?"

'"If you feel like that, you know what you can do," he sneered at me.

'"Why don't you just stop being an idiot?" I asked him.

'"Just stop doing the drink and the dope. Clean yourself up! No one else does it!"

'I only found out afterwards that everyone else *was* doing it,' says Mick, ruefully. 'My eyes were closed to all that. I just wasn't seeing what was going on.'

Even after Marc went off the rails, Mick stuck by Marc until the end. How was he able to bring himself to do that?

'I loved him,' says Mick. 'It's as simple as that.'

The Slider was finished in just five days, after which the band moved on to Rosenberg Studios, Copenhagen, to record additional sessions. Flo & Eddie's back-ups were done at LA's Elektra studios the following month. Marc then gave his full attention to their forthcoming Wembley concerts . . . and to Ringo Starr.

You know that you've made it when they start making movies about you? This was precisely the glamorous world of broad-spectrum celebrity to which Marc Bolan aspired. He must have been pinching himself when Ringo first proposed the idea of a film based on and featuring footage from one of T. Rex's pandemonic live concerts. The film, according to Ringo's extravagant vision, would take them the rest of the year to make, and would include studio scenes featuring Elton John and Ringo himself, to augment T. Rex's Wembley concert footage.

'We'd hang out,' recalled Ringo, in a Hard Rock Café interview. 'I wrote [his own single] "Back Off Boogaloo" because [Marc] came to dinner, and that's how he spoke.

'So I said to him one day, "Why don't we do a movie?" He was very proud of his poetry. Every time he came to say hi, he'd say, "I'm the Number One-selling poet in Britain!" It was as important to him as his music.

'Anyway, I said, "Let's make a movie. I'll bring the cameras and everything else. You bring yourself. And that's what we'll do." And we did. We had a lot of fun. Especially with the sketches.'

Ringo had chosen the locations already: Apple's Savile Row Studios, Tittenhurst Park (at that time the home of John Lennon and Yoko Ono), and Denham studios in Buckinghamshire. The whole thing would have a *Magical Mystery Tour* meets *Imagine* meets *Alice In Wonderland* flavour. This, the zenith of T. Rextasy as the 'official' successor to Beatlemania – after all, he had a genuine Beatle's blessing – was, if only he'd known it, Marc's finest hour.

By the time *The Slider* was being torn off the shelves by eager fans in July 1972, both Beep Fallon and Bob Harris were out of the picture. But the show must go on, and on it went. A short, riotous UK tour confirmed Marc's deepest fears: that to continue to perform live with fans behaving uncontrollably at his gigs was simply asking for it. He feared for his safety. He began to suggest in interviews that he was planning to withdraw from public life; that he intended to drop out, turn his back on rock stardom and become a complete recluse. But who put that idea into his head? Was he following the earlier example of Bob Dylan, or had he been talking to David Bowie again? The bond between them was as strong as ever, despite the obvious jealousies. Just twelve months later, having performed his 'Ziggy' track 'Lady Stardust' (said to be about Marc) on stage at the Rainbow Theatre while Bolan's projected image pouted from the backdrop curtain, and after paying homage to T. Rex on 'All The Young Dudes' (which Bowie wrote, then gave to Mott the Hoople), David would retire Ziggy Stardust and the Spiders from Mars, and would be pulling a Greta Garbo of his own.[4]

With fan attention in London now out of control, Marc and June were forced to abandon their Little Venice flat – where fans were writing all over the walls, depositing paraphernalia and harassing the neighbours – to a less-accessible top-security apartment in

Marble Arch. Their full-time entourage now consisted of roadie Mick O'Halloran and minder/driver Micky 'Marmalade' Gray. Jeff Dexter was on hand most days, too, doing 'bits of everything'.

Money, it seemed, was no object. As well as the 'Rolls Royce Bentley', they now owned a purple Jaguar and a red Ferrari, which June adored. Marc would soon acquire a purple Mini 1275 GT runaround, which had formerly belonged to Steve O'Rourke, manager of Pink Floyd.

Even Tony Visconti was amazed by the collection of guitars that Marc had amassed: 'a Les Paul '48, a Les Paul Special 1961, a 1958 Fender Stratocaster, a Fender Custom Telecaster, two Japanese acoustic guitars (an Aria and an Astoria), a Gibson Special and a 1969 Epiphone.' There was also a bespoke Zemaitis, as played by Ronnie Wood. By Tony's reckoning, most of those guitars would change hands today for between £60,000 and £100,000 – and that's without them having been owned and played by Marc Bolan.

Nicky Graham, a former member of hard rock band Tucky Buzzard, worked in the Main Man offices and played keyboards for Bowie on and off throughout 1972 on the *Spiders* tour. He went on to become A&R manager at CBS Records, where he signed The Clash. He produced hits for The Nolans, Bros, Ant & Dec, Shakin' Stevens, Barbara Dickson and Bonnie Tyler, and conceived – with former Wizard (Bahamas) executive Brian Dunham – the Marc Bolan musical *20th Century Boy*.

'Marc Bolan never existed,' Graham maintains. 'He was Mark Feld's "Ziggy Stardust". He invented his own personal Pinocchio, and brought him to life. Mark never needed a Svengali. He was his *own* Svengali. Managers, to him, were notional; which is why, perhaps, he had so many of them. They were there to do the business and the money, nothing more.'

★ ★ ★

Addicted to his superstar lifestyle, and having somehow 'forgotten' to hit the road to promote his new album and single around the UK, he barely noticed that *The Slider* itself was on the slide already – a chilling prediction of the direction his career was to take.

There was, by chance, a second random meeting with American singer Gloria Jones that summer. Gloria had flown into London as part of Joe Cocker's impressive road-show, and was performing in a festival at south-east London's Crystal Palace. Joe treated his backing singers to an evening up at the Speakeasy club one night after the show, their party pitching up at its discreet doors just as Bolan and his entourage stepped out to get into Marc's Bentley. They recognised each other and said hello, Gloria remembers. Nothing came of the encounter at the time. Everything would.

It was Jeff Dexter who came up with the manager who would prove the most loyal and enduring. Tony Howard had long been a friend of the Bolan inner circle, but kept himself to himself. Few knew the extent of his music business credentials.

A reporter for the *NME* in the early Sixties, Howard found himself working with the manager of the Pretty Things in a new agency, and by 1965 was the exclusive booker for avant garde club Blaises – choosing bands like The Byrds and The Ike & Tina Turner Revue, and allowing unknown guitarist Jimi Hendrix to sit in with jazz/rock keyboard and organ player Brian Auger. Three years later he was booking artists into the Speakeasy, Revolution and UFO. Tony Howard had been one of the first to hear potential in psychedelia, and signed Pink Floyd and other underground cousins to the Bryan Morrison Agency. After Beatles' manager Brian Epstein died in 1967, and his company merged with Bryan Morrison's, Howard and his colleague Steve O'Rourke (Pink Floyd's manager) moved to NEMS.[5] Between 1969 and 1973, he ran The Speakeasy out of NEMS while continuing to book acts: Jeff Beck, Fairport Convention, T. Rex and so on. After the sale of NEMS in 1973, he went on holiday.

'I'd just been in Greece with Tony, who was the booking agent from Bryan Morrison days,' recalls Jeff. 'Things were getting out of hand in Doughty Street. It was just Chelita and June running the show now, and they were run ragged. It was obvious they needed more. I wasn't in a position to get too involved at the time, although I did come on board later as tour manager.

'I talked with Chelita and said, "Look, Tony's just back off holiday, he's all refreshed, why don't we get him to be manager as well as agent?" Chelita said, "I told Marc that as well, but he doesn't want another straight manager from the business."

'I then spoke to Marc and June – you always had to talk to June, because she was the boss . . .' for a while longer, at least. 'I explained what had been happening over the last few years with NEMS and the Bryan Morrison agency,' Jeff goes on.

'I told them that they could do a lot worse than Tony Howard. He was the most honest, truthful person they could ever deal with. A true professional. Tony was one of those people who wouldn't ever do anything that wasn't correct.'

They continued to voice their misgivings, having had little luck with managers, but decided eventually to trust their old friend's advice.

'I made the introduction and they had a couple of meetings,' said Jeff. 'It was up to them. At one of the meetings Tony said, "Well look, I can understand what you've been through, and I can see why you're anxious. Rather than me signing you, then, you sign me. I'll be your man." Marc went – and June went – "We sign *you*?" "Yep," he said. And they got it.'

It marked the beginning of the end of June's superglue hold on Marc. Thus did the struggle for command commence. But it would be fair play: no sneaking round to the rival's gaff with an envelope stuffed with fifties this time.

'The arrangement made sense,' says Dexter, oblivious of any wrong-doing whatsoever on June's part. 'Tony Howard had foresight', Jeff goes on. 'He knew how paranoid Marc and June had become about business and finances (perhaps June more so than Marc). He was a very sharp and clever bloke. "Uncle Grouch", as we called him, was the font of all knowledge to us.

'It was Tony who hired a new driver for Marc, to take a bit more pressure off, and make sure Marc was always safe. His name was Alphi O'Leary.'[6]

Alphi and his brother Laurie were a pair of bluff Eastenders with connections to the London underworld. Laurie had once managed a group called 'Mickey Finn & The Bluemen' – the reason that T. Rex's Micky originally left out the 'e'. In 1963, Laurie was appointed manager of Esmeralda's Barn, a high-profile Knightsbridge nightclub owned by the Kray Twins. Come 1966, he had graduated to Sybilla's Club in Mayfair, whose board of directors included George Harrison and DJ Alan Freeman. Regular customers Frank Sinatra, Mick Jagger and John Lennon were entertained there by fellow artists such as Joe Cocker, José Feliciano and Chuck Berry. Two years later, Laurie found himself in charge of the Speakeasy, where every name of the era gathered to jam. It was there that he had a hand in launching the careers of many artists, including Bob Marley, Elton John and Cockney Rebel. Laurie became tour manager to a variety of visiting American acts, Marvin Gaye, Otis Redding and The Drifters among them.

He was appointed personal manager to Doris Stokes, amid outraged claims that the much-published, world-famous medium relied on 'plants' in the audiences of her live shows – in order to give the impression that she was in touch with the dearly departed. After her death in 1987, Stokes's role was assumed by her namesake – clairvoyant Doris Collins – who also happened to be managed by Laurie O'Leary. Laurie and Doris Stokes would loom large, albeit briefly, in the life of Phyllis Feld about a year after the death of her son. Doris gave Phyllis a reading, which she also wrote about, in which she described Marc singing the words to the pop song 'Tie A Yellow Ribbon Round The Old Oak Tree', and made various other personal references.

Laurie O'Leary having been so close to people in the Bolan camp, however, it seems likely that he tipped old Doris off.

Laurie's brother Alphi, a gentle giant who was given to the biggest bear hugs and who was fiercely loyal to his friends, watched over Marc until an accident forced him to retire from driving.

With his tattooed arms, ruddy cheeks and ever-ready smile, everybody loved him, recalls Jeff Dexter.

The T. Rex operation would shortly move to new premises, at 69 New Bond Street, in London's Mayfair. Howard would remain Marc's manager until the end. While some have dismissed him as a 'yes-man', those in the know explain that Howard's *modus operandi* was subtle, and could be deceptive.

His softly-softly approach with Marc, and his instinct for balance – letting the big-shot rock star think that he was getting his own way all the time, while orchestrating situations to ensure that what Marc was getting was what was best for him, was masterly. Not everybody got his way of doing things. This was mostly their loss.

★ ★ ★

August 1972 saw them all back at the Château d'Hérouville, for the recording of 'Children Of The Revolution', and to experiment with tracks for the next album, *Tanx*. 'Solid Gold Easy Action' happened to pop into Marc's consciousness while they were down there, which was a bonus. But other aspects of the visit were not so good.

Firstly, Tony Visconti's relationship with Marc had cooled to the point that the pair could barely stand each other in the studio. There had for some time been issues over contracts and money. New lawyers had been given *carte blanche* to trample all over agreements that June and Marc had approved with Tony, sometimes on little more than a handshake. There is a suggestion of disingenuity and double-crossing on June's part. To affable, principled, laid-back Visconti, this all seemed a disloyal move.

Tony began to sense an insincerity and possible dishonesty in dealings. He describes candidly in his autobiography how he knew that his friendship with Marc was now over, and that he was finding both his behaviour and his persona increasingly intolerable. Tony was only 'biding his time' by continuing to record with Marc, he admits, until he could find a way of extricating himself that would not cost him. The considerable amount of booze and drugs that Marc, the formerly vehement non-drug-taker, was now ingesting – while denying to himself and others that he had become dependent – was key.

Secondly, Château owner Michel Magne was now way out of his depth, trying to run an efficient and profit-making ship. Despite d'Hérouville's popularity as a residential recording venue, Magne couldn't keep pace with expenses. Both the property and its music facilities had deteriorated drastically. Staying abreast of ever-changing technology required massive investment, while recording equipment required constant parts replacement, service and repair. Magne was facing eye-watering maintenance and legal bills. The business was haemorrhaging money. Exhausted come autumn 1972, an increasingly desperate Magne resorted to renting out his premises to a studio syndicate. There was even talk at one point of Virgin or Trident purchasing the place outright, but nothing came of it.

Whatever the overview, Marc was devastated that his favourite retreat in the world was now a mere shadow of its former self. He moaned about everything, his complaints mostly falling on deaf ears. That was just 'Marc being Marc', as Mick O'Halloran puts it. But he had to admit, the place was not as clean and well-kept as before. External plaster was crumbling and in need of renovation, while its dilapidated interiors were blighted by woodworm and peeling paint. Not even dead light bulbs had been changed – a full-time job in itself for a *bricoleur* in such an extensive property. Vast swathes of the grounds were now a tangle of overgrowth, but the *jardiniers* were long-gone. His 'home from home' was not at all as Marc remembered it. This upset him very much.[7]

Could even June tell how deeply the Château's deterioration affected Marc psychologically? The substance dependency that he continued to deny, both to himself and others, was blurring his perspective while accentuating every emotion. Thus, the Château's stark decline was a metaphor for personal experience. It reflected what Marc himself was going through. This tangible reminder of something once glorious but now on the wane was the thing he was neither ready nor willing to face.

It was with the intention of creating their own Château d'Hérouville that Marc and June decided to find themselves a country house. June conducted an extensive search with Sir Mark Palmer, Her Majesty the Queen's godson. This led to them buying, that October, the Old Rectory at Weston Under

Penyard in the Welsh Marches, on the edge of the Forest of Dean. They had like-minded friends in the neighbourhood: the Ormsby Gores;[8] Alexis de la Falaise, a furniture designer who had appeared in Andy Warhol's *Tub Girls*; mover-and-shaker Martin Wilkinson, and Sir Mark himself: a colourful figure who, as one of the first pioneering New Age travellers, lived in a gypsy caravan.

'All lovely, alternative, drop-out rock'n'roll toffs,' remembers Jeff Dexter. 'Marc was their "prophet". They all had a copy of *Prophet, Seers & Sages* . . . and they were all learning guitar. They strummed them under their druid cloaks! All thanks to Marc. Because of us, particularly Sir Mark Palmer, they all wanted to speak with a Cockney accent. There was this yearning in such people to attach themselves to somebody or something which could give their lives meaning.

'We'd come from different places,' adds Jeff, 'but that didn't matter. These people loved the Stones, for instance. They loved the glamour of what we were doing. Their parents and grandparents had all been through the mad 1920s/1930s debauchery. Our aristo friends just wanted a piece of that too, but in a modern way.'

With plenty of land to develop stables and create studios, the grade II-listed 17th century vicarage with Roman foundations and a ruined castle tower, purchased from the Church of England, was to be their retreat away from the madding crowd.

The house was a bargain, being in an advanced state of disrepair. Restoration work was carried out on its oak floorboards, plaster ceilings and large staircase, and some funky fittings were installed – including a raspberry-coloured bathroom suite off the master bedroom. There was even the requisite rock star bathtub: a double, with gold taps.

A library was created on the ground floor, with French windows leading out to the lawn. Marc is believed to have chosen the rectory for its view of May Hill, a landmark which can be seen from miles away. He would certainly have found The Hill's pagan and classical associations enchanting, harking back as they did to the things which had inspired and informed his earliest poetry and songwriting. As such, May Hill – *The Beltane*, no less – could have been 'welcoming him home'. Its copse of trees, which the Hill appears to 'wear', like a crown, is said by locals to 'denote a coven of crones, left there after a spell.' Druids, dragons, unicorns, warlocks . . . not hard to imagine the like lurking there, especially after the odd glass of wine, or at nightfall.

'May Hill is certainly a bewitching place, swirling with mystery,' said the celebrated political sketch writer and journalist Quentin Letts, who once visited the house with a view to buying it as a family home. 'Bolan would surely have enjoyed the view of it from the rectory's upper windows. West, towards Wales, there are panoramas of the Black Mountains.'

Described by John Masefield in his poem 'The Everlasting Mercy', May Hill is where composer Gerald Finzi's ashes were scattered.[9] Morris dancers also gather there each May Day with hundreds of well-wishers, to welcome the dawn – a ceremony which dates back several centuries.

The Feld Bolans never moved in officially – although Marc remained its legal owner until 1977, when Tony and Nina Leach bought it from the Wizard Group/Warrior Music, shortly before his death. They returned it to the market 26 years later, asking £1.25 million.

The facade of the rectory still bears an impressive white shield, engraved with the motto of Oxford University: 'Dominus Illuminatio Mea': 'The Lord is my light.'

14

The Heat's On, Mister

The most important decade yet in the cross-over of African-American music, the Seventies had soul for a heartbeat, funk for nerve, and a new pop-jazz rhythm fizzing in its bloodstream. Berry Gordy stood the first round with the launch of his Tamla Label in 1959, then Motown in 1960.

The corporation played a vital part in the racial integration of popular music, reflecting social changes and tastes and launching gigantic careers – Diana Ross's and The Jackson 5's not least. Dionne Warwick, Stevie Wonder, Gladys Knight & The Pips and countless others surfed the crest of this wave, while Barry White, Donna Summer and their funky soul-mates got set to pour the black into disco.

Marvin Gaye's smooth offerings *What's Going On* and *Let's Get It On*, and Stevie Wonder's superlative *Music of My Mind*, *Talking Book* and *Innervisions* were the albums of the moment. Marc, ever mindful of the latest trends, soaked all this up, and was fascinated. He wanted in, sensing again another new direction that the charts were about to take. He began experimenting, with a view to harnessing a few black elements of his own.[1]

September 1972 had seen T. Rex depart for Canada, ready to flog again their flagging American tour horse. With Marc still kidding himself that he could crack the US, an air of desperation pervaded the trek. Gig reviews were far from ecstatic, while their domestic star was demonstrably on the wane. Little wonder that the exuberant backing vocalists conferred upon them at notorious rock promoter Bill Graham's Winterland concert venue in San Francisco were fallen upon as welcome distraction. Those singers were Stephanie Spruill, Oma Drake,[2] and Gloria Jones.[3]

T. Rex, performing on the same bill as Poco, and The Doobie Brothers, rode roughshod all over Graham's cherished stage with their elaborate set.

'When Bill arrived and saw his stage covered in stuff, he completely freaked out, and demanded to have "all that shit removed!"' remembers Jeff Dexter. 'It was a hideous falling-out, which proved catastrophic to the tour. Arguing with such a major American promoter was a disaster. It was hugely hurtful to everyone, not least Tony Howard.'

'Marc was impressed by Gloria from the off,' remembers Marc's roadie, Mick O'Halloran. 'She was very talented musically, and Marc picked up on that. It was what first attracted him to her, there was nothing else on his mind at that point. He was just very impressed by the relative success she'd had in America – especially since it was the thing he continued to crave the most. Marc was definitely still in love with June when Gloria first was on the scene,' Mick says.

'It was written all over him. They had chemistry, you could feel it. But they drifted, as some couples do. There were things getting in the way – not least, the brandy, the Champagne and the coke. I carried on trying to talk to him about all that. I was probably the closest one to him at that point. But he wasn't going to listen to me.

'As always, it was all about timing,' he adds. 'June wasn't there. Gloria was. She took him to a couple of do's. Invited him round to meet her mum and dad. No one thought anything of it. She had something that Marc really wanted for himself, and that made her an object of fascination for him. She was working with a lot of big artists and musicians – Gladys Knight, Ike and Tina – and maybe it went through Marc's head that she could help get him get involved with people like that. It would have been a very Marc thing to do. That, I'm sure, was what drew him to her initially. After a time, things kicked off between them, as these things do.'

Gloria Richetta Jones was born in Cincinnati, Ohio, in 1945, the daughter of a Pentecostal minister, and was two years older than Marc. She sang and played piano from an early age, showing such promise that her family relocated to Los Angeles when she was 7, with a view to getting her into the movies. She co-created her first Gospel group The Cogic Singers while she was still only 14, a line-up which also featured Billy Preston[4] and which achieved relative fame.

At 19, she was picked up by songwriter Ed Cobb, who signed her to his Greengrass Productions. Cobb wrote and produced her first hit record, 'Heartbeat Pts 1&2', toured her across America, and landed her many appearances on US television.

Her most famous recording was the 1964 Cobb-penned number which remains her signature: 'Tainted Love'.[5]

Like her fellow 'Young, Gifted and Black' soul sister Marsha Hunt, Gloria had starred in *Hair* the musical, but in Los Angeles. It was a meeting with singer Pam Sawyer that led Gloria, already the mother of a young son, Walter, to begin writing for Motown Records, where she worked with The Four Tops, The Commodores, The Jackson 5 and Gladys Knight & The Pips.

Gloria and Marc fell in love unexpectedly. It took them both by surprise.

'An interracial couple is nothing shocking today,' Gloria tells me, when I catch up with her in Los Angeles. She is staying with her son Rolan, on a visit from her home in Sierra Leone. She moved to West Africa from South Africa a few years ago, in order to 'help the children'. She is creating there, slowly, the Marc Bolan School of Music and Film. It may seem an unlikely place to do it, but she has her reasons. There are no buildings, the School meets in borrowed premises. It relies on charitable donations, and progress is one-forward-two-back, all very hard. But Gloria is galvanised by every delivery of second-hand musical instruments. There is a vague sense that she is punishing herself, but she evades the question. What you can't knock is her spirit and determination. She is doing work that she knows Marc would have wanted. It's what spurs her on. From Los Angeles, this visit, she travels to Cleveland, Ohio for meetings with the curators at the Rock and Roll Hall of Fame. She tells me that their museum has long planned a section dedicated to the memory of Marc Bolan – but that they haven't got any artefacts to put in it. To all fans in possession of guitars, clothes, recordings, photographs and other personal property stolen from Marc's and Gloria's house after his death: even if you paid good money, you know where to send it.

'Marc and I weren't thinking about each other in terms of a "relationship" when we first started, Gloria tells me. 'It was about music. There was an element of Soul creeping into Marc's electric sound at the time, which I found very interesting. It gave us something in common. I think he was looking at all kinds of ways to update his brand of music, keep it flowing and alive. He was still looking to do something which would win him an American following. That constant change and longing to keep improving himself, be a better and better musician, was the thing I admired about him the most.'

Other musicians were experimenting too, Gloria points out.

'This was nothing unusual. David Bowie went on to do R&B, for example. The only problem was when the fans didn't want you trying different things, when they wanted the music to keep on sounding the same. That's when it stagnates. You've got to keep moving, keep taking risks.'

Tony Howard was now installed, and starting to impose his particular brand of management.

'They were lucky to have him,' remarks one high-profile industry executive, who prefers to be nameless.

'So many managers at that time were complete arseholes: utter bullies who would stop at nothing to succeed, not so much for their artists, but for themselves. As for the fans, the spending public, 'screw them!' was the attitude. Tony Howard wasn't like that at all. He respected the fans. He understood completely that they were the ones who turned an artist into a star in the first place.'

Bands and those who organised and represented them were all feeling their way in the early Seventies. Lacking decent precedents and without specific rules to guide them, everyone made it up as they went along. Specialist showbusiness lawyers were not as ubiquitous as they are today. Not every manager had his artist's best interests at heart. Many were double-crossed, undersold or ripped off – not least Marc Bolan and David Bowie.

At the height of his fame, Marc had already had so many managers, agents, record labels, publishers and distributors that 'rights' to his work were scattered all over the place, with too many separate factions 'owning' a bit. Napier-Bell, one of the more scrupulous, if occasionally mischievous, operators in the business, was one of them. Having paid for those early recording sessions himself, he did have a genuine right to them.

'I remember Kit Lambert receiving a rather provocative letter from one of Marc's managers, suggesting that it was no longer in order for them to have a share in the rights to his recordings,' Simon tells me.

'Kit never took such things lying down, he always retaliated, and good for him. He rang me to ask whether I had any of the original recordings I'd done with Marc. As a matter of fact, I did. Why not release them? I agreed with Kit to lease them to Track Records. Kit had an idea to put out an album, *The Beginning of Doves* – of *course* cashing in on Marc's fame, but isn't that what the music business is all about? Marc's management were not happy, unsurprisingly, and tried to prevent the release.

'The reason for this was that they had just signed some amazing new contract with EMI. They'd had to assure EMI as part of the deal that there were no old tapes kicking around in cupboards or on shelves which could be released in competition with his new recordings.

'Kit braved it out, released the record, and earned Track a writ. The ensuing court case was a bit of a farce, but who really needed lawyers? We sorted it out ourselves with Marc, all quite amicably. It was he who paid for dinner at the Savoy Grill!'

'Marc loved being a star,' says Eric Hall, who by the 1970s was something of a star himself, in record promotion and publishing. 'He loved it so much. I think *I've* got a big ego: his was *huge*. He loved being friends with Ringo Starr, popping out for a drink with Paul McCartney, going off sailing with George Harrison and Ringo in the South of France, getting up to no good with Keith Moon.

'He was in his element. To him, having some of the biggest names in showbiz as his closest pals was proof that he'd made it.

'But he was still just Mark Feld from Stoke Newington with me,' Eric insists. 'We'd still meet up together just the two of us and go for something to eat: Harry Morden's in St John's Wood, Graham's fish restaurant in Poland Street or one of our other old haunts.

'When he used to come and see me at ATV music off Berkeley Square, we'd go to an Italian we liked, Serafino on Mount St.

We'd still get out for our bit of fish, some chopped liver, a bowl of soup. You never lose that. You get that famous, you've got to remember who your friends are. Marc didn't always remember, and he left a lot of people behind, it's true. But he was never like that with me.

'On a Friday,' recalls Eric, 'I'd have a songwriter's day, when I used to take the writers out for a lunch. He found out about that, Marc, because he'd follow me everywhere. He'd turn up, sit down and join in.

'I wasn't even his publisher, he just wanted to come! Even when he was a big, big star, he'd love to join in with whatever I was up to. He'd sit here now and have this bit of chicken with us, no airs and graces. You'd have loved him. Everyone loved him. He was good company, too. Life and soul, very funny, he was. Made people laugh, which gave him pleasure. He had a really generous heart, Marc. He was special.'

As Eric and I eat lunch together at Shoreditch House in his old stomping ground off Bethnal Green Road, he happens to hear two couples on the adjacent table discussing T. Rex. Eric can't resist leaning over and telling them who he is – in a nice way – and of his lifelong Bolan connection. All four seem amazed.

'Things like that always happen,' grins Eric. 'That's Marc. He's never far away.'

In December 1972, T. Rex embarked on a successful ten-day tour of Japan – where Marc also took the unprecedented step of producing his own work. The experiment at EMI's studios there resulted in the single '20th Century Boy', to be completed on their return by Tony Visconti. Back in London, everyone psyched themselves up for the pre-Christmas release of *Born To Boogie*: the concert film directed by and starring Ringo Starr, which was marketed by The Beatles' Apple Films label and distributed by Apple Corps.

Its premiere was held, unfathomably, at the somewhat low-rent Oscar's on Brewer Street in Soho – a cinema perhaps better suited to the softcore offerings of Sylvia Kristel as *Emmanuelle*.

The 'funny little film' as Dexter describes it was attended by Ringo, Elton, Marc and June, of course, Tony Visconti, Eric Hall, and the members of T. Rex. Jeff recalls being called away for some reason, and missing it. Its reception was exactly what they didn't want, media reaction more whimper than bang. While die-hard Bolan fans flocked to see it, and loved it regardless because it depicted their beloved Marc, even some of those described it privately as 'a wank'. It fell short of the interest of most regular cinema-goers, and would today be dismissed as a 'straight to video'. Nor was it sold in America, to the production team's (Ringo's) lasting disappointment. To his public, Marc gushed proudly of 'his' movie with all his customary exuberance. Behind closed doors, as he sat pondering the implications, he was gutted.

'20th Century Boy', one of T. Rex's most recognisable tracks, made its brazen appearance in the New Year, 1973. Its chart reign was short, with strange new album *Tanx* bringing up the rear. By now, his drug-taking and drinking had taken their toll. Marc was looking terrible. While the pumped-up face and general weight-gain were almost certainly down to his booze intake, the sallow skin, limp hair and empty eyes were thanks to drugs. Where was June to keep her husband out of trouble, as she had always done? Some say she was confronting demons of her own.

'I think the over-indulgence was just generic then, for most of them – including June,' comments Jeff Dexter. 'You have to realise that some cope much better than others. I can't say exactly what happened, but relations had become a struggle between them.'

The gulf between the pair continued to widen. As we know,

Marc even hooked up with his former girlfriend, Terry Whipman, perhaps seeking solace and security in her arms.

In June 1973, Marc, Tony Visconti and the members of T. Rex, accompanied by backing singers Pat Hall and Gloria Jones, decamped to Musicland Studios in Munich to commence work on the *Zinc Alloy* album.[6]

June's decision to remain in London was asking for it; but she seemed oblivious, caught up in some alternative rock'n'roll zone of her own. Part of Marc still wanted her there, for support: not least because his relationship with Tony Visconti was on its last legs now: *Zinc Alloy* was to be the final album that Marc and Tony would record together. But the greater part of Marc – his heart, his psyche, his deepest soul – was already falling in love with Gloria.

'When Marc and June's marriage began to disintegrate, I felt betrayed,' admits Mick O'Halloran. 'Not by June – but by Gloria. And she knew that. I think it did affect my relationship with her later, to some extent. I tried not to let it. End of the day, I was still the hired hand. I missed June, though. We always kept in touch.'

Gloria is, understandably, reluctant to discuss this. I must say here, I admire hugely her ability to accentuate the positive. She talks, instead, of where Marc's head was at the time.

'He wasn't "terrified of fame slipping away" as people have said,' she insists. 'Marc was philosophical. He accepted that not all his fans were willing to go with him on the whole journey. You had Gary Glitter, David Cassidy, The Bay City Rollers all jumping around at that time. Young fans are fickle, and they are growing themselves. They always want the Next Big Thing. Marc understood that. He was already thinking, quite naturally, that he wanted to take his music into other areas, and create new sounds. We talked about this a lot. Performers today seem to be able to grow and move more easily with their fans. It wasn't like that back then.'

As for the personal habits that were clearly bringing him down at the time, she remains reserved.

'People have always exaggerated,' she says simply, perhaps in denial as to the level at which Marc was now damaging himself.

'Marc was a famous rock star. When you're on the road for years and years, you become a kind of touring machine. You gradually start neglecting yourself. I never discussed his drinking with Marc. Maybe I should have. But it was rock'n'roll. Nowadays, the rockers are all drinking tea. They are more concerned about health and diet. They take care of themselves. Today's artists are very aware, and much different. In the Sixties and Seventies, you didn't think about the harm you might be doing to yourself. There was nothing sinister about it. You just did whatever was going, because everybody else did.'

'Marc was all over the place on this one,' remembers Bill Legend, referring to the sojourn in Munich. 'The leader we'd known and loved, the one who made us laugh and told us what to do, the one who asked our opinion then usually did it his way anyway, because he always knew what he wanted in the studio, was nowhere. It was obvious what was going on, but he seemed too gone to care. I did worry for him. He seemed completely detached from the rest of us, as if he didn't even know us at times.

'We all did our best, we got the job done, we got our money, but there was a very sour after-taste. Everybody's confidence was knocked.'

A poorly-thought-through six-week stadium tour of the US and Canada was next on the agenda, supporting American rockers Three Dog Night. Eye-shadowed, uber-glam rockers versus middle-of-the-road hunksters in grubby jeans, best-known for hot-selling cover versions of other people's numbers: what audience could be expected to get both? Marc, however, was still so desperate for fame in the land of the free – which after all had worshipped The Beatles, so why not their natural and indeed 'official Beatles-endorsed' successor? – that he was jumping at everything. He was forgetting, or not facing, the fact that America had already lost its heart to Ziggy Stardust. To add insult to injury, Led Zeppelin were touring the US at the same time, and commanding every available column inch. With a freshly-polished pout and the tenacity of a limpet, Marc soldiered on.

'That tour wasn't Tony Howard's fault, as it has been portrayed,' says Dexter. 'Marc was the problem, throughout. He wouldn't listen to reason. He was too loud. He wanted to be louder than everyone else. The American bands have one thing in common: when they go on the road, they demonstrate stage craft. You're on tour, you work out and put together ways of delivering your music each night – unless you are a brilliant, blinding musician and you just don't need anything extra.

'Otherwise, you have to be showbiz. You have to have a regular set. You have to have it all planned, rehearsed, and as tight as can be. Marc was rehearsed – but then he became a monster. He wouldn't settle in. Each show got worse. Tony and Mick O'Halloran were both there, and neither of them could do anything with him, at that point. He wouldn't be told.

'It didn't help that alliances in the group changed somewhat when Micky Gray became a personal roadie. Things became distorted.'

'It was strange, playing with Three Dog,' Marc told New York journalist and author Michael Gross, in 1974.

'Although they're very nice people, musically we weren't that compatible. We did tend to wipe the floor with them a bit. The audiences were fantastic, so that's the only thing I can judge the tour by. Then we did five dates in England, which doesn't sound like very much, but I hadn't played there in over two years. It was very successful, but a bit freaky because it was more like Beatlemania than when I had played before. I found myself still a teenage idol!,' he gushed, as if willing it.

T. Rex continued gigging across Europe, Japan and Australia. Marc himself clung doggedly to the plot.

'I'd had enough in the end,' admits Bill Legend. 'Tony Visconti and I quit at about the same time, and for about the same reasons.'

Tony and his family moved to France and built a recording studio: his own Château d'Hérouville, in essence, which was rubbing his former charge's nose in it a bit: Marc wasn't anywhere near ready to build his. There, Visconti mixed Bowie's *Diamond Dogs*. Bill made his way back to Essex for a kip. T. Rex would never sound the same again.

Although a few maintain that Bill was fired by Tony Howard at Marc's behest, Bill insists that his departure was his own decision.

'I saw the beginning of the end about a year before I went,' he tells me. 'We were down in Australia when I snapped. That was it. I didn't say a lot, I just asked for my passport back. There was nothing to lose: I was only on a wage, and I'd only had one £10 rise the whole time I was with T. Rex. The guys all went back from Brisbane to Sydney. I went home.'

In London, in their spacious new premises at 69 New Bond Street, Tony Howard and his team were still trying to make sense of Marc's and T. Rex's tangled business affairs. With Bill Curbishley and The Who on the ground floor, T. Rex in the middle and Steve O'Rourke and Pink Floyd upstairs, there was more than enough work to go round. Jeff Dexter, who would later manage Hawkwind from the same premises in 1975, reports the coming and going of a seemingly endless stream of lawyers and accountants, while old companies were dissolved and new holdings established – including a series of offshore accounts designed to 'modify the tax bill'. What was not disclosed at the time was the fact that a considerable amount of this capital-juggling pertained to the pending collapse of the Feld Bolan marriage. Steps were taken to ensure that June couldn't make a claim on most of it. Such measures were to prove disastrous in the end.

'For example,' reveals Dexter, 'a lot of bad investments were made. Buying art, for instance.

'Who was doing all this buying? One of the accountants. He was buying up arts for the future, he said. He supposedly had a department in his firm which was purchasing artworks for a lot of people in the business. Rather than put their money in the bank, they would own these works that would double or triple in value over the years, which they could then sell. Turned out few people had even heard of any of these artists. The artworks all turned out to be pieces of shit!'

There weren't that many millions at stake, insists Dexter, contradicting decades-old speculation and conspiracy theories.

'There *were* millions – but not *millions* and millions.'

Where did all the money end up?

'In the Bahamas.'

Who got it?

'The trustees. The faceless trustees. No one really knew who they were at the time,' says Jeff. 'You saw signatures. There were a couple on one document which I recognised. One of my oldest friends is a signatory on another set of trustees' papers. It was all set up in America.'

No one could have predicted how horribly wrong this would all go. Although some fingers still point at Howard with regard to

Bolan's 'Missing Millions' all these years after Marc's death, Jeff Dexter insists that his late friend Tony was made a scapegoat, and had been the innocent party.

'I wish he *had* got it all!' exclaims Jeff.

'He was the one who actually deserved it! No one else lasted that long, or was as good to Marc. He deserved to get some money for that. He got nothing.'

Dexter knows where the bodies are buried. A full list of names, dates, lawyers and locations exists. He and a handful of relevant individuals own copies of it. While a couple of investigative television documentaries, including Channel 4's *Marc Bolan's Missing Millions*, have sought to explore the financial mystery, no lawyer has ever sanctioned full disclosure. No newspaper editor has dared run a complete exposé. No publishing lawyer would permit me to do so here. Reader, please make up your own mind as to why.

'I'd have opted out years ago without June,' Marc had told the then *Evening News* pop writer John Blake, in an interview published in May 1973. Was he trying to convince himself, one wonders?

Blake, now a highly successful publisher with best-selling titles by glamour model Katie Price, her pop star ex-husband Peter Andre, and the late reality TV star Jade Goody, has little recollection today of the revealing exchange, in which Marc protests too much his love for his wife, and declares marital bliss to be the antidote to all life's ills.

'Marriage is a great basis for sanity,' said the coke-snorting, brandy-vodka-and-Champagne-swilling, junk-food-munching multi-millionaire rock star, who was now out of control and clearly teetering on the brink of marital collapse. The irony was not lost on Blake, a popular, brilliant and sabre-toothed hack who nevertheless was gentle on him.

'I'd always liked Marc,' said John, a former colleague and a long-standing friend, when we met again recently at a Fleet Street wake. 'You don't kick them when they're down, do you. You just hug them.'

There were said to have been a couple of half-hearted attempts at reconciliation. June had been with Marc in Milwaukee in July, for the start of the Three Dog Night tour. Business recalled her to London, but she did go back – to Seattle, where she learned what had been going on with Gloria. She left in a huff.

Marc returned to London in September. The story goes that he tried to reason with June.

I'm not convinced.

'I'm not sure that he did, either,' remarks Jeff Dexter. 'He did kind of lose everything in June, and part of him must have been devastated to lose her. But he pushed her out. I don't know why. Something happened. She was out.

'It was partly to do with the new management regime. Tony had to do Marc's bidding. That was his job. Tony also adored June, and he would not have tried to stitch her up.

'It comes down to "orchestra wives". Although June knew the business, at the end of the day she was "just Marc's wife". She never had the professionalism of Tony. He was eleven years older, and a very clear, sharp thinker. He was a sage to all of us. People used to come to him with their problems. He'd always have the answers. He was a very clever bloke, a lovely man.

'But June and Tony were never really going to see eye to eye . . . and Marc saw, through Tony, a new style of doing things. He was breaking out, in a way.'

Perhaps Marc now felt that he had been under her thumb for too long?

'I think Marc was a lesser person without June,' Dexter

counters. 'Just as I don't think his music was ever as good without Visconti. You always need someone to rein you in. Tell you whether it's good or not. If everyone tells you that everything you do is great, you lose perspective. You think you don't have to listen anymore. That was where Marc was now.'

Despite his new-found 'freedom', Marc must have grieved for her. June had been his rock: his mother, his sister, his lover, his nurse, his muse. She had been there from the beginning, she knew him better than he knew himself. At least, she had always told him she did.

There were business matters to attend to in the Bahamas. He took time out for a relaxing beach holiday. No one remembers what happened next . . . except Gloria, who joined him there.

'I was in Nassau with Marc at that time,' she admits. 'What can I tell you? Marc's marriage was over. He was so happy, that holiday. We both were. We were very much in love.'

The Marc who emerged from the colony bore little resemblance to his former self.

Gone were the porcelain complexion, the scrunch of ringlets, his androgynous air of wanton fragility. Marc's skin was now tanned a deep bronze all over. His locks had been cropped closer to his scalp than he had ever previously worn them. He looked 'harder' in a way – more 'butch', and, dare I say it without wishing to cause offence, more 'ethnic'.

Was he meeting Gloria in the middle here? His visual style was edging closer to that of those making the soul-based music then dancing all over the charts. In an interview with *Disc* magazine dated October 1973, during which he was quizzed about his 'new look', Marc explained that he had just been on holiday with his wife June, and that she had been the one to cut his hair. Some have even claimed that this was a 'final act of revenge' on

June's part – though who can imagine Marc allowing her to do such a thing? Besides, by all accounts, June was never vengeful.

'The haircut story is not true,' says Gloria.

A possible explanation for his strange remarks in *Disc* is that, deep down, a part of Marc still cherished hopes of a reconciliation with his wife. The shearing could have been a red herring. He might have been carefully throwing the journalist off the scent. A published split is a marriage done for, as every divorced celebrity knows. Whatever the truth, the result was an image wholly at odds with the Bolan the teens knew and loved. Some raved about Marc's make-over, while others cried over it. For the fans, it would take some getting used-to. For his wife, it was the end.

Especially saddened by the demise of their marriage was their new publicist, former rock writer Keith Altham.

'I liked June a lot, and I was sad to see her go,' Keith admits. 'She was a very feisty and interesting woman. She had seen the potential in Marc right from the start and obviously the relationship between them meant that she was always going to work harder for him. He was the love of her life, anyone could see that. I always thought she was really special. One of the real forerunners of women's lib. She had to fight that whole male-dominated bullishness in the industry, which took some guts, and she did it with style. She did it for Marc. She was bloody good for him: always put him first.'

You don't know what you've got 'til it's gone? Keith agrees.

'I used to love going round to their place in Little Venice to do interviews, when I was still a journalist,' he remarks. 'They were a lovely, homely couple together. She would make spinach pie or some other nice vegetarian dish. They were both veggies, at least Marc was at that point, he did change later; and she was always cooking. Looking after her man. She adored him. But she was also tough. She'd been an agent. She was clever – but not ruth-less – and had good instincts. I'm not sure at what point she started moving in on his image and things, but I know that she had a lot to do with it. Who really knows what goes on behind closed doors? I don't think anyone could single out a specific thing that went wrong between them. But of course, Gloria was on the scene by this time. June found out, and that was the last straw. I was upset when I heard about it.'

Others remember the split as a gradual process: fuelled by the power struggle between June and Tony Howard, not helped by the fact that Tony was now also managing Gloria's career.

On the 'up' side, in September that year, Big Biba opened – a vast department store-sized boutique in Kensington, where Derry & Toms had once been. The Art Deco building's fifth-floor Rainbow Room restaurant was as big as the Savoy and seated four hundred people. It buzzed with trendiness. Sunday lunches were an extraordinary experience: a veritable Who's Who of London's showbusiness scene. Everybody table-hopped, and everybody knew everybody else.

'This was the most glamorous London had ever been,' recalls Simon Napier-Bell. 'Everyone loved the place. You could pitch up for dinner and find yourself next to Barbra Streisand or a Pointer Sister. Or you could drop in late for some caviar and Champagne, and be gulped into a party bubbling Princess Margaret, Mick Jagger, Andy Warhol and Liz Taylor . . . or the *real* aristocracy', he adds with a wink, 'David Bowie and Marc Bolan.'

Not a Myth Left

What the Rainbow Room's celebrity-infested dazzle did not reflect were the true colours of the country at large.

Many reasons are given for the UK's depression during the Seventies, but it boiled down to money. Miles of newsreel recorded the immigration of thousands of British passport-holding Asians who flocked here from Uganda to escape Idi Amin. Aspirational, ambitious and hard-saving, the lifestyles they created in Britain cast a shadow over homegrown workers, not least the 300,000 men hacking at the coalface. They wanted what the corner-shop keepers were having. They wanted televisions, cars and holidays. It didn't seem much to ask, in return for toiling in the most punishing conditions imaginable. Miners' union boss Arthur Scargill galvanised them into protest. They had not been out since the General Strike of 1926, but now they meant war.[1]

Prime Minister Edward Heath, in power since 1970 with an aim to continue building on the Harold Wilson years, would not play ball. In February 1972, pickets encircled the power stations. A state of emergency was declared. Power cuts closed offices, factories and schools, and the three-day working week was imposed. When agreements were reached, the strike was called off, and miners' wages soared. They became, for a moment, the highest-paid faction of the working class. This reversed within the year, however, when the majority of the workforce caught up – while the Arab-Israeli war sent oil prices rocketing and rendered coal even more valuable. The miners saw renewed opportunity, increased their demands, and in February 1974 were striking again. With Britain now on the verge of economic collapse, Heath called a General Election he thought he could win – but was ousted. Wilson returned, in the dourest and most 'Yorkshire' of moods, and kept the country even more miserable than it had been under his predecessor.[2]

Little wonder that all this began to be reflected in music, as well as in street culture. It was the gloomy climate of Britain during the mid-Seventies which led to the emergence and brief domination of punk: down-beat, dreary, politically-obsessed, and throbbing with the anger of the nation, which was the point of it. In such a climate, glam rock's days were numbered. Even the dealers were forced to adapt accordingly. Popular drugs went from uppers – sulphate and cocaine – to downers, mainly Xanax (alprazolam) and then heroin: thanks to a vast, bargain influx from the Middle East, cheap enough for anyone to afford.

Writer Nick Kent recalls in his memoir *Apathy for The Devil* an occasion just before Christmas 1974, when he called on a drug dealer friend off the Edgware Road. People were lying on cushions on the apartment floor: including an urchin-like man. Marc.

'He looked a lot bulkier than the elfin figure he'd cut back in his glam messiah days,' wrote Kent.

'His physical deterioration . . . coincided with a marked dip in his popularity here in the UK. His records weren't setting the charts on fire anymore. Most of his old fans had shifted their allegiance to David Bowie.'

They all got talking in the den.

'I found [Marc] pleasant enough,' Kent reflects. On the surface he was woozy and effete, but at heart he was a canny little hustler who knew how to turn on the charm . . . He also had a lively sense of humour, and good taste in heroes. Syd Barrett was an obsession of his, and he'd read my piece on the guy, earlier in the year.'

When Kent told Marc that Syd had run to fat, Marc apparently flinched in recognition. They swapped anecdotes about Bob Dylan, of whom Bolan remained a huge fan.

The times they hadn't a-changed that much. Not really.

With his once close friend Bowie now soaring, thanks in no modest measure to the efforts of Tony Visconti, and with his wife over a rainbow too far, Marc had free rein. His first mistake was bringing Gloria to London – leaving behind her small son, who stayed with her family in Los Angeles, and causing her to dump her contract with her record company.

His second was moving her into the Bilton Towers, Great Cumberland Place apartment. The ghost of June inhabited every room. Gloria was uncomfortable. They moved on, to a flat in The Avenue, St John's Wood. Paul and Linda McCartney on Cavendish Avenue were now their neighbours. Gloria and Marc started writing songs together, but neither could settle. Gloria missed her son Wally too much, causing the couple to jump back and forth often between London and Los Angeles.

It was in LA that Marc first began to work with Gloria's brother Richard, a coalmine of a man with gospel flair and a baritone boom. Marc 'adored' Richard, says Gloria, and had plans to launch him as the next Barry White. At MRI Studios, they did sessions with Motown legend Sylvester Rivers – known for his work with Barry, Johnny Matthis, Aretha Franklin – and with other notables such as Ray Parker Jnr., Ollie E. Brown and Scott Edwards.

'Marc was a really warm and friendly guy. We had an immediate and personal connection', Rivers tells me. 'It was a really *fun* experience. What I liked about him especially was that he didn't take himself too seriously. There were good vibes, he seemed very at home in Los Angeles. It was a good reminder that it doesn't seem to matter, the location, the time. When musicians get together, they can make music anywhere. What's more, Marc had a real affinity for the Detroit sound, which had arisen out of an industrial city and which resonated with him deeply.

'I think Marc cherished the idea of "making it in America" because it's a much broader market place', Sylvester opines. 'It never happened for him during his lifetime. I often wish that America will eventually wise up to Marc Bolan. What people tend to overlook is that when it comes to the proverbial "hit single", there are so many elements involved beside the music. Bands as big as The Beatles and K.C. & The Sunshine Band had records that had to be released and re-released before they became hits. Music and promotion go hand in hand, the balance is a delicate one. If a record by someone as talented as Marc fails to become a hit, it cannot be his musical fault. There was no weakness in his music.'

Richard Jones's big career never happened, either at home or in the UK. But this exposure to soul and black culture was reshaping Marc's music all the time. He felt at home on the West Coast. Working with Gloria, Richard and their many friends – not least Ike and Tina Turner – gave Marc a new lease of life.

It has long been rumoured that it is Marc playing the guitar solo on 'Nutbush City Limits'. Gloria herself maintains that it is.

'Lesley-Ann, he was *on* it. What happened was, Tina and I

were good friends. They booked me for a back-up session. Marc came with me. Imagine him getting out of the limo and carrying his little Orange amplifier – he took his Les Paul and his amp everywhere.

'We go into the studio, I introduce them, Marc and Ike hit it off, they are really getting along. Ike plays Marc the riff he has come up with. Marc listens. Ike looks. Then Marc goes, "All right, Ike, I'm ready." He pops his knuckles and stretches his fingers. Ike puts the track up and Marc starts playing. Tina and I look at each other in amazement. We withdraw, and leave them to it.

'Extraordinary though it sounds, I can assure you this happened. You never heard that exact sound on Ike recordings. He let Marc do what he wanted to do. It is definitely Marc, I promise you.'

BBC Radio 2 producer Mark Hagen doubts this.

'The consensus seems to be that nobody's ever heard Tina say this', he assures me. 'It was allegedly said in a Radio 1 interview that Steve Wright did, but Steve doesn't recall her saying it either. Everybody does seem agreed that Marc played on one of their B-sides, though'.

He is referring to the B-side of the 'Sexy Ida' (parts 1 and 2) single, June 1974, on United Artists.

'I tend to agree that Marc would shout it from the rooftops if he'd played on "Nutbush",' says Tony Visconti. 'But he never really came forward about playing for David Bowie's 'Prettiest Star' and 'London Bye Ta Ta'. He did play on Ringo's album, I can hear that it's Marc – even when it comes over supermarket speakers – but I don't think Mac said much about that. I am not sure. Anyway, I am only vaguely aware of 'Nutbush'', he says. 'I probably only heard it once.'

Later, having listened to it again, Tony gets back to me.

'Just heard it on YouTube,' he says. 'Apart from the riff resembling many a T. Rex song – which borrowed heavily from '50s rock'n'roll – that is not Marc's style or his tone. It sounds like Ike to me. It could be that Ike humoured him by letting him play a take or two, but it probably didn't make it to the mix.'

Marc and Gloria continued to live as jet-setters. They jumped from continent to continent, recording wherever practical, with Gloria tearing herself in half to maintain her own career. Marc even attempted to revive his proposed rock-opera *The Children of Rarn*, but nothing came of it. Tony Howard having recently signed a new US deal with Casablanca through Warner Brothers, Marc was determined to have one last crack at America.

Nick Kent was among the many who failed to see the point, believing that Marc was too arrogant ever to make it there.

'He was simply too ethereal and too aloof for their earthly tastes.'

Not that it stopped him. But that two-month tour was a resounding so-what. The acceptance of this broke his spirit, in some ways. Marc would never work in the States again. Still he thumbed his nose at the critics with his album *Light of Love*, as it was known in the US, but which was reworked and re-released in the UK as *Bolan's Zip Gun*. With too many conflicting influences, most found it baffling. Had Marc at last lost interest? Gloria says not.

'He was experimenting!' she exclaims. 'Everyone else was doing it. His music was a mix, his life was a mix. He was a glam rocker. He would become a punk rock star. He was free, because he was a person of the arts. He did not ever pay attention to the kind of people who seemed to think they could dictate rules as to how other people should live. Who were they to tell the rest of us? We were agreed on that one!

'He hadn't had the chance to have a full, formal college

education, so he was getting his education about life and the world for himself. He wasn't hung-up about it. He wasn't intimidated by people with heavyweight academic qualifications. That was not the path Marc took.

'He was a true artist who was very straight and clear about who he wanted to be, and about where he wanted to be. He loved it all, he soaked up life. He had so much energy, because he absorbed from everything. He was so excited, every day, like a little boy. I never once thought that Marc was jaded by it all.'

Nevertheless, he was obviously frustrated by the reception he received on the US tour.

'Marc started having a go at Gloria,' admits Mick O'Halloran. 'More than once, I saw the girl with a black eye. His rage used to boil over, and he'd whack her. It was as if he was angry with himself, and he was taking it out on her. It was awful, at times.'

That December, Marc and Gloria rented a bungalow in Benedict Canyon, with the intention of consolidating their relationship and creating stability. All too soon, Marc fell in with the old drinking gang: Richard Joncs, Harry Nilsson, John Lennon, and his old muckers Keith Moon and Ringo Starr. There were nights when Gloria felt so afraid of her lover that she turned to God in desperation; on one occasion, she begged her minister father to come. He arrived armed with a crucifix, and prayers were said over Marc, which may have been a bit extreme. What he needed was an exit route from boozing and partying, not exorcism.

From January 1975, Marc and Gloria spent a year in tax exile, to avoid monstrous debts to the Inland Revenue. Tony rented him an apartment in Monte Carlo, which was clearly intended as a permanent residence: Marc had most of his belongings and

Bentley shipped to Monaco, where Ringo and Maureen Starr were their occasional neighbours. Despite its proximity to London, it was an odd choice of destination for someone like Marc. Neither he nor Gloria could ever get into the 'groove' in Monte Carlo, because there wasn't one. Marc never considered the Principality 'home'. He found the locals 'a bit too old-money and boring'. There was no one to party with. It wasn't what you could call a rock'n'roll town, and he had never felt more isolated. The hippest thing in the Casino at night was the clinking of European crown jewels. The cocky boy from Stoke Newington was not at home in such a stately and contained environment; it must have given him the urge to drop his aitches and spit in the street. Despite the stretched blue views of the Mediterranean, the elegant architecture, the palm trees, the mild winters, the dry summers, the soaring Alps, the London Boy felt a very long way from home.

'They were allowed back thirty days each year', remembers Jeff Dexter. 'They'd come in for three to five days at a time. While they were here, they'd be doing business stuff. You'd talk to the accountants, the lawyers, maybe do an interview or two, and a couple of photo shoots.

'I'd go down to the Portobello Hotel or wherever they were staying, and eat dinner with them. But it wasn't "all back to mine" by then. Things had changed.'

Were he and Marc now detached from each other's friendship?

'I only ever detached myself from the madness of T. Rextasy,' declares Jeff. 'Marc was still Marc. But you had to put up with all the other stuff. Rock stars like to misbehave and show off. Harry [Nilsson], Moonie, Ringo and "Fat Reg" [Elton John] together were a handful. There was that competitive edge between those making the scene, to out-do, out-shout and out-insult each other.

'That didn't really appeal to me,' he admits.

'I'd join the party and have a laugh, but then I went home. I was busy. Managing – I'd lost America, but I had Isaac Guillory and Peter Sarstedt – and producing. I was still running shows and MC-ing at the Roundhouse.

'That was not my time with Marc. I'd get him back, though.'

Given that his life at that time was so disjointed, and that he was living in self-imposed exile, it would perhaps have made sense to hang on to what was tried and trusted; the people and things in his life which represented stability. Marc did otherwise. A new kind of recklessness had been consuming him since he lost June; he appeared to be willing himself to become someone else. He made rash if not irrational decisions now: offloading his loyal bandmate Mickey Finn without a backward glance. Mickey himself would later insist that it was mutual.[3]

Like his home town, the charts were now a foreign country. They did things differently there. Marc would return to London when his time was up, but was reluctant to do so without 'product'. He was convinced that there were endless albums and hits in him yet. There undoubtedly were. Back and forth to Los Angeles they travelled, as he wrote, recorded and gave interviews until he bored himself – which was saying something. He began to imply to journalists that T. Rex were no more. But he *was* T. Rex: so what was he trying to say?

16

Measuring the Stars

It could have been curtains, had Marc not heeded a concerned physician's advice. With the drug-induced heart rate of a person more than twice his age, it was time to take stock. Gloria and Marc repaired to a chi-chi southern French clinic for a fortnight's rest, around Easter 1975 – and got more than they bargained for While Marc's M.O.T. turned up little that diet and exercise couldn't fix, Gloria's diagnosis turned out to be pregnancy.

While a September due date would suggest that Gloria knew sooner, consider the lifestyle they were living at the time. Still, less time to be pregnant was less time to worry about it, as far as she was concerned. As for Marc, he was going to be a father for the first time, and he was ecstatic. Tearing into overdrive, he rushed Gloria back to the Château with the current T. Rex line-up – bassist Steve Currie, drummer Davey Lutton and keyboard player Dino Dines – to cram in further recording, where, as if in celebration, he promptly sank back into his debauched rock star ways. Marc was still fantasising about his *magnum opus* rock opera, and was behaving as if he were running out of time. He toyed with a concept called *Billy Super Duper*, about a punk kid from the 25th century – not a million miles from the characters which comedian and writer Ben Elton would dream up, in the late 1990s, for the musical *We Will Rock You* – as a vehicle for the music of Freddie Mercury and Queen.

April saw the band back in Germany. Thanks to Marc's appalling behaviour, owner and producer Reinhold Mack banned the band in perpetuity. By May, Gloria and Marc were in London, in a rented Fulham house on Holmead Road. Both were anxious for their baby to be born in Marc's hometown, Marc's parents were conveniently close by in a flat in Putney, and Gloria needed time to prepare.

Their unborn baby brought them luck. Babies do. Just six weeks later, Marc's 'frog song', 'New York City', had made it onto the charts. Had he and Macca been talking again? Just a few years later, Paul McCartney would be hitting the charts with a 'frog song' of his own – albeit the somewhat more polished and choral 'We All Stand Together', from the 1984 Rupert Bear film. What McCartney's project wouldn't boast, mind you, was his EMI promotions man (Eric Hall) leaping about the stage or studio in a frog suit, wherever they performed it.

Manager Tony Howard is said to have despaired when Marc announced his intention to hit the road again. Even more so when Marc specified a handful of good old-fashioned seaside towns. But the mini-tour went ahead, and was a minor success. It must have made for some entertaining sights, too, whenever the band piled out of the mini-van with their instruments and fell head-first into the venue, leaving Marc to help Gloria, in a delicate condition, from the limo which was bringing up the rear. Less a climb-down for the hot-shot rock star, this was rather a clever coup. The fans adored it and were putty in his hands, made up to find themselves drinking with their idol in the bar afterwards; while Marc felt he was well on his way to re-establishing a rapport with his audience. America knew where it could stick it, for now. He'd started with a home-grown audience, and he would finish with one . . . not quite what he'd had in mind.

★ ★ ★

'I met June Bolan a couple of times,' remembers Cliff Wright, who was now driving for Marc. 'She started turning up to rehearsals for that tour, at the Tunnel in Great Suffolk Street, Waterloo. Even though she and Marc had broken up, she'd come. I assume she met Gloria there too, a few times. I was just the new kid on the block. I didn't take much notice, I just did my job. I suppose it was a bit strange, though Marc never said anything.

'I used to drive him around in the Mini a lot. We'd go to pie'n'mash shops. There was one on the Old Kent Road called Bert's that he liked. He'd wait in the car, I'd go in for the pies. He knew he'd get mobbed if he was recognised.

'We did the pie-run often,' smiles Cliff, appearing to yearn for one, as we pick over a shared pub sandwich. 'A lot of the time it was fish and chips, too. He'd always rather have a pie than a big swanky dinner up West. He was down-to-earth, no airs and graces, a real East London boy.

'And he had the most amazing laugh,' says Cliff. 'I'll never forget it. A real fruity, rascally, "I've had yer knickers off, Missis" laugh. Like John Lennon in *A Hard Day's Night*: full of innuendo and sarcasm. He was a full-blooded geezer all right.'

Marc might have underestimated the looming power of pre-punk, but only for a moment. As soon as he perceived what was going down on the streets, he perfected his masterstroke. Why shouldn't he have been the one to have invented all this in the first place? In which case, why couldn't he relaunch himself as founding father of the latest 'new movement' now?

Thrilled to have their teen idol back in their midst, Marc's fans were now back and out in force. A hardcore band of them followed him from home to office to recording studio, almost daily. There are plenty of them still reminiscing about it on the Internet. They also swarmed in healthy numbers whenever he pitched up to film another episode of the surreal *Supersonic*, for TV producer Mike Mansfield – which he did often during that period. It was during a rehearsal for one such show, on 26 September, that Gloria went into labour.

It was all in the name. A stay at Anouska Hempel's elegant boutique hotel Blakes, on Roland Gardens, South Kensington, had inspired them. Then Marc remembered David Bowie's child, Zowie. Rolan Seymour (after American sci-fi/horror movie series *Friday Night* presenter, Larry Vincent, aka 'Sinister Seymour') Feld Bolan would, like Zowie, boast an instant rock'n'roll name. Zowie Bowie and Rolan Bolan: they should have packed them off to a studio together that instant, and recorded their lambkin gurglings for posterity.

All was coming together now. Marc could barely believe his luck. Inspired to write at an astonishing rate, he was penning poetry again, with a view to publishing another collection, *Wilderness Of The Mind*. He began to fill his notebooks with songs and scenarios for a Lionel Bart's *Oliver!*-meets-King-of-the-Mods extravaganza: a full-blown London Opera, based on the Jewish-London childhood they had shared.

Bart, long the toast of the West End and Broadway, had fallen on hard times after the failure of two obscure and ambitious musicals. He'd been licking his wounds among his rock star friends, drinking heavily and taking LSD.

'Never invest in your own musicals', is Sir Tim Rice's take on what happened next. 'If the work is any good, the investors come running.'

But Bart couldn't resist making the classic mistake, even parting with future rights to past triumphs, including *Oliver!*, to raise money to fund new shows. By 1972 he was bankrupt, and had fallen into a two-decade abyss of alcoholism and depression. A collaboration on a London Opera with Marc would have given him hope.[1]

Two of Marc's *London Opera* compositions, 'Funky London Childhood' and 'London Boy', were given air-time on the *Today* show on Thames TV that October, where Marc occasionally stood in as its host. Whenever he was about to do so, he'd go ringing round his friends, coercing them to come and appear on the show with him. Keith Moon, Angie Bowie and Roy Wood, the former ELO star who had now launched a new band, Wizzard, were all recruited in this way. The *London Opera* – sadly, because it could have been good, with such background to draw from – never saw the light of day.

'Marc was everywhere again, the media and the public were lapping him up and he was loving it,' remembers Keith Altham. 'He was always great copy and the press always wanted more.'

It was Keith's own collapse in the office one day which prompted an act of infinite kindness and selflessness from Marc. The story is taken up by Alan Edwards, who at the time was Keith Altham's office junior, but who went on to PR some of the biggest names in rock: from the Stones to McCartney to David Bowie, whose publicity he manages to this day. Alan has nothing but praise for Marc, remembering him as 'a warm, generous and lovely man to work with. A proper star.'

'Keith himself was something of a star by this time,' says Alan, 'having handled all the big acts at Woodstock. Keith knew everyone, had seen it all and was now Keith Altham International – which in reality was just him, me and this French book-keeper a couple of times a week.

'He was taken ill at our offices in Marble Arch one day. He hadn't had a heart attack, as we first thought. He was rushed to hospital, leaving only me to man the phones and run the show. I was 17, 18 years old at the time, I barely knew which way was up. The phones didn't stop ringing, and I was getting very stressed.' Keith explained to me later, 'I was under a huge amount of stress. And we were moving offices. My blood pressure was through the roof, which is why I collapsed.'

'A member of the Moody Blues called up, at one point. "Where's Keith?"

'"Terrible news," I said, "he's been taken ill and rushed to hospital."

'"That's all very well," the guy snapped, "but we've got an album out next week!" Nice.

'The next call was Marc. "Hi," I said, "before you ask, I'm afraid that Keith's been taken ill, and is in hospital."

'"Wow, man," Marc goes, "that's so uncool. That's a drag, man." He says goodbye, and hangs up.

'Twenty minutes or so later, Marc appears at the office door, in a glitter jacket, eyeshadow, the whole look. He smiled, rolled up his sleeves and got stuck in, and spent the rest of the afternoon answering phones for me.'

The more he thought about it, the more Marc was convinced that science fiction was the future, so to speak. What he had failed to deliver with *The Children Of Rarn* would now be encapsulated in *Billy Super Duper*. After a fast-turnaround Baby's First Christmas with Gloria's family in LA, he was back and banging on about it the following spring. But it was mostly all talk, never seeming to leave the notebook. Marc's belief in his own, big-blown fantasies hit an all-time high. At least he'd managed to finish off the long-time-coming *Futuristic Dragon*, which he'd been working on since 1974.

That sixth T. Rex studio album, released in January 1976 to

predictably mixed reviews, was aimed at re-establishing him as a chart superstar. The LP would climb only as high as Number 50, but it was a start. Marc was undeterred. He was also pleased to bits with the album cover artwork, for which he had gone back to illustrator George Underwood, Bowie's old eye-watering playground foe. He sat down with Tony Howard to plan an ambitious UK tour. He and Keith went into publicity overdrive, landing column inches in everything.

Marc declared himself to be born-again, a drink-and-drugs-free zone. It wasn't true. Some of the worst behaviour ever seen by his guitar roadie and driver Cliff Wright, a teenaged family friend of Tony Howard's who had been drafted in to replace Alphi O'Leary after a serious accident, was, he says, exhibited by Marc during the 'Dragon' tour.

Now that Gloria was back on the road with the band, Rolan was cared for by his paternal grandparents, with the help of a professional nanny. Phyllis and Sid were devoted to the baby, and rarely let him out of their sight. He brought new meaning to their lives in their twilight years. Phyllis remarked more than once that it was 'like having Marc all over again . . . like going back.'

Marc continued to guzzle every venue dry.

'But he was funny with it', insists Sally James, who had struck up a friendship with Marc after she interviewed him for her London Weekend Television show *Saturday Scene*, in 1976.

Sally, a trained actress, had played various roles on Yorkshire TV when her agent responded to a request for 'a denim-clad girl to present links between programmes'. She presented *Saturday Scene* for four years, before joining *Tiswas*. Sally was 'the new Cathy McGowan'. Marc adored her.

'The following year he was presenting his own TV

programme, the *Marc* show', she says, 'and I got to know him quite well then.'

'He'd come down to the London Weekend studios quite often. *Saturday Scene* was very popular at the time: there wasn't much else to *be* on. Even when he wasn't on the show, he'd sometimes just turn up! We used to do the programme live at first, but then it changed to a pre-recording on a Friday night. So the after-show in the bar later was a bit of a free-for-all, and people were in the habit of popping in. Not many did if they weren't actually appearing but Marc was quite fond of doing so!'

He'd come on his own, says Sally, or with Eric Hall. Often, they would all go out to dinner.

'Mike [Smith, her husband] and I got to know Marc well. We went to his house a few times.

'I never met his wife June, she was long off the scene by then. Gloria Jones didn't seem to be around much. Even when she was in London, she didn't socialise a lot. But Marc loved to. He was so incredibly easy to talk to, we got on like a house on fire. He was full of everything and wanted to know about everything. He was just like a sponge.'

Sally will, she says, never forget his reaction when Rolan was born.

'He was such a proud dad, it made your heart melt. He'd jump around, going, "I cut the cord! I cut the cord!" I'm almost certain that he didn't! That would have been a very unusual thing for a father to do in those days. But that was exactly the kind of thing Marc used to say. I never met Rolan, sadly but I *felt* as though I knew him. Marc never stopped talking about his son. It was delightful, really. It made you want to hug him.

'As for the showbiz scene, he loved it all. *Loved* it. He was truly convinced that he was going to be a massive star again. I do believe that he had what it took to be able to do it.'

★ ★ ★

Yes sir, that's my baby: Marc, Gloria and baby Rolan Seymour Feld Bolan, born 26 September 1975.

Baby Rolan with grandparents Phyllis and Sid Feld, 1976.

Marc with fan Caron Willans, The Royal Clifton Hotel, Southport, 13 February 1976.

Backstage at Lyceum Theatre, London, 18 February 1976, during 'Futuristic Dragon' tour. Phyllis and Sid Feld, Marc with publicist Alan Edwards.

Marc and Gloria,
March/April 1976.

Matinee idol Marc during his 'Bolantino'
phase, promoting single 'Laser Love',
September 1976.

Mike Mansfield's *Christmas Supersonic* TV show, filmed at the Theatre Royal, Drury Lane,
London, 19 December 1976. The frog is Eric Hall.

Actress Susan George, Marc, and Linda and Paul McCartney at the after-show party for Rod Stewart's gig at Olympia, London, 21 December 1976.

Marc with 'Cockney Rebel' Steve Harley and *Top of the Pops* producer Robin Nash, late 1976/early 1977.

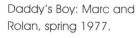

Daddy's Boy: Marc and Rolan, spring 1977.

Marc with Billy Idol at the *Dandy in the Underworld* launch party, The Roxy, Covent Garden, 2 March 1977.

Marc with Siouxsie Sioux at the Music Machine, Camden, May 1977.

Richard Young captures Marc with The Ramones at the Roundhouse, London, June 1977.

The *Marc* TV show, Manchester, August 1977. L-R: 'Beep' Fallon, Jeff Dexter, Marc, Johnnie Fingers and Bob Geldof.

Marc with Sally James at final recording of *Saturday Scene* TV show, 3 September 1977.

David Bowie and Marc during filming of the final *Marc* TV show, 7 September 1977, nine days before his death.

The Mini. 'Easy as picking foxes from a tree …'

Marc's death certificate.

Glorious swan song: 'In life, in death, in love', read the message from Marc's manager Tony Howard.

With a valuable friend: 'Byron' Bowie mourns 'Shelley' Bolan, there for him to the last.

Phyllis Feld and Rolan,
October 1977, a fortnight
after Marc's death.

Rolan Bolan with
Harry and Sandy
Feld at the *Born
to Boogie* DVD
premiere, 2005.

Danielz of 'T.Rextasy' and Eric Hall.

'Deeb' and Jeff Dexter,
Glastonbury Festival, 2000.

Steve Harley and Rolan Bolan at London's BBC Radio studios.

December 1972. Baby, I was born to boogie. R.I.P.

In May 1976, Marc took a deep breath, grabbed Gloria and allowed himself to be driven to Wembley, where the 'Thin White Duke' was in six-night *Station to Station* residence at the Empire Pool. The superstar turned end-of-pier piss-artist paying homage to the fellow mod he'd once massively outsold: it took some guts, that. Marc chose not to see it that way, and good on him. He celebrated, instead, the success of the global superstar who had always been and would forever be his friend.

Besides, as he was fond of banging on about, he and Bowie were in serious discussion now, about a film project which would launch them both into the stratosphere . . . neatly side-stepping the blinding and incontrovertible fact that Deeb was already there.

Steve Harley fell in with Marc in 1976. The Cockney rebels became close friends.

'We met with Cliff Richard,' he tells me. 'Marc was already a superstar or should I say, he'd *been* a superstar, and was planning to be again. He would have done it, too.

'I only knew him for about eighteen months, but we spent a huge amount of time together. This was during a time when Gloria kept going to Los Angeles for long periods, because she was producing The Commodores. They'd moved into a late Victorian villa on Upper Richmond Road.

'Quite a modest house, considering; he had a lot of money at that point, but he wasn't spending it on property, that's for sure. I liked that house, however, I was there a lot. It was never finished.'

While Gloria was away, the mouse was inclined to play; but he couldn't do much for himself.

'I don't think Marc would have been capable of checking himself in at an airport,' declares Steve. 'And he absolutely hated being on his own. He's in that house, and all he's got around him is basically a shell, with plumbers, carpenters and builders coming and going. Not that they appeared to be doing much: whenever I was there, they *weren't* there . . . as is the builder's wont. I'd say "Marc, I wouldn't stand for this. I wouldn't put up with it. *Why* isn't that job finished yet? *Why* does your friend come round and have to sleep on a camp bed?" It was just a mess in there. Guitars all hanging about. I can imagine Gloria coming home each time and wanting to rip her hair out, because nothing had been done.'

Marc often asked Steve to stay over.

'I only did once,' he says. 'I didn't enjoy it. I was used to comfort. Even at that age, I was a little bit beyond camping out. If I'm gonna do that, I'd like a tent!'

While he clearly adored Marc, it is Steve's memories of Gloria which are the most telling.

'When Yvonne [Keeley, the Dutch pop singer who was his girl-friend at the time, who sang on "Make Me Smile, Come Up And See Me" and who had a worldwide hit of her own in 1978 with "If I Had Words"] was away working, and Marc was off on tour, I used to take Gloria to dinner. It happened several times. Totally platonic. We were mates. I liked her a lot. She's such a musician's musician. I learnt from her. I was picking her brains all the time – about production, backing singing and so on. I like women, as you know. I like women's company, and she was a good man's friend. She didn't flirt. So there was never any suspicion.

'You could dine out safely with her in London's finest restaurants, and there was never any stress. Everyone knew I lived with Yvonne, and Gloria was famous as Marc's girlfriend. It was all cool. No innuendo for the press to pick up on. I enjoyed her.'

Were Gloria and Marc good soul mates, did Steve think?

'Can't comment,' he gruffs. 'I know too much about life to presume. To me, though, they were built for each other. She was obviously his crutch. I should have thought she was massively important in his life. She knew how to mother him, but she knew how to respect him at the same time. She kept his self-confidence at a high without letting his ego run riot. She knew how to balance Marc – which took some doing, I can tell you.'

Gloria says much the same about what Marc did for her, I tell him – which Steve likes.

'She once told me, "He was my best friend",' Steve says. '"He could always see when my face looked bored."

'"Come and write a song, Glo," he'd say.

'They saw each other as a comfortable old pair of slippers. I like to think that they'd still be together now. No one can know that. But I hope so.'

Marc played guitar for Steve on a track called 'Amerika the Brave', for the *Candidate* album.

'Came out 1978,' Steve affirms. 'He plays his Les Paul. I paid his fee, but he wouldn't take it. He plays fantastic electric guitar for me on that. I was recording at the original AIR studios, above Oxford Circus, where I used to work quite a lot . . . and Marc was recording what turned out to be his last album. I sing the harmonies on the choruses of the song 'Dandy In The Underworld'.

One of the things Steve loved most about his eccentric friend was his gloriously uncontrollable imagination.

'At times you'd look, you'd listen, your jaw would drop. "Is he on fantasy island?," you'd think. Should I stop him mid-sentence and say, "Marc, this is bullshit," or should I let it go? Because he was so entertaining, and so sincere. He was a mass of contradictions. We'd sit together with a bottle of Remy Martin and a gram of coke, when Gloria was way. Time and time again, this happened. Just the two of us, a couple of acoustic guitars, play till four o'clock in the morning, we were happy.

'We'd talk about the week's sales. His new single was out, my new single was out – both on EMI – and I knew the figures, because we'd get given them.

'In those days you were talking 10–50,000 sales each day, 45s. And he would have – and don't get me wrong, it was brilliantly amusing, I am not mocking – it's essential that you get this across, yeah? Because I adored him. It was so entertaining to hear him rattle off the day's figures of a T. Rex single. I'd be thinking, "It's *one tenth* of that! He's put a zero on!" I knew that, because I knew what *my* sales figures were! And they told me what yours were at the same time. So, I'm sorry!

'But I never told him that. I'd never diminish him. I wouldn't dream of deflating his ego. Never. Except sometimes for a belly laugh, I would prick his superior bubble. Just occasionally. I say that with nothing but respect.'

It had reached a stage, Steve remembers, when he couldn't tell the fantasist out of drama school from the genius of *A Beard of Stars*.

'*That's* the album,' he enthuses. 'I'd have to check myself sometimes. Who am I talking to! Is this the genius of whom I have long been in awe? We'd become mates. He suddenly had feet of clay. It's true that you never want to meet your heroes.

'But Marc was different,' he says. 'As Ezra Pound said to T.S. Eliot, "Bugger the biography, read the poetry."

'He never let me down, and I would never let *him* down. I would have gone out of my way for Marc. I did do. Jesus, I miss him to this day. I want to phone him up now!'

Encouraged by his Top 20 hit 'I Love To Boogie' that July, Marc continued to pour energy into Gloria's recordings, as well as those of her brother, Richard Jones. When Gloria went on the road to support Bob Marley & The Wailers with Gonzales, for whom she had written the hit single 'I Haven't Stopped Dancing

Yet', Marc was happy to tag along and be her partner. He did it with pride. Gone was the egocentric madman who had needed to hog the headlines. Fatherhood and romantic stability had softened him. His priorities were straight.

'Although he and Gloria were always fighting!' laughs Cliff Wright. 'I remember once walking out of a studio to get the teas and coffees, and walking back in to Gloria laying into Marc. He was going, "Glo! Glo!" She looked at me and went, "Chile [child], you'll never know!"'

Were they in love?

'Yes, definitely,' says Cliff. 'You don't fight the way they did if you're not in love.'

Meanwhile, 1976 was the year of punk – when harmony gave way to cacophony, and musical sentiment caved in. This was exactly what Marc had been waiting for. The hastily-restyled Godfather of Punk threw himself at the bandwagon, making it his own. Launching *Dandy in the Underworld* at a hallowed punk temple was a canny move. Covent Garden's the Roxy ensured the attendance of punks galore, Billy Idol and The Damned not least. He may not have had any Sex Pistols but at least he had a Beatle and his Missis on standby, in case the whole scene got out of hand. Paul and Linda seemed mildly bemused by it all.

One thing led to another. The unlikely Damned were enlisted as willing support for the *Dandy* tour – notable for the fact that Marc had got his act together, had turned his back on booze and drugs, was up and out running every morning, would you believe, and taking the early bedtime bath.

The former superstar had turned a corner, pulled his socks up, and was ready to go again. No stopping him now.

Fade-out . . .

By summer 1977, Marc had come full circle. Pared down, on peak form, and having faced the errors of his ways (or at least giving the impression that he had), he now appeared to exude vigour and valour from every pore.

Dandy in the Underworld, which he claimed privately to have written in tribute to his roadie Cliff Wright's notorious Great Train Robber father, who had died recently, was not a hit single. Cliff clocked the calendar; realising that Marc must have written the song before his estranged father's passing, he was still deeply touched.

'He knew what I was going through – that I hated my dad for what he'd done to me and my mother, but that I would still suffer at the loss of the father I'd never had,' Cliff explains.

'He wasn't an emotionally articulate person, Marc. He felt stuff, he took everything to heart, but he couldn't sit and chew the cud with you about your feelings. Blokes don't do a lot of that anyway. But he'd feel like he wanted to do something. A bit like a little kid who sees you upset about something, can't compute that, doesn't know what to do about it – so he comes up and give you his teddy bear or his Dinky toy.

'This was the kind of thing Marc did. The intent was there. He always wanted you to feel good about yourself or your situation.

So he stretched the truth. So what. The point was that he cared. He had this big, generous heart. He came across as selfish, at times. He could also be brilliant at putting others before himself.'

Marc's star must have been in the ascendant. His domestic profile was certainly on the rise. *Record Mirror* offered him a regular column, which he got Keith Altham to ghost. Even better, producer Muriel Young wanted to give him his own TV show. In a first-series run of six episodes for Granada Television with an option to renew, Marc would present the latest acts, and jam with them too.

The punks came running: Billy Idol, Paul Weller, Bob Geldof. Filming took place in Manchester, at Granada's own studios.

'I saw it a few times, and I thought, "Oh dear me no!" remembers Judy Dyble. 'He wasn't a terribly good host to his guests. He seemed to hog it a bit. By then, he had changed his musical style radically. He was always aware of the changing palette of people's interest.'

Jeff Dexter was happy, that summer: he had his old friend back. 'With Alphi gone after a bad accident, and Mick O'Halloran having had a stroke and being off the scene', he says, 'there was hardly anyone left, that summer of 1977.'

'I was around all the time,' says Cliff. 'I was with Marc, and Gloria when she was in London, pretty much 24/7. I'd drive Rolan round to Marc's mum and dad, and Marc to studios, radio interviews, shopping, or up to EMI, to kick some butt.'

'Things felt strange,' says Jeff, nonetheless. 'I knew it at the time, but could never put my finger on it. Tony had opened a taxi account for Marc, with Berryhurst Cars. Gloria didn't like driving the "Roller", as we called it, but she was happy in the Mini. But then, she was also away a lot. She and Rolan were in LA. So for much of the time that summer, it was just Marc and me. It was just like old times. We were two silly young boys again. Going out to dinner at the White Elephant on the River, coming home and taking the piss. And of course he was in great shape by then. He'd got really quite fit. He'd been running on tour, he'd been eating properly, he wasn't drinking . . . he didn't drink the whole summer, as far as I'm aware. Until . . . but I didn't know at the time . . . he drank on the last TV show, with Bowie.'

Between them, Jeff and Marc had pulled off an amazing coup: persuading David Bowie to fly in from Switzerland, where he had made his permanent home, to perform on the final episode of the *Marc* show. It was a massive favour for a couple of little mates, who could hardly believe their luck. The big-shot rock star was due in by plane on 7 September. The oiks got on the puffer, and headed north.

'When David arrived, Marc said to him, "This is Cliff." To me, it was, "Look after David for the day, whatever he wants," says Cliff Wright.

'Marc gave David a Fender Strat: a Sunburst with a maple neck. We set up an amp and cab [speaker cabinet] in the studio for him, and they recorded "Heroes" for the show. This was going to be the first airing of the single on British TV. I thought David could have let Marc play on it with him, to be honest.

'David also wanted a bottle of red and a bottle of white. By the end of the day, Marc had got so pissed off that he wound up drinking both of them himself.'

'The morning of that show was fantastic,' remembers Jeff. 'What you had to do in those days was make the backing track in the studio. It was Bowie with his old band, and Marc. Together again, in the recording studio. They were playing off each other, and really enjoying it. Their hearts were out. The friendship was intact. It was beautiful. This is the morning.'

Is there truth in the rumour that they were discussing recording an album together?

'They were talking about *all* kinds of things, the early part of lunch,' Jeff affirms. "They would definitely have done something. I was watching Deeb, he was in his element. He was in a strange place, in some ways: although he'd had great success, he loved that thing of the London Boys, just him and Marc together. And of course me being a London boy too, we were all loving it.

'Everyone did a run-through, we got the timings, we made the notes – but it didn't go as if it's the show, because the show went out live. So this was the rehearsal, really.'

But after lunch, proceedings took a turn for the worse.

'While we were off having our lunch,' says Jeff, 'the gang had arrived from CBS – including Coco Schwab [David's companion, who was doing everything for him at the time]. They'd brought with them their own security team. There was also a bunch of journalists, accompanied by Keith Altham.'

Tony Howard had just flown back from a six-week holiday in Greece, in time for the last show.

'I drove to the station to pick him up,' says Jeff. "How's it been?" he asked me on the way back, "all crazy?"

'I said, "Marc's been as good as gold, everyone's been doing their thing, it's been a breeze. Eric Hall has behaved like a diamond, he's been entertaining everyone, he's dealt with all the poofs, it's been fantastic." Tony's going, "Oh Jeff, I'll have to leave you in charge more often in future. I can't believe it. No aggro?" None at all.

'We walked back into Granada, and went to go into the studio. This big arm comes across:

'"Closed session!"

'"Who are you?" I said to the torso to which the arm was attached.

'"I'm Bowie's security."

'"Well what fucking right have *you* got . . ." I said. I turned around, and there's all the television crew and the boss of the union, having this big discussion. "We've been thrown out of our own studio!", they said.

'I knocked the security guy out the way, telling him, "You can't do that!", and there's Tony going, "I thought you said it was all love and light . . ."

'We get Coco.

'"How dare you!" I say, "do you realise what you're doing? This is *their* show, not yours. It's not yours, David!" I said to him, when I saw him. I lost it. And then Marc lost it. Marc didn't know that the floor manager, who had been thrown out the studio as well, was also the head of the union.

'So it was all off. We were called upstairs to the big boss's office and read the riot act. Marc's in tears, David's slinking off. It looks finished. But then Marc goes, "We've got to do this." And David says, "Well I didn't even know I *had* a crew throwing people out: what's going on?" So because of David and Marc being grown-ups, everyone goes back in the studio and finishes the rehearsal. The other bands had been run through, and suddenly everyone's jolly. Obviously some alcohol has appeared from somewhere.'

Thanks to Union regulations, the programme was not allowed to over-run. When Marc fell off the edge of the stage, therefore, to David's great amusement, there was simply no time to stop and go again. The programme was not fit for public consumption. That didn't stop the producers transmitting it during the week after Marc's death. It can be found on YouTube.

With Gloria just back from Los Angeles, and over her jetlag, 15 September was slated as a night out.

'Earlier that day before we went out to dinner, Marc did interviews at the 69 New Bond St offices, and then he came home,' remembers Gloria. 'We got ready, and we went out together – first to the Speakeasy, and then on to Morton's in Berkeley Square.'

In 1997, during an interview for a German television show, the 6'7" tall British-born blues, folk and rock singer Long John Baldry insisted that he had been the last person to see Marc. Baldry suggested that he had interviewed Bolan for a US production company, before Marc 'drove away' and had the accident.

While we know that Marc never drove, there is some truth in the claim by the popular artist who had worked prolifically with Alexis Korner, The Rolling Stones, The Beatles and Rod Stewart, launched the band Bluesology with keyboard player Reg Dwight (later Elton John) in 1966, and who had a hit record in 1967 with 'Let the Heartaches Begin'.

'Long John Baldry had moved to Canada, but came back to England in 1977 to do a series of interviews which I had set up for him for a syndicated show, *The History of British Rock*,' explains Anya Wilson.

'Hazel Griffiths at 69 New Bond Street was doing Marc's PR, and I arranged through her for them to meet.

'The interview took place in Muswell Hill, at a house which Baldry rented from Rod Stewart's brother. Marc was driven to the house, dropped off [driver Cliff had been given the night off], and was later picked up by Gloria. Her brother Richard was with them. This interview, which was the last that Marc ever gave, was broadcast in Canada.'

'This was their first night on the town since Gloria got home,' confirms Jeff Dexter. 'Because obviously when you come back from America you're jet-lagged. She had a young kid in tow, and a big brother to feed. So it was their first night out. It was actually a pre-arranged night with me, for Marc to come and listen to two songs performed at the Speakeasy by The Lightning Raiders, guests of Alfalpha, who had the residency there throughout the year. I'd played Marc a couple of their songs on cassette, and he liked them. He wanted to hear them play live.

'But unfortunately he arrived totally pissed. They'd been out somewhere earlier, or they'd been drinking at home. They were supposed to get to the Speak at about 11pm, just as Alfalpha were kicking off. Shortly after they came, Marc tried to get up and play with them. But he was too drunk to talk. Arseholed on Champagne.'

Off they went to Morton's in Mayfair, leaving Jeff behind at the Speakeasy.

'No point in going with them,' he shrugged. 'I wasn't going to get any sense out of them that night.'

Jeff Dexter never saw his friend again.

Morton's was buzzing when Marc's party arrived – to find Eric Hall waiting for them. Tony Howard was joining them, as was Keith Altham, who, in the event, got held up by The Damned.

'I was too tired, I didn't want to stay long,' says Eric. 'Marc didn't want me to leave. He was on a roll, the life and soul that night. He had Gloria back, he was on the up again, he was happy. In the end, I went to the Men's, then escaped by the fire exit door, and drove home to Essex. He wouldn't have let me go otherwise. I have wished every day since that I'd stayed.'

Before long, Richard Jones noticed the pretty blonde woman in the corner, singing and playing piano. She was a regular employee of the club, and her name was Vicky Aram. Before she knew what was happening, Vicky found herself being talked into going back to the house with them, to discuss the possibility of recording together.

'It didn't occur to me that there was anything untoward in accepting an invitation from them', says the still-chic mother-of-three – whom I tracked down on the internet, after finding an extract of a small self-published book she had written about her childhood in the north of England. An unusually intuitive woman who appears ridiculously young for someone well into her seventies, she even drew up my astrological chart.

'Artistic people do not live by conventional rules,' says Vicky. 'We go with the flow. It wasn't shocking to be going home with them. I wasn't at all impressed by glamour or stardom. I met this kind of people all the time. I also knew my husband would not worry if I didn't get home until late. I worked every night at Morton's until 2am.'

When Marc and Gloria left the club, they went to find the Mini while Vicky drove Richard in her own car – a dark green Ford estate. Not familiar with the part of London they were going to, Vicky needed to wait for Gloria, and follow her.

'Richard was in a panic that night. Who knows why. Did he feel that something odd was going to happen?'

There have been rumours all these years that 'the blonde from Morton's was going back to Marc Bolan's to spend the night with Richard Jones.'

'Not true!' Vicky exclaims. 'I was 42 then! I'm 77 now. I was happily married with three children. My husband was an eminent architect. We spent our time with fantastic, artistic, bohemian people. That was not the kind of thing I did.'

What happened next?

'We drove off, and I kept losing sight of Gloria, whom I was supposed to be following. Her car was scuttling around corners like a little purple beetle. Richard fell asleep, so he could not guide me. I lived in north London, I didn't know the part of London they were headed for. Pretty soon, I had no idea where we were . . .'

As Vicky steered her car over the Queens Ride hump-back bridge towards dawn, that Friday 16 September, the wreckage of the Mini lay ahead of them. The car had crashed, not into a sycamore tree as has always been reported, but into a steel-reinforced concrete post.

It was the impact with the post which killed Marc instantly. The tree took the blame.

Richard Jones was at first hysterical. Vicky had to calm him down, then get him to remove Marc and Gloria from the car, as she feared it might explode. She had him lay them on her mother's old air-raid shelter blanket, which she had taken from the boot of her own car.

'Gloria's head, her neck, the blood . . . her head seemed to be on the floor,' Vicky says. 'Marc was in the back. Someone said afterwards that they thought they saw a body on the bonnet, but I don't think that was the case. That might just have been in transit – Richard lifting one of them out, as I was laying the blanket down, say.

'Marc had already departed. He didn't seem remotely hurt. He looked totally at ease. He just looked like a sweet little boy, lying there on my mother's blanket. It was Gloria whose body was broken and crumpled. She was in terrible pain.

'One car went past. I asked Richard if I should flag them down, but he didn't want me to. They didn't stop, either. I think the driver of this car later put up some lousy stuff on the internet.'

'I wasn't there when the police came,' Vicky says. 'I was down at the crossroads, where I had driven to look for a phone box and call an ambulance. The emergency services told me to remain there until they arrived.'

Why has she never before divulged all these details?

'I was a respectable married lady with three children,' she says quietly. 'People would not have understood why I was there.'

Vicky knew that the mouth-to-mouth and cardiopulmonary resuscitation that Richard was administering were in vain. But there was no stopping him. He pressed on, his efforts hampered by heavings from Marc's stomach, ejecting blood and fish-smelling vomit all over him.

'Richard was later very angry with the ambulance people that they didn't have special revival equipment with them. He felt that Marc's life could have been saved,' Vicky says.

All was pitch black out there on the road, except for a shimmer of moonlight. It was extremely cold at that hour. Richard and Vicky stood shivering.

'It was silent, no sound at all,' she remembers. 'As far as I knew, we were in the middle of nowhere. I had no idea that there was a row of houses just below where the accident took place. No one came out. Now that I know the location, I think, how extraordinary.

'I went back to the scene when the ambulance came. Richard got back in my car, and we followed it to St Mary's Roehampton hospital. From there, I called my husband. "Don't worry," he said, "I heard it on the news."'

David Hardman, Police Constable 522T, was reported as having been sent from Barnes police station to the scene of the accident 'within minutes'. His report, filed at 5.58am, stated that the car had not been driven at excessive speed. In his opinion, the driver was neither drunk nor on drugs. There was reason to believe that a wheel had been removed from the Mini in order for a puncture to be repaired, a few days before the crash. The car was later examined by mechanic Colin Robson of local garage Wardo Autos. It could not be ruled out that the wheel nuts had not been re-tightened sufficiently, that the wheel had come loose, and that this had affected the steering.

Safety crash barriers were installed at the site after the crash. There had been accidents at the spot before. The traffic-calming speed bumps did not appear until 2007.

'I can see myself this minute,' says Harry Feld. 'I was on the buses doing overtime, so I'd started at half past four in the morning.

When I got to the depot at North End in Portsmouth, a guy came up and said "I've got to relieve you, you've got trouble at home."

'I got in my car, drove off, and it came on the seven o'clock news, just then – that Marc had been killed. It wasn't their fault at the depot. The police had rung from Roehampton to Southsea, where I was living, and they thought I'd already been told.

'That is a feeling that you never want,' says Harry. 'I thought well, I've got to get home. I picked myself up and drove. I had to go up and identify him, which was all I could think about at that point. I went to Mum and Dad's to get Mum and go up the hospital, because they didn't want her to go on her own. After that, we went to Marc's house, and there were the "suits" there, business people, discussing it all as if Marc never existed. It upset me. They were discussing my brother as a product. His name wasn't mentioned at all.'

There are many things he can't prove which Harry says he knows happened.

'His house was ransacked the day Marc died. There were a couple of fans who wrote to someone in Birmingham, who immediatcly contacted me. I went round to theirs and got some of the stuff back. They'd taken suitcases of clothing. They said they didn't take any tapes, but I wonder. When we got back to Marc's house after identifying him, there were already six guitars gone out of his music room. They crop up on *Antiques Roadshow* to this day.

'Those guitars just vanished,' says Harry, 'and I don't believe that was fans. The only people there that day were business people. I don't know who exactly, but I'd like to know how they got in. It was private property. Anyone in there without permission was trespassing.'

A surprising number of people appear to 'own' Marc's personal belongings today, which by rights ought to have been returned to Gloria and Rolan.

'This is what Mum, Dad and I always thought,' Harry says. 'Why have they got them? Even Marc's Rolls Royce Bentley, which my dad had been looking after: that went too. Seven years after Marc died, we saw it advertised for sale. It had been painted pink.'

Could Marc have been saved, does Harry believe? He shakes his head.

'Oh no, no. He was dead, right there,' he says. 'When the car crashed, Marc was on the passenger side. The stone pillar on the side came in, and hit him in the head. He was somersaulted over. They told us every bone in his body was broken. The consultant told my mum that if he'd lived, he would have been brain-damaged. All you could see was like a tiny bullet mark in his temple. His face was untouched. But with so many internal injuries, he could never have survived.

'It was strange,' says Harry, 'when we got to the hospital. There was this book on his bed: Nijinsky, the Russian ballet dancer. A biography. I never found out what it was doing there. It was no use to Marc by then.'

'June,' says Jeff Dexter. 'She would have been the one to leave that there. That was such a June thing to do. She did tell me that she'd gone down to see Marc in the mortuary.'

Why would they allow her in?

'Their divorce had never been finalised,' Jeff says. 'June was still his wife.'

'I was sent to see Gloria in hospital,' says Cliff Wright. 'Tony and Jeff asked me to do it. I had to go in and tell her Marc was ok. I had to stand there and lie to her. I felt awful. It was a big ask of a young kid whose dad had just died that year. But Jeff and Tony wouldn't have got away with it. She'd have known immediately.

'As it was, I'm sure she smelt it. We were "family", we all saw each other every day. Poor thing was pumped full of morphine, and high as a kite. She could only communicate by pen and paper, and she wrote to me, 'Is Marc ok? They won't let me see him.' I told her he was fine, and on another ward.'

'When I heard about the crash, I felt responsible,' Anya Wilson admits sadly.

'I felt terrible personal guilt, for a very long time. It was because of me that he'd gone to Muswell Hill to do that interview. He may even have got drunk there: not that I could ever tell whether he drank a lot, or whether alcohol simply affected him more than it did most people. Whatever it was, I felt for a long time that it was all my fault.

'T. Rex was a huge thing in my life,' she reveals.

'I enjoyed them and the music so much. I have an abiding memory of being in the green room at the Old Grey Whistle Test with Bob Harris once, and Marc coming in with Harry Nilsson. They'd been on the booze, they were drinking buddies. Marc looked at the monitor at one point and said, "Oh look, there's another John Peel protégé!"

'"I remember when *you* were a John Peel protégé!" I said to him.

'Marc stared at me. "Anya, you're my lady," he said. I feel so saddened by that memory. Marc was a very smart man. He was mixing with such excellent writers. He and David Bowie, my other maestro, were compatriots. Both were very much on the wave of growth. The music of both artists blew me away. How fortunate in a lifetime, to get to work with two such amazing people.

'I know, in my heart of hearts, that Marc would have developed wonderfully, and have gone from strength to strength.'

★ ★ ★

The funeral was held on 20 September, four days after Marc was killed. It was much worse than Jeff Dexter had anticipated.

'Gloria still didn't know that Marc was dead', he says, 'She'd been unconscious all this time. That morning, we didn't have time to get to the hospital to tell her – we did it the next day, not *on* the day, as is always reported. We got up at six o'clock, pulled the security men together, got the flowers, and then went straight to EMI.

'They had given us a big room to organise everything from. All the people being bussed to the funeral were going to go together from Manchester Square. Marc's family didn't come to EMI. They went straight to the crematorium with the funeral directors.'

Then June turned up.

'It was terrible,' Jeff relates, 'because she was now on the outside. She'd been *persona non grata* for practically two years before this happened. Both around the office and in and around Marc's life – although it was said that they'd seen each other a couple of times. I believe it, too.'

June was, understandably, in a terrible state. Nobody wanted her there.

'For me it was heartbreaking,' says Jeff, 'in threefold. Because I knew what June did for Marc. I knew what Marc did for June, and what they did to each other. So it was horrible.

'She was on the outside, and had been painted as the bad girl. But she was broken-hearted. It was too much for her. Tony and I walked her back to the lift. It was Tony who had to say, "June: you cannot be here." She broke down, of course. He explained – because he had a great heart, our Tony – all the reasons why she should not be there. But of course, he also knew the reasons why she *should* be there.

'I walked her out the door.'

★ ★ ★

June made it to Marc's funeral anyway – enlisting the help of Scotland Yard, as she later claimed, whom she persuaded to drive her to Golders Green crematorium. The scene which ensued was heart-rending. Throughout the service, Marc's mother and brother sobbed uncontrollably. The place was besieged by grief-stricken fans. The spectacle of them wailing while jostling to get to celebrities was distressing and bizarre in equal measure. Loudspeakers had been set up, so that the fans who had gathered outside could listen to the service. Tony Visconti for one was angered by proceedings, feeling that the hysteria made a mockery of the occasion. He did notice June, who managed to smuggle herself in, and was seated not far from him and Mary Hopkin. Cliff Wright saw her too.

'Outside,' he remembers. 'She was just standing there afterwards, helpless and alone among the crowd. Then David Bowie came past in his limo. June spotted him, and called out to him, "David! David!" Bowie opened the door, and let her in.'

'I'd travelled there in a limo with Rod [Stewart], remembers Steve Harley. 'Bowie was sat right in front of me – the only time I ever met him. Rod was staying at the Intercontinental on Park Lane. We were going back there to have our own little wake. We asked David to join us. He didn't come.'

In the hospital, Gloria Jones's head was as swollen as a basketball. Her jaw was wired, she couldn't speak or eat. She'd broken both her feet, and one of her legs. No seat belts. She had lost her partner, her baby's father, her livelihood and almost her life. She'd lost everything she owned, too, thanks to a series of break-ins at the couple's home, which was stripped of even her underwear.

'I went to see Gloria in hospital,' Vicky Aram tells me. 'I saw her and Richard a few times afterwards. Lovely people. They sent me flowers. As far as they were concerned, I'd saved their lives.'

Although rumours did the rounds of 'criminal charges', and headlines were dominated by claims that Gloria would be 'done for dangerous driving', there was never any arrest, nor any charge. Gloria was free to return with her son to Los Angeles. She was penniless. She scooped up Wally and Rolan, retreated into her family, and set about rebuilding her life and career. She got married, eventually – to music industry executive Chris Mitchell.

'Gloria vanishing out of our lives, and taking Rolan away, was hard on everyone,' reveals Jeff Dexter. 'Because there was real love for her too – not just June. I'm not sure Gloria ever knew that.

'When I used to DJ in the ballrooms, one of the records I played often, which I loved and which touched me deeply, was "Heartbeat" by Gloria Jones. I knew that record long before I ever knew the woman. Gloria's voice is incredible on that. Whenever she sings "Heartbeat", I hear my heartbeat too.'

Cliff Wright was accused of having been responsible for the break-ins. It is good to be able to set the record straight here.

'The morning of the accident, Tony Howard asked me to go down to the house and protect the place,' Cliff says. 'He was fearful that the fans would break in, and hold vigils or something. Fans were always going nuts. They nick stuff from graves, don't they?

'The fans always knew where we were going, too, they followed us about. They'd phone studios, and get there before us. They'd book into the same hotels, and be in before we arrived. I was distraught myself, but I did as I was told. Went round to Tony's, got the keys, turned up, went all over the house checking windows and doors and stuff. Then I locked and chained myself in, and just sat in the front room, strumming on one of Marc's guitars. I must have dozed off. After a while, I heard a terrible racket at the front door – like someone trying to kick the door in. They had keys, and the chain was rattling. I thought it was burglars.

It was actually Richard Jones: covered in blood and vomit and angry, understandably.

'He had no idea who I was,' says Cliff. 'He kept going, "Who the fuck are *you*?" He must have thought I was a fan who broke in. I told him. He said he just wanted to wash and sleep. He was in a bit of a state, so I made him a cup of tea. We sat down and he told me over and over what had happened. How he'd tried to save Marc. He thought, in the darkness, that Marc was covered in engine oil. It was actually blood. I then made my way up to 69 New Bond Street to take the house keys back. There was no way I could have been the last person in the house. I didn't even know it had been turned over.'

'Hawkwind were going on tour that day,' says Jeff Dexter. 'I still had to get that show on the road, get everybody up to Manchester. Cliff came in to help me.'

'I remember him coming in,' says office secretary Gill Abrahams. 'We were all in the office together fielding calls.'

One of the most heartbreaking calls that morning was from the garage who had been repairing TOF262, Marc's Bentley, saying that it was ready for collection.

'Gill burst into tears again,' says Jeff, 'telling the caller "it's too late. Marc's dead."'

'The shock and feeling of desolation was overwhelming,' Gill goes on. 'We couldn't believe it, none of us. It was one of the most awful days of my life. Everyone was crying. We were all just stunned.

'Wizard Artists had an account with Moyses Stevens, the Mayfair florists, and it was from them that Tony Howard ordered the white swan tribute to Marc.

'A couple days after the funeral, the accountant Ian Taylor came back to the office from the bank, saying that the accounts were frozen. There was no money. No way of paying wages, bills or anything else. That swan was just one thing that was never paid for.'

'I never set foot in Marc's house again,' says Cliff. 'But had he lived, I know I'd be working for him now. Not many days go by when I don't think about him. Whenever I drive past the tree, which is quite often, I pull over. I go, "How you doin', mate?" and I tell him what I'm up to. He probably knows.'

The inquest into Marc's death was held at Battersea Coroner's Court on 28 November 1977. Vicky Aram gave evidence as a primary witness, despite the fact that she had been quite seriously injured in a car accident herself, only the night before, on her way home from work at Morton's. The cause of Marc's death was stated by Registrar R.A. Hedge as 'shock and haemorrhage due to multiple injuries consistent with road traffic accident. Passenger in a private motor car which collided with a tree'. Verdict: 'Accidental'.

June Bolan would cut an unfocused figure in the years to come, despite a couple of relationships and a baby daughter. Former journalist David Hancock remembers her as a 'stumble-drunk, using a pub a couple of friends of mine ran, north of the M25.'

Jeff Dexter recalls that she got a job with an accountancy firm, eventually, and that she once came to his home to see him. The hours they spent together that day didn't go down too well with Mrs Dexter.

'When I met her again in the 1990s,' says Caron Willans, 'I thought that she came across as a little bit sad. I don't think she ever thought that she and Marc would split up. She always used to talk about her and Marc getting back together, didn't she? But to me, he always seemed so happy with Gloria and Rolan.'

'David Bowie is not my godfather,' says Rolan Bolan, who could not have been more helpful in the preparation of this book.

'A lot of crazy stuff has been written and said down the years. I can assure you he's not, though.

'Nor did he pay for me to go to school. I've never met him.'

'What happened was, David put some money into a fund for Rolan,' explains Gloria. 'He did it so that we could live; and he did it without being asked. It was simply that he loved Marc. He wanted to look after us. He didn't say anything, and he didn't have to. It was from his heart.'

To Ringo Starr, Marc's original Beatle buddy, did the honour of godparentship fall.

'I had a christening,' Rolan says, and Ringo gave me a silver egg dish. I still have it. I've been close to his kids, for which I've been grateful.

'But in a way, it's like everyone's your godfather when you're in my situation. There were a lot of great people who'd been close to my dad. Like John Entwistle: I met him in LA, right before he passed away. "I lived near the tree", he told me. It was fascinating to hear stories about The Who and John's Children on the road.'

All these years later, Rolan is still trying to make sense of his father's financial affairs.

'The Wizard [Bahamas] company no longer exists,' he confirms.

'It was acquired by the Spirit Music Group in New York, with whom I am working now. But "rights" are still all over the place.

I'm still looking for questions to be answered. There are still many things that we need to sort out.

'It was at the 20th anniversary celebration in the UK of my father's death that I first started to take an interest in the business side. I think it was seeing so many fans there, and such huge interest. I was spending some time with my Uncle Richard. One day he turned around to me and said, "It's time for you to become a man, Rolan, and find out what really went on." I've been trying to find out ever since. It's not at all that I'm desperate for fortunes I haven't worked for. All I'm looking for is freedom. To know who I am.

'My father was a very proud Englishman. A real London Boy. People related to that in him, coming as it did off Beatlemania. It is a huge legacy, and I shall do my part to preserve it for as long as I can.'

His name does get him through the door, whenever he wants to do something, Rolan admits.

'But after that, I still have to prove myself. My name is the one thing my dad left me which no one can take away from me. It's my connection, and I'm proud of it.'

Is Rolan happy with the way his father is regarded today?

'Oh, sure. There's a song, there's something for everyone. His music was and remains so special. I meet his fans all over, and I'm so thankful for their devotion. People everywhere are still discovering him for the first time, which is amazing after so much time has passed.

'His music follows me around, too, you know: I can walk into a car dealer's and "Get It On" will come on the radio. "You're so cheesy, Rolan!," they go. "Did you tell them to do that?"'

To the many who believe he is rolling in Bolan millions and living the high life in LA, Rolan says this:

'I make my own living. So does my Mom. There are some royalties [to Rolan and to the PRS for Music Members' Benevolent Fund] but there are no huge funds. It's all gone. The people who took the money know what they did with it. What's left is a great story of music, of love, and of a piece of time when everything stood a little differently. We all need to remember where we came from.

'I take strength from what my father went through, in order to be with my mother. There was true love there. Being a product of their love, the racial and background differences and so on, is something I'm really proud of. I continue to work on putting his legacy straight, and I am finding myself as a musician. You can definitely hear both my Mom and Dad in me.

'The most important thing is that my Mom raised me to know that he loved me very much. To the fans, he was, is, and will always be Marc Bolan. To me, he's just Dad.'

To lose your father before you are old enough to know him is to be hit by a blow that could knock down walls. Rolan could have wasted his life as an angry young man, wallowing in bitterness and recrimination. He has weathered it all with dignity and pride. He was never your average rock kid, granted. That's not nothing. I can think of a few who could do with a leaf from his tree. Perhaps the best bit is that he doesn't believe Marc owes him a living. There may not be the millions that are rightfully his, but listen to the legacy.

Marc remains twenty nine for all time. We who are left grow old. The band plays on.

Post-script

I heard that my children told their father I was writing a book about Marc Bolan.

'Did I ever tell you my Marc Bolan story?' my former husband, Gerard Shine, asked me, when he came to pick them up.

He hadn't.

He proceeded to.

In 1987, Gerard was the director of an appeal for the new Bournemouth Hospital. Fund-raising was an all-encompassing effort. It included an event at the local bingo hall one evening, attended by an enthusiastic crowd. The following day, local newspaper the *Bournemouth Echo* received a somewhat unortho-dox pledge. A gentleman called Larry Mitchell, who described himself as a 65-year-old retired undertaker from Tottenham now living in the Bournemouth area, said that he had directed Marc Bolan's funeral in September 1977. For reasons he either declined or was unable to explain, he had retained the clothes Marc was wearing on the night he died. He wanted to offer them as items to auction, to help raise money for the hospital appeal.

The *Bournemouth Echo* immediately assigned a journalist to the story. She telephoned Marc's brother Harry, then living in Portsmouth, and a front page splash ensued.

'*BLOOD MONEY FOR HOSPITAL*' blared the headline, on 7 December 1987.

'*Macabre mementoes – the blood-stained clothes of tragic pop star crash victim Marc Bolan – may be sold to raise cash for Bournemouth's new hospital. Retired undertaker Mr. Larry Mitchell hopes the ghoulish gear will attract international interest and net thousands of pounds at auction.*'

What did you do?' I asked.

'Well, there was no way we were going to accept something like that to raise money for the hospital, of course not,' Gerard said.

'Some things are beyond the pale. The local radio station 2CR got involved, there was quite a to-do. I wrote to Harry Feld, distancing the appeal from the macabre proposition, apologising for any understandable distress, and reassuring him that we would be having nothing whatsoever to do with it. I remember Harry contacted me a few days later. He was very understanding and extraordinarily nice about it all.'

I called Golders Green Crematorium, where the staff are impressive record-keepers. Despite the fact that we were talking 35 years ago, they were able to inform me within minutes, from their log books, that Marc's funeral had been organised by the Jewish Joint Burial Society, who then sub-contracted to a firm of funeral directors. This was for a simple reason: not only must a Jewish death be registered according to the requirements of English civil law, but the observation of traditional Jewish rites is imperative. Once the relevant burial society has been appointed, it organises both the collection of the deceased and the *Taharah* – the ritual cleansing and preparation of the body for its final journey. Special prayers are recited during the procedure, beseeching God to lift the soul into the Heavens and to eternal rest. The body is then wrapped in plain white *Tachrichim* (shrouds), symbolising the spiritual and the sublime over the physical and the material. Together with the officiating Rabbi – in this case, Henry Goldstein – arrangements are made for a funeral service and the ensuing burial or cremation. While cremation is not the traditional Jewish practice, it is often preferred. An organisation such as the Jewish Joint Society ensures that, even when burial is not taking place, all other rites are respected – which may not be possible if conducted by a general undertaker.

The elderly administrator at the Jewish Joint Burial Society on Victory Road in London's Leytonstone district remembered Larry Mitchell very well.

'Mitchell's in Tottenham,' Mr Colin Joseph confirmed. 'They ceased trading years ago, they no longer exist. Larry retired, closed down his business, and moved to the south coast.'

I called Harry.

'It's all true,' he confirmed – as incredulous as I had been that my ex-husband had been involved.

'My mum and dad were very distressed by it all. As if they hadn't suffered enough. A young journalist rang up to warn me about what this old undertaker was trying to do. She gave me his address and telephone number. I phoned him and said 'I'd like to see you about these clothes you're selling.' I got a reporter and a photographer along from the *Portsmouth Evening News* – not because I wanted publicity, but just to come along and be witnesses.

'When this Larry Mitchell came round, he was with a news agency bloke who thought he had an exclusive. He was livid when he saw the other journalists in my house. "This isn't for any story," I told him, "this is just between me and him." Larry went back out and got the clothes from the boot of his car. I had a feeling there was a good deal more in that boot.'

There they lay, in Larry's little suitcase: tiny garments that Harry had never imagined he would see again. A silky shamrock-green satin shirt with some sequinned wording on it: Harry thinks the letters of his name, 'M-A-R-C'; a red vest; a pair of narrow-hipped black velvet trousers, and his child-size socks.

'I felt sick, to be honest,' said Harry.

'These were the clothes they'd taken off Marc in the mortuary. When we were preparing for his funeral, Mum picked out some things that she wanted him cremated in – you know what mums are like. In fact, they take those off you too, and just wrap you in a shroud. In the Jewish faith, when you are cremated, you go out the way you came in.

'"But I remember telling you in the undertaker's office," I said to Larry Mitchell, "whatever you've got from the hospital, whatever came with my brother, can you please destroy it all. Why didn't you?" He couldn't answer me. I said, "Well, I'm going to do that now."

'Before anyone could move, I had the clothes on a sheet of metal in the garden, and was pouring lighter fuel on them. I burned the clothes in front of their eyes. Mitchell's jaw hit the floor. He got quite agitated, and stood chanting Jewish prayers in Hebrew as Mark's stuff went up in flames. This was a sacred moment to him. Mitchell was Jewish too. Marc's blood was all over those clothes I was burning, so this was like a second cremation for him.'

'"There you go, and *out* you go," I said. "No one's going to have them now."'

Larry Mitchell never understood what he was supposed to have done wrong.

'I sincerely felt it was an excellent opportunity to keep the memory of a wonderful performer alive, and also contribute to a worthy cause,' he said at the time – his words quoted in the *Bournemouth Echo* the following day.

'I can believe that,' says Gerard.

'Although it was difficult to understand why he hadn't dealt properly with the clothes at the time, my impression was not that he was some grasping, manipulative type, just a poor old boy who'd lost the plot a bit. He'd simply found the bag of clothes in a store room when he was clearing out his premises on his retirement, and hadn't known what to do with them. He couldn't exactly throw them away. When our appeal came up, he spotted what he thought was a chance to do something good with them. I don't believe there was any malice involved, nor that he had intended to upset Marc Bolan's family in any way. He just hadn't thought it through.'

What became of the ashes of those garments?

'We had a lovely white rose bush – a replica of the one for Mark – and he *was* "Mark" again, to me – at Golders Green Crem,' Harry told me. 'I dug a hole under the bush, and I buried the ashes there. I felt I had to respect what had happened in my garden. If it *had* been a sort of second cremation, then this was another resting place.

'One last resting place for my brother that was just for us. That had nothing to do with anybody else.'

Chapter Notes

FADE-IN . . .

1 Legendary New York recording studios on W 44th St, founded 1968. The first studios to introduce a relaxed, cosy recording environment complete with home comforts designed to encourage creativity. Jimi Hendrix spent three months there in 1968, completing the album *Electric Ladyland* which he had started at Olympic Studios, London. Record Plant mixed the tracks recorded at the Woodstock Festival in 1969, and was the first studio to mix quadraphonic sound. Further Record Plants were opened in LA, 1969, and Sausalito, 1972. The New York studio closed down in 1987.

2 Not on the day of the funeral, as previously reported.

3 Dexter Jeffrey Bedwell was Jeff Dexter's real name. David Robert Jones is David Bowie's.

CHAPTER ONE: MUSIC OUT OF THE MOON

Les Baxter's 'Music Out of the Moon' was a popular recording of 1947 – the year of Marc's birth. According to fellow astronaut Michael Collins, 'first man on the moon' Neil Armstrong took into space, for the moon landing in July 1969, a 'cassette of strange electronic-sounding music' that was later identified as 'Music Out of The

Moon'. A musical innovator and a major contributor to the 'Exotic Movement', Baxter is credited with changing the musical taste of America with this album, on which he collaborated with Samuel J. Hoffman. It was the first recording to feature a Theremin, played by Hoffman – an early electronic musical instrument with an eerie sound. It also gave the American space programme an uncanny Russian connection: the instrument had been invented by Russian physicist Leon Theremin. A 'space oddity' linking two London-born musicians born the same year: Bowie and Bolan.

1   Rolling Stone Ronald David 'Ronnie' Wood, Reginald Kenneth Dwight (Elton John), Brian Harold May of Queen, Michael Lee Aday (Meatloaf), David Albert Cook (David Essex), Ian Scott Anderson of Jethro Tull, Michael John Kells 'Mick' Fleetwood of Fleetwood Mac, Gregory LeNoir 'Gregg' Allman of The Allman Brothers, Jeffrey 'Jeff' Lynne of The Electric Light Orchestra, and Eagles Donald Hugh 'Don' Henley and Joseph Fidler 'Joe' Walsh, to name a few.

CHAPTER TWO: DROP A NICKEL IN
From the lyrics of 'Jukebox Cannonball' by Bill Haley and The Saddlemen, later The Comets. This 1952 song is an early example of rockabilly, and features a reference to 'old Carnegie Hall' – the hallowed venue which Marc longed to play, and where he would perform in February 1972.

1   The hand-me-down term would be picked up by funk-disco outfit Heatwave in 1977 for their hit 'Boogie Nights', featuring the keyboard wizardry of Rod Temperton ... whose greater claim to fame was the title track on the biggest-selling album of all time: Michael Jackson's 'Thriller', in 1982. The irresistible trivia here, if you'll allow, is that The Jacksons

enjoyed a hit with 'Blame It On The Boogie' in 1978 . . . as did the song's main originator, British singer-songwriter Mick Jackson, no relation. The two versions went neck-and-neck on the charts, the music press frothing about The Jacksons' 'self-penned song'. It wasn't, though. I blame it on the boogie . . .

2 Edmond O'Brien later won an Oscar for 'The Barefoot Contessa', and starred in many other films: 'The Man Who Shot Liberty Valance' and 'The Wild Bunch' among them.

CHAPTER THREE: NO DICE, SON

From the lyrics of Eddie Cochran's immortal 1958 hit 'Summertime Blues'. Marc would record a minimalist acoustic cover of one of his favourite tracks – probably inspired by The Who, who played 'Summertime Blues' during their earliest live concerts until 1976 (they have not performed it since bass player John Entwistle's death in 2002). The Who served up the song most famously during their 1967 US tour, from which the acclaimed early recordings were made. That tour included their legendary June 1967 date at the Monterey Pop Festival. The B-side of T. Rex's first hit single 'Ride a White Swan' was their version of 'Summertime Blues'.

1 The age of consent was reduced to 18 in 1994. This was equalised in 2000 to 16 for both homosexual and hetero-sexual activity in the UK.

2 Irena Sedlecka also created the famous statue of Freddie Mercury on the edge of Lake Geneva in Montreux, Switzerland.

3 The Day the Music Died would later be immortalised in Don McLean's epic encapsulation of rock'n'roll, 'American Pie' – the ground-breaking 1971 hit in both America and the UK which has become an all-time classic.

CHAPTER FOUR: CALL HIM A MAN

From the lyrics of 'Blowin' In The Wind', recorded by another of Marc's great idols, Bob Dylan, in 1963.

1 Frontman of popular tribute act T.Rextasy.
2 Available to download on iTunes.
3 The former Tornado George Bellamy is the father of Matthew Bellamy, of British rock band Muse.
4 Warren is said to have later 'sold' his contract with Mark to his landlord, in order to settle an unpaid rent bill. The landlord, David Kirsch, was allegedly visited some time afterwards by an irate Phyllis Feld, who complained that Kirsch had done nothing for her son, and demanded that he destroy the contract. The tapes recorded during Mark's 'Toby Tyler' sessions were 'lost' for a quarter of a century. After they were found, in 1991, they sold for several thousand pounds and were released on CD in 1993.
5 The film, based on the 1966 novel by Leslie Thomas, starred Hywel Bennett and Lynn Redgrave. The soundtrack was by Ray Davies of the Kinks. David Bowie cut his hair very short to audition for the movie, but failed to land a part. O'Hara went on to stage Shakespeare for the now-defunct Portobello Festival, and bought a famous Notting Hill pub, the Malvern, for £1 million in 2003. He made a small fortune when he sold up within four years – to a property developer who built ten luxury apartments on the site, total sales value £4 million.

CHAPTER FIVE: FACES LIKE A POEM

From the lyrics of Donovan's 1965 album track 'The Ballad of A Crystal Man', on his second album Fairytale: *'Read your faces like a poem'.*

1 The writer whose book *Yea Yea Yea* became the 1966 Norman Wisdom film *Press for Time*.
2 The 1962 Western starring John Wayne and James Stewart.
3 The 1972 film adaptation starred Richard Burton, Elizabeth Taylor and Peter O'Toole. In 1988, 'Fifth Beatle' George Martin produced an album version with much of the dialogue sung – the music composed by George himself, with Elton John and other contributors – and featuring Anthony Hopkins. This was performed live in the presence of His Royal Highness Prince Charles to mark the 1992 opening of George Martin's new AIR Studios, Lyndhurst Hall, London. The performers included Tom Jones, Harry Secombe and Catherine Zeta-Jones.

CHAPTER SIX: NOMIS
Referring to Simon Napier-Bell, famous songwriter for the likes of Dusty Springfield, manager of The Yardbirds and John's Children, briefly Marc's manager and companion. Years later, SNB founded a studio facility in West London known as 'Nomis Studios'.

1 The musical was adapted for the screen in 1966. Its most famous, Newley-penned song, popularised by Sammy Davis Jnr and Tony Bennett, was 'What Kind Of Fool Am I?'
2 Re-made in 2004 with Jude Law.
3 With music by Australian group The Seekers, composed by Dusty's brother Tom Springfield.
4 He was later played by Phil Collins in the film.
5 Bolan kept faithful to the theme, as evident from the lyrics of T. Rex's November 1971 Number 2 hit single 'Jeepster': 'Girl, I'm just a vampire for your love . . . I'm gonna suck you'. The song clearly borrows from Howlin' Wolf's 'You'll Be Mine', and also echoes Roy Orbison's 'You're My Baby'.

He acknowledges Howlin' Wolf in the fade-out to his third UK Number 1, 'Telegram Sam', from the 1972 album *The Slider*.

CHAPTER SEVEN: EVERYTHING'S SPINNING

A line from the Napier-Bell-penned lyrics to John's Children track 'Smashed, Blocked' – smashed being mod slang for drunk, blocked being 'pilled-up': out of one's brains on amphetamines.

1 The Action evolved their style through psychedelic to folk rock. Lead guitarist and vocalist Alan 'Bam' King would later form Ace. Phil Collins cites them as one of his all-time favourite bands, and performed with them for their 2000 reunion. 'For me, it was like playing with The Beatles,' he said. John's Children are credited with having exerted a huge influence over punk rock. Their singles are among the most highly-prized Sixties collectables. 'Smashed, Blocked/ Strange Affair' made the US Billboard Hot 100, and a couple of Top Ten local charts in Florida and California.

2 A controversial novel published in 1959, exploring both Jewish and Christian themes, its central premise being that art can eliminate hatred and war. It was the first in the author's 'Danziger Trilogie'. Adapted for the screen in 1979, it landed that year's Palme d'Or at Cannes, and the Oscar for Best Foreign Language Film.

3 In August 1971, Shankar would front, together with George Harrison, the world's first international benefits gig, the Concert for Bangladesh at New York's Madison Square Garden. This was mounted to raise money and awareness for refugees following the 1970 cyclone and atrocities during the Bangladesh Liberation War.

4 Pink Floyd were due to appear, but had to cancel because Syd Barrett was incapable of performing.

5 Brother Reg Watkins developed a lucrative business manufacturing only the second British-made solid electric guitar, and the family went on to create the Watkins Rapier guitar – manufactured in their thousands and sold all over the world.

6 Adam Faith also rejected the song, which was eventually recorded by Gerry and the Pacemakers, produced by 'Fifth Beatle' George Martin. It went to Number 1. The Beatles' version was not released until the group's 1995 Anthology 1 album.

CHAPTER EIGHT: SOLID SILVER GENI

From Tyrannosaurus Rex's debut album My People Were Fair ... *the track 'Dwarfish Trumpet Blues', the lyrics of which feature a reference to a 'solid silver geni (sic)' – which could be another name for Tony Visconti.*

1 Peregrin without the 'e', though it is commonly mis-spelt, even on their own record sleeves – possibly the result of some secretary's carelessness. A 'peregrine' is a falcon. Steve did eventually start signing himself 'Peregrine Took', with the 'e' – perhaps having resigned himself to the fact that people were always going to get it wrong! The Who have always had the same problem – only Keith Moon had a surname that was easy to spell. John Entwistle made fun of all this by naming his second solo record 'WHISTLE RYMES'!

2 Peel's death in October 2004 was 'The day the music died' according to the London *Evening Standard*. 'Teenage Dreams, So Hard To Beat' were the words engraved on his headstone, from Irish punk/new wave/glam-rock-lovers The Undertones' 1978 hit 'Teenage Kicks'. Some consider the song to have been inspired by Marc Bolan's 1974 single 'Teenage Dream', from the album *Zinc Alloy & the Hidden Riders of Tomorrow*.

3 Boyd worked with many folk/folk rock artists, returning to the US at the end of 1970 to produce for Warner Bros with responsibility for film music – including the soundtrack of Stanley Kubrick's *A Clockwork Orange*. He now works and lives in London.

4 Napier-Bell still speaks of Marc with nothing but fondness.

5 The Move's single 'Flowers In The Rain' was the first record ever played on BBC Radio 1.

6 Hare Krishna chanting also featured in the stage musical *Hair*, in which Marsha Hunt, a brief flame of Marc's, appeared.

7 David Gilmour joined Pink Floyd in December 1967. Barrett left in April 1968, due to deteriorating mental health. After Floyd, Jenner and King managed a string of other bands. King had Ian Dury in the early Eighties, while Jenner looked after Billy Bragg and Eddi Reader. Barrett died from pancreatic cancer in 2006, aged 60.

CHAPTER NINE: DAZZLE DAWN MAN

From the track 'The Pilgrim's Tale', on the B-side of the third Tyrannosaurus Rex album Unicorn *– their first to be released in the US.*

1 Ironically, T. Rex's September 1972 Number 2 hit single about teenage rebellion, 'Children of the Revolution', on which Ringo Starr plays drums, was rumoured to be pro-communist propaganda!

2 Among the earliest signings for the Apple label were American singer James Taylor, Beatle-esque Liverpool group The Iveys, and the Welsh *Opportunity Knocks* TV talent contest winner, Mary Hopkin – who had a huge hit with 'Those Were The Days', and who would soon become Tony Visconti's wife. Mary sang on the 1971 T. Rex demos

'Cadilac' (sic) – a B-side, with 'Baby Strange', on 'Telegram Sam', and on 'Truck On (Tyke)'.

3　David Stark attended most of the free Hyde Park shows. Thirty two years later, he co-wrote a brief history of them with Jeff Dexter.

4　Like the 1950s American high school rock'n'roll 'Sock Hops', but without the dancing – referred to in Danny and the Juniors' 1957 single 'At the Hop'.

5　Her Majesty the Queen, as Princess Elizabeth, was born in 1926 at 17 Bruton STREET – NOT in the same house that became the Revolution Club during the Sixties, as has been stated!

6　It was 1950s Beat poetry that kick-started the 'Liverpool scene', that gave rise to The Beatles – during a time when the city was described by US Beat poet Allen Ginsberg as 'the centre of the consciousness of the human universe.' Henri, McGough and Patten's joint compilation, 'The Mersey Sound', 1967, now a Penguin Modern Classic, has been described as 'the most significant anthology of the 20th century' for having delivered poetry to new audiences.

7　Named by John Peel after his nanny, Florence Horne, whom the family nick-named 'Trader' after the famous adventurer.

8　In *The Lord of the Rings*, Peregrin Took is a Hobbit, also known as Pippin; a friend of Frodo Baggins, he becomes Thane of the Shire after his father's death. The characters Pearl Took, Pimpernel Took and Pervinca Took are his older sisters.

9　In 1966, one of the first psychedelic songs, first released on Donovan's Epic (USA) LP *Sunshine Superman*. The song has been covered widely by artists including Julie Driscoll, Stephen Stills, Robert Plant, Lou Rawls and Joan Jett, and was the inspiration for the name of Joe Boyd's production company Witchseason Productions.

CHAPTER TEN: EAGLE IN A SUNBEAM

From the lyric of T. Rex's first hit 'Ride a White Swan'.

1 In Los Angeles, Gloria Jones and Meat Loaf were performing in the West Coast production of *Hair*.

2 Marsha became a novelist, and acted with the National
   Theatre and the Royal Shakespeare Company. She survived
   third-stage breast cancer, and went to live in France. She is
   said to still be engaged in her 'life's work': a biography of
   Jimi Hendrix.

3 Jagger's first daughter, Karis, born in November 1970.

4 Caroline Coon is an English writer, artist and political activist, who founded Relcase – a legal service for young people
   charged with drug possession. She became a top rock writer
   at the *Melody Maker* in the late 1970s, and went on to
   manage The Clash.

5 Finn originally styled himself 'Micky' without the 'e', insists
   Jeff Dexter – there was another musician called Mickey Finn
   around at the time. But his name was so often assumed to be
   a pseudonym, based on the American slang for a drug-laced
   drink (named after the 1903 Chicago saloon bar manager
   first accused of spiking booze in order to steal from his
   customers) that Finn gave up and let them spell it how they
   liked! The 'inner circle' called him 'Fingers'.

6 This group is known as 'The 27 Club' because of the age at
   which they all died. It also featured many other, lesser-known
   rock musicians. They were joined by Nirvana's Kurt Cobain
   on 5 April 1994, and by Amy Winehouse on 23 July 2011.

7 Not 'THE Hype', insists Jeff Dexter, who also maintains
   that the outfit were never actually a 'band', as such. They
   just assembled to play a few gigs. The posters from those
   gigs confirm that Jeff is correct.

8 After Tony produced Morrissey's highly successful 2005 album *Ringleader of the Tormentors* in Rome, Morrissey wrote in the foreword of Visconti's biography: 'There are many respected bores of Tony's generation, nursing memories and resentments and never letting the trapped listener forget – but Tony isn't like that. He doesn't pick over the Saxon remains of T. Rex; the time is always now. He is a noble example of the self-flogger who knows that the song doesn't end just because it's over. Musical notations are images, and the Visconti style is timeless and lionised and is therefore for evermore.'

9 'Star' was David's nick-name for his girlfriend. He would later, Angie claims, write another song about her: 'Golden Years' (1975), which appears on the album *Station to Station*. The rock movie *Velvet Goldmine* is reckoned to be loosely-based on her relationship with Bowie – which he once described to this author as 'like living with a blow-torch'.

10 Referring to The Beatles' 1966 LP, a massive UK and US hit which marked a turning point in the group's career. Featuring the tracks 'Eleanor Rigby', 'Here, There & Everywhere' and 'She Said She Said', it is recognised as one of the greatest achievements in pop music history.

11 (There you go, Steve, it's in print now. It's official.)

12 Stained orange to simulate the Gretsch 6120 once played by his guitar hero Eddie Cochran.

13 Marc would opt for a similar hat himself, come his 1972 album, *The Slider*.

14 'Ride a White Swan' was kept off the top slot by 'Grandad' – a sentimental novelty by actor Clive Dunn, of long-running TV series 'Dad's Army'. Co-written, ironically, by future T. Rex bass player Herbie Flowers, it had been marketed as the sure-fire 'Number One Christmas single' of 1970 – but missed out thanks to a strike at the EMI pressing plant.

CHAPTER ELEVEN: COSMIC ROCK

From the lyrics of 'Hot Love', T. Rex's debut Number One single.

1 'The Ugly Duckling', composed by Frank Loesser, was sung by Danny Kaye as Andersen in the 1952 film *Hans Christian Andersen*. The original 'duckling' story, 'Den grimme ælling', was published in November 1843.
2 The third being sport!
3 Bill takes some tracking-down, with the assistance of Danielz, to his latest home in California. He usually declines to be interviewed, but made this worthwhile.
4 When Eric Clapton adopted pseudonym 'Derek and the Dominos' in 1970, in order to release the LP *Layla & Other Assorted Love Songs*, his record label retaliated by putting out pin badges revealing that 'Derek is Eric'.

CHAPTER TWELVE: GIRLS MELT

From the line 'girls melt in the heat', lyrics of 'Telegram Sam'.

1 Burt Bacharach, Neil Diamond, Bobby Darin, Gerry Goffin & Carole King, Ellie Greenwich & Jeff Barry, Neil Sedaka, Phil Spector and Ben E. King were some of the countless who made names in the Brill Building hit factory on Broadway and 49th St., north of Times Square. Among those hits were 'Yakety Yak', 'The Locomotion', 'Breaking Up Is Hard To Do', 'It Might As Well Rain Until September' and 'River Deep, Mountain High'.
2 The prophetic 'California Dreamin'' had been a hit for The Mamas & The Papas in 1965. They split in 1968, reuniting in 1971. Cass Elliot continued to record and perform until her death in Harry Nilsson's flat in Shepherd's Market, London's Mayfair, in July 1974, aged 32. Four years later, The Who's Keith Moon died at the same age, in the same flat.

3 *Billy Elliot* the feature film was released in 2000. The stage musical opened in London in 2005.

4 Rock writer Nick Jones described Secunda as 'a Svengali figure who bridged the gulf between the old-style Tin Pan Alley music biz people and the hippie underground.' After his relationship with Marc was terminated, Secunda managed Steve Peregrin Took for a while, then went into rock biography publishing in California. He died of a heart attack in February 1995, aged 54.

5 The English-American folk rock band, perhaps best known for their Number One hits 'A Horse With No Name' and 'Sister Golden Hair'. Seven of their albums were produced by 'Fifth Beatle' George Martin.

6 In September 1972, rock manager Tony Defries formed a company called MainMan Management, through which he masterminded Bowie's rise to superstardom. Defries also managed Lou Reed, Mick Ronson, Iggy Pop, Luther Vandross and John Mellencamp. It's often said that Defries took the title of his company from a line in Bolan's 'Telegram Sam', but this could be chicken-and-egg: 'Telegram Sam' was not released as a single until 1972.

CHAPTER THIRTEEN: STING LIKE A BEE

Famous line from prize-fighter Muhammad Ali's doggerel, which Marc borrowed for his lyrics to the single '20th Century Boy'.

1 Showaddywaddy were brightly-dressed 'Teddy Boy' 50s/ early 60s revivalists, famous for such covers as Eddie Cochran's 'Three Steps To Heaven' and 'Under the Moon Of Love', originally produced by Phil Spector for Curtis Lee. They enjoyed 23 hits in total, including 10 Top Ten singles and a Number One.

2 Don McLean wrote 'Vincent' ('Starry Starry Night') in autumn 1970, while reading a book about van Gogh. 'The print of "Starry Night" stared up at me,' he said. 'Looking at the picture, I realized that the essence of the artist's life is his art. And so, I let the painting write the song for me.' The year Marc first recorded at the Château near the site of van Gogh's death, 'Vincent' was Number One in the UK (Number 12 in the US). Coincidentally, it was the song that toppled Marc's last major UK hit 'Metal Guru' from the Number One slot, on 17 June, 1972.

3 Better known as French novelist George Sand.

4 'Lady Stardust' written by David Bowie from the album *The Rise & Fall of Ziggy Stardust and the Spiders From Mars* (1972). The song is believed to have been about Bolan because its original demo title was 'He Was Alright (A Song for Marc)'. Bowie played the song on the BBC radio show *Sounds Of the Seventies* with Bob Harris, on 27 May 1972, broadcast on 19 June 1972. This recording was released in 2000, on the album *Bowie At The Beeb.*

5 Brian Epstein's and The Beatles' company, named after 'Eppie's" original Liverpool record shop, North End Music Stores. 'Eppie' is known to Jeff Dexter and the inner circle as 'Leggy Mountbatten', in homage to popular Beatles' spoof 'The Rutles: All You Need Is Cash'.

6 After Marc, Alphi became Eric Clapton's personal assistant for the next twenty years. He died of cancer in 2002.

7 Sound engineer and musician Laurent Thibault assumed management of the studio in June 1974. Legal and financial disputes mounted during the sale of the Château in 1984. The studio closed for good on 25 July 1985, a year after Magne committed suicide. Thibault and team were ejected from the premises, which fell dormant for many years. The

Château has since been acquired for renovation as a 'major studio facility', rumoured to be set for relaunch in 2013, with 'a waiting list of artists seeking to compose and record in this venue so steeped in rock history.' The industry does not believe this, however. Modern recording methods and digital technology have rendered redundant the traditional large, residential studio. Few believe that the legendary 'Honky Château' can ever rise from its ashes. That is perhaps as it should be. The Château and studio as they were during Marc's time there can be seen clearly in the DVD of the making of Elton John's album *Goodbye Yellow Brick Road*.

8 The Ormsby Gores were the children of the 5th Baron Harlech, Ambassador to Washington during the Kennedy era. In 1974, Alice found her 33 year-old brother Julian shot dead in his flat, having apparently committed suicide. Alice, a heroin addict, died penniless in a Bournemouth bedsit, the day before her 43rd birthday. Alexis was the father of model Lucie – who married Marlon Richards, son of Keith Richards and Anita Pallenberg.

9 Finzi, an apple-bobbing Englishman of Italian and Jewish heritage, was a well-known composer during the 1930s, who wrote songs based on the poems of Thomas Hardy, and of William Wordsworth – who had lent his name to Marc's old school. His cantata 'Dies Natalis', on the meditations and poems of 17th century poet and preacher Thomas Traherne, is Finzi's most celebrated work.

CHAPTER FOURTEEN: THE HEAT'S ON, MISTER
From the lyrics of 'Teenage Dream'.

1 One early 'racial integration anthem', the fanciful 'Melting Pot' by Blue Mink (October 1969), predicted a harmonious

world embracing every race and creed, 'churning out coffee-coloured people by the score.' The song was written by Roger Greenaway and Roger Cook, the latter also performing in the group – which included singer Madeline Bell, and bassist Herbie Flowers: an eventual member of T. Rex. A US cover of the song, 'People Are Together', by gritty soul singer Mickey Murray, arrived too soon for American sensibilities. It was allegedly 'killed' by black DJs in the South, fearful of losing their jobs if they played it on air – despite its 'call to all mankind to join together and love one another'.

2   Oma Drake's Christian name is often misspelt, with an 'H'.

3   Although some accounts identify a fourth backing singer – Julia Tillman – Gloria Jones's unpublished autobiography states that Tillman was not present – confirmed by photographs of those gigs, which show clearly that there were only three backing singers including Gloria.

4   Billy Preston toured Germany with Little Richard, where he met The Beatles before they'd made it. He would later be signed by Apple Records, and recorded with the Fab Four – he is co-credited on 'Get Back'. He appeared on several Rolling Stones albums, had a Top Ten hit with Syreeta Wright in 1980 – 'With You I'm Born Again' – and toured with Ringo Starr, Steve Winwood and Eric Clapton. He performed in London for the 2002 concert for the late George Harrison. He died in 2006.

5   During the 1980s, the song earned Gloria the epithet 'Northern Queen of Soul'. Marc Almond, himself a huge Bolan fan (hence the Christian name) heard her recording in a club in the north of England, and re-recorded it with Soft Cell. It gave them an international Number One in 1981. The following year, in the US, it set a then Guinness World Record for the longest consecutive stay

– 43 weeks – on the US Billboard Hot 100 chart. Gloria's best song for Gladys, 'If I Were Your Woman', was Grammy-nominated in 1971.

6 Famous for having been the hub of producer Giorgio Moroder's disco-era success. German producer Reinhold Mack co-created the studios with Moroder. Deep Purple, The Rolling Stones and notably Queen recorded there. Mack confirms that he worked with T. Rex, by all accounts these were not the happiest of recording sessions.

CHAPTER FIFTEEN: NOT A MYTH LEFT

From David Bowie's 1975 'Young Americans', featuring the line 'Not a myth left from the ghetto'.

1 During which the author's great-grandfather, iron miner Daniel Jones – a follower of Scottish socialist James Keir Hardie, a founder member of the Independent Labour Party and a vociferous activist – was banned from working in every pit in South Wales in perpetuity. He became a barber instead, and continued to hold political 'salons' in his front room.

2 The miners' strike depicted in the 2000 film *Billy Elliot* took place in 1984–5, during Prime Minister Margaret Thatcher's regime – *not* during the strikes described above. Its soundtrack was composed primarily of T. Rex tracks – 'Cosmic Dancer', 'Get it On', 'I Love To Boogie', 'Children Of The Revolution', 'Ride a White Swan' – which ironically were chart hits just before or during the miners' strikes of the 1970s. The film also featured The Jam's 'Town Called Malice', 'Walls Come Tumbling Down' by Weller's Style Council, and 'London Calling' by the Clash.

3 Mickey rekindled his love affair with Sue Worth: the

girlfriend he appears with in Marc and June's wedding photo, who had dumped him for playing away from home. They were married after Marc's death, in 1978, but it failed to last. 'Fingers' later worked as a session musician for The Blow Monkeys and the Soup Dragons. He died, penniless, of alcohol-related illness in January 2003. He was 55.

CHAPTER SIXTEEN: MEASURING THE STARS

From the track 'Chrome Sitar' on T. Rex's album 'Futuristic Dragon', the lyric features the line 'measuring the stars'.

1 In May 1977, about 4 months before Marc died, *Lionel,* a musical about the composer's early life, opened in the West End. It closed after 6 weeks, losing £250,000 – close to £1.5 million today. Bart had clearly had his day. But he lived to see his work back in the spotlight. In 1994, impresario Cameron Mackintosh, who owned 50% of its rights, revived *Oliver!* on the West End stage. Bart died from cancer in 1999, and joined his friends Keith Moon and Marc Bolan at Golders Green Crematorium. *Oliver!* was revived yet again in 2009, after UK TV series *I'd Do Anything,* found both its 'Nancy' and its 'Olivers'.

A NOTE ON THE COVER

Marc was photographed by Neal Preston in Los Angeles in 1973. When he and Cameron Crowe walked into his hotel room to do the interview, Marc was sober. Out came the wine, and out came the nipple.

'I love the matter-of-fact look on his face, as if he knew it was the world's most attractive nipple,' notes Preston.

Marc Bolan's Life and Times

INSPIRATION & DESTINY
George Gordon, 6th Baron (Lord) Byron, poet, 22 January 1788 –19 April 1824 (died aged 36). 'Mad, Bad and Dangerous to Know'.

Percy Bysshe Shelley, poet, 4 August 1792 – 8 July 1822 (died aged 29).

Jean Nicolas Arthur Rimbaud, as **Arthur Rimbaud**, French poet, 20 October 1854 –10 November 1891 (died aged 37).

Khalil Gibran, Lebanese-American poet, writer & artist, 6 January 1883–10 April 1931 (died aged 48).

René Magritte, Belgian surrealist painter, 21November 1898– 15 August 1967 (died aged 68).

Salvador Domingo Felipe Jacinto Dali i Domenech, Marquis de Pubol, Spanish surrealist painter, 11 May 1904 –23 January 1989 (died aged 84).

INFLUENCES & IDOLS

3 January 1892

John Ronald Reuel Tolkien CBE, author, poet & professor, born to English parents in Bloemfontein, Orange Free State (now Free State Province), South Africa. The father of modern high fantasy literature, world famous for *The Hobbit, The Lord of the Rings* and *The Silmarillion*, Tolkien's influence over Bolan's own writing is immense.

27 October 1914

Dylan Marlais Thomas, Welsh poet & writer, born in the Swansea uplands, Glamorgan. Achieved great fame in the US through public readings of his own works, remarkable for their musicality. His marvellous Welsh accent is as admired as his poetry. Thomas claimed that the poems which influenced him most were the 'Mother Goose Rhymes' read to him in childhood.

7 April 1920

Robindro Shaunkor Chowdhury (Ravi Shankar), musician, born in Varanasi, United Provinces, Indian Empire. First visited Europe as a dancer, became legendary sitar virtuoso, three-times Grammy Award winner, and India's most esteemed musician.

12 March 1922

Jean-Louis 'Jack' Kerouac, American poet, novelist & Beat Generation co-founder, with Allen Ginsberg and William S. Burroughs. Born to French-Canadian parents in Massachusetts, US. An 'indie-celeb' and pioneer of the hippie movement, Kerouac's writings had a profound influence on Bob Dylan, and, later, on Mark Feld.

8 February 1931
James Byron Dean, American actor, born in Marion, Indiana. Achieves iconic cult status through starring roles in just three films: *East of Eden, RebelWithout a Cause* (both 1955) – the latter defining the classic 'troubled teenager' and making Dean a symbol of his generation – and *Giant'* (1956). His personality and screen performances resonated deeply with Mark.

5 December 1932
Richard Wayne Penniman, later **Little Richard**, American rock'n'roll musician, born Macon, Georgia, US.

8 January 1935
Elvis Aaron Presley, American musician, the King of Rock'n'Roll, born Mississippi, US.

3 October 1938
Ray Edward 'Eddie' Cochran, American rock'n'roll pioneer & rockabilly star, born Minnesota US.

24 May 1941
Robert Allen Zimmerman, later **Bob Dylan**, American folk, blues & rock'n'roll musician, born Minnesota, US.

19 October 1945
Gloria Jones, American singer, songwriter & producer, born Cincinnati, Ohio, US. The future soul queen will bear Bolan his only child.

8 January 1947
David Robert Jones, later **Davie Jones/David Bowie**, English musician, born London, on Elvis Presley's 12th birthday.

MARK
1947
30 September
Mark Feld born, second son of Phyllis and Simeon (Sid) Feld, in Hackney Hospital, London. (Elder brother is Harry.) The family home is a rented flat in a Victorian building, 25 Stoke Newington Common.

1951
April
Jack Kerouac finishes, in NYC, what will become *On The Road*, his largely autobiographical masterpiece describing road-trip adventures and relationships with other Beat figures. Mark will become a devotee of Kerouac and other Beat poets.

1952
September
Mark begins school at Northwold Road State Primary School, Stoke Newington.

1953
9 November
Dylan Thomas dies in New York. His body is returned to Laugharne, in Wales, where he had made his home, to be buried in the village churchyard.

'Ours was a drink story, not a love story,' wrote his widow Caitlin. 'Our one and only true love was drink. The bar was our altar.'

1954

Elvis Presley, aged 19, records first single 'That's All Right' at Sam Phillips' Sun Studios, Memphis.
Embarks on first US tour.

1955

Little Richard launches new chapter in rock'n'roll with debut 'Tutti Frutti'.

30 September (Mark's 8th birthday)
Movie star James Dean, 24, killed in a car crash in California. He was driving his own Porsche Spyder.

1956–7

Eddie Cochran features in musical movies *The Girl Can't Help It* (with Little Richard in a cameo) and *Untamed Youth*, which influence Mark hugely.

Elvis Presley breaks through with a string of hits: 'Heartbreak Hotel/I Was the One', 'Blue Suede Shoes', 'I Want You, I Need You, I Love You', 'Don't Be Cruel/Hound Dog', 'Love Me/When My Blue Moon Turns To Gold', 'Love Me Tender/Any Way That You Want Me', 'Blue Moon'.

Little Richard hits back with 'Long Tall Sally', 'Rip It Up', 'Ready Teddy', 'Lucille', 'Good Golly Miss Molly', 'The Girl Can't Help It'. Rock'n'roll has arrived.

Ravi Shankar tours Europe and the US, bringing classical Indian music to an international audience, most notably thanks to associations with Russian Jewish American violin virtuoso Yehudi Menuhin and, during the mid-1960s, Beatle George Harrison.

1956
30 September
Mark receives his first guitar, a 9th birthday present from his parents.

1958
Cliff Richard, 'Britain's answer to Elvis', releases his fifth single 'Move It', the UK's 'first authentic rock'n'roll song'. Written by Ian 'Sammy' Samwell, the song establishes Cliff's superstar status. He adopts similar dress and hairstyle to Presley, but can't quite match his stage presence. Mark's roster of idols continues to grow.

August
Eddie Cochran's first major chart hit 'Summertime Blues'.

September
Mark enrols at William Wordsworth State Secondary Modern School, Hackney, London.

1959
Mark and tailoring student Jeff Dexter meet in a menswear store in Dalston, and become lifelong friends.

3 February
Eddie Cochran's close friends Buddy Holly and Ritchie Valens, with the Big Bopper, are killed in a plane crash while touring the US. The 'Day The Music Died' will be immortalised in Don McLean's epic 1971 encapsulation of rock'n'roll, 'American Pie', a huge hit in the US and UK and an all-time classic.

Summer

At age 12, Mark joins his first pop group, alongside singing teen sensation-to-be Helen Shapiro.

1960–73

The dawning of the counterculture of the Sixties, which begins as a reaction to US military intervention in Vietnam. It will affect recording artists and their song writing for years to come.

1960

17 April

Eddie Cochran, 21, dies in road accident in Wiltshire, UK, during his British tour. He had been a passenger in a Ford Consul mini-cab, en route to the airport for a short visit home to the US. Earlier on the tour, while performing in London, Cochran's distinctive Gretsch guitar was carried for him to his car by Mark Feld.

1961

Feld family leave Hackney for a prefab in Summerstown, Wimbledon. Mark is registered at Hill Croft Secondary School, which he attends briefly before leaving education for good.

October

Bob Dylan releases first, eponymous album. Initiates civil rights/ anti-war stance, predicting route that contemporary popular music will take.

1962–4

Mark becomes a fixture of Soho's mod mecca, and briefly a sought-after male model. He and his friends are interviewed and photographed for a somewhat condescending feature on mod culture, 'Faces Without Shadows', in *Town* magazine (September 1962).

In south-east London suburb of Bromley, Davie Jones (Bowie) is also posing earnestly as a mod.

Mark meets clubber-about-town Allan Warren, accepts an invitation to share his flat at 81 Lexham Gardens, Earls Court/Gloucester Road, where he stays for six months. Inspired by Bob Dylan, Mark begins to develop own style as a poet and folk singer/guitarist.

1962
Mark's friend Jeff Dexter, aged 16 and now a high-profile scenester, dancer, singer and DJ, becomes the Beatles' stylist.

June
The Beatles' first recording session at EMI's Abbey Road Studios, with producer George Martin. Although Mark is not especially a Beatles fan, their global phenomenon and all-pervading musical influence become his yardstick and ambition.

1963
Mark meets barrister Geoffrey Delaroy-Hall, who becomes his first manager. At 15, Mark is too young to sign a contract. His mother signs the management agreement for him. The pair also begin a relationship.

March
Bob Dylan releases *Freewheelin' Bob Dylan* LP, featuring 'Blowin' In The Wind', a huge hit for Peter, Paul & Mary, which Dylan

sings with the trio at the Newport Folk Festival that summer. Dylan begins relationship with Joan Baez, appears at her concerts and headlines at New York's Carnegie Hall. Mark resolves to headline the hallowed venue himself one day.

Mark meets Joe Meek, Britain's first independent pop producer, famous for his work with Tom Jones, Rod Stewart and for having rejected The Beatles with a view to launching a singing career. Whether or not they record the song 'Mrs Jones' and possibly others together is disputed.

Mark and Jeff Dexter attend a screening of Cliff Richard's *Summer Holiday*. Mark leaves the cinema telling Dexter he's going to be a singer. Dexter demolishes the idea, the friends fall out, but resume their relationship later. Dexter becomes an important part of the T. Rex entourage.

1964
Teenaged singer/pianist Gloria Jones discovered in Los Angeles by songwriter Ed Cobb. Signs with his Greengrass Productions. Records first hit 'Heartbeats Pts 1 & 2', written/produced by Cobb. Jones tours US, performs on many US TV shows, rapidly achieves high profile. 'Heartbeat' becomes R&B classic, later recorded by Dusty Springfield, Spencer Davis/others. Jones records other tracks for Upton Records, notably Cobb's composition 'Tainted Love' – eventually discovered by Marc Almond/ Soft Cell, who have a Number One worldwide hit with it in 1981 – when Gloria is proclaimed 'Queen of Northern Soul' in UK.

Mark works as a model for the Littlewoods mail-order catalogue and similar publications.

February

The Beatles kick off The British Invasion of the US, gifted instant coast-to-coast TV exposure. They perform live on *The Ed Sullivan Show*, are watched by 73m viewers.

August

The Beatles meet Mark's idol Bob Dylan in NYC. He has become a recluse, using bodyguards and drugs to protect himself from the outside world. Dylan introduces The Beatles to cannabis.

28 August

'All At Once', written by George Bellamy, recorded at IBC Studios, London. Two takes mixed to 1/4" tape. This is most likely Mark's first-ever recording.

Late 1964/early 1965

Dylan's *The Times They Are a-Changin'* makes him hero of the protest movement. LP fails to chart in the US. Single reaches Number Nine in UK.

Mark records demos at Regent Sound Studios, Denmark Street and at Maximum Sound Studios, Dean St, Soho. Briefly adopts pseudonym Toby Tyler. Lands audition with John Burgess, EMI/Columbia at Abbey Road Studios. Burgess hears nothing unique in Mark. Declines to sign him.

Mark meets American actor Riggs O'Hara, whom he later dubs 'The Wizard' and weaves entire mythology around. Moves into O'Hara's flat in Lonsdale Road, Barnes, where TV actor James Bolam also lives. O'Hara and Mark travel to Paris, the inspiration for many Mark stories. O'Hara gifts him a small statue of Pan, re-named 'Poon', which Mark keeps as his muse.

Mark works as a cloakroom attendant at Le Discothèque club, Wardour Street, Soho.

1965
Leaves O'Hara, moves back to his parents' home, Wimbledon.

12 March
Scottish singer-songwriter Donovan, the 'British Bob Dylan', debuts with single 'Catch the Wind'. It reaches Number 4 in UK (and Number 23 a few months later in the US). Achieves popularity on TV show *Ready, Steady, Go!* and re-records the song for his album *What's Bin Did, What's Bin Hid*. Mark influenced greatly by Donovan's success.

29 May
Mark photographed marching with Joan Baez, Donovan and Tom Paxton in CND rally.

MARC
1965
Summer
Mark meets freelance publicist Mike Pruskin, moves in with him in a flat in Manchester Street, close to EMI's world-famous offices.

Changes name to Marc Bolan, for which there are several possible explanations.

Begins first serious heterosexual relationship, with Terry (Theresa) Whipman. Continues to play the field.

Strikes first professional deal, with agent Leslie Conn, who introduces him to Beatles' publisher Dick James and young hopeful David Jones (Bowie). Bolan and Bowie become lifelong, off-on friends.

August
Meets American producer Jim Economides, who introduces him to Decca A&R man Dick Rowe ('the man who turned down The Beatles').

9 August
Lands recording deal for one-off single.

14 September
Records three tracks, including 'The Wizard' at Decca's West Hampstead studios

19 November
'The Wizard' single released, fails to chart. Performs for Glad Rag Ball, London School of Economics, at Wembley Empire Pool, alongside The Who, Donovan, The Hollies and others.

30 December
Returns to studio to record four new songs.

1966
Spring
Economides records Marc independently, with session musicians including bass player John Paul Jones, future Led Zeppelin star.

Begins to hustle music journalists around Soho pubs. Meets rock writer Keith Altham, his future publicist.

Still living at home, Marc writes prolifically in what is much later described as his 'dyslexic' hand: diaries, poetry, songs, love letters, short stories, plays. Angels, dragons, trolls and unicorns abound, J.R.R. Tolkien's *Lord of the Rings* proves a major influence.

Allan Warren, former flatmate and manager, 'sells' contract with Marc to landlord David Kirsch as settlement for unpaid rent. Marc's mother visits Kirsch, demands he destroy the contract.

Summer
Marc works on his voice, experimenting to perfect distinctive vibrato sound.

3 June
Decca Records release single 'The Third Degree'.

29 August
Beatles give final live concert, Candlestick Park, San Francisco.

September/October
Marc meets famous songwriter/manager Simon Napier-Bell (Dusty Springfield, The Yardbirds) who is enchanted by his sound and image. Napier-Bell records 14 demos in De Lane Lea Studios, Kingsway; becomes Bolan's first formal manager. The pair become lovers, while Marc remains involved with Terry.

Re-records De Lane Lea demo 'Hippy Gumbo'. Napier-Bell pulls strings to achieve release on EMI/Parlophone.

25 November
'Hippy Gumbo' released on Parlophone Records. Flops, but whets appetite of DJ John Peel.

13 December
Marc performs 'Hippy Gumbo' for *Ready, Steady, Go!* alongside The Jimi Hendrix Experience – Hendrix's debut. Show is broadcast three days later.

1967
Napier-Bell introduces Marc to his act John's Children (formed 1964). Marc joins the band.

Marc records 'Jasper C. Debussy' at Advision Studios, Gosfield Street, with Nicky Hopkins (piano) and John Paul Jones (bass).

Journalist Keith Altham interviews John's Children for the *New Musical Express*.

April
John's Children support The Who on outrageous German tour and are asked to leave.

En route home from Germany in Napier-Bell's car, they attend Ravi Shankar gig, Luxembourg. Marc is enchanted by the Indian music and simple, dignified presentation.

John's Children play further gigs back in England.

May

Ravi Shankar opens branch of Kinnara School of Music, Los Angeles.

5 May

John's Children release Bolan-penned 'Desdemona'. 'Risque' single earns ban from the BBC.

Band record further material.

June–July

Monterey International Pop Music Festival, world's first official rockfest, takes place over three days in Monterey, California. Featuring major performances by Jimi Hendrix, The Who, Ravi Shankar, Janis Joplin and Otis Redding.

The Beatles release magnum opus *Sgt Pepper's Lonely Hearts Club Band* and revolutionise the record business.

The Summer of Love: 100,000 hippies descend on San Francisco's Haight-Ashbury district. A 'hippie revolution' ensues.

Napier-Bell introduces Marc to David Platz at Essex Music publishing company (involved with Who manager Kit Lambert's Track label). A deal is signed. Marc leaves John's Children, launches Tyrannosaurus Rex with Steve Peregrin Took.

7 July

Scheduled release of 'Midsummer Night's Scene'. Single was withdrawn, but some copies got out. Now one of rarest singles in the world.

Radio London DJ John Peel continues to champion Marc's unusual sound. The pair become friends.

Simon Napier-Bell books sessions in South Molton Street. Tyrannosaurus Rex record demos for Track Records.

August
Marc and Steve rumoured to have worked as street buskers when money runs out.

September
Tyrannosaurus Rex join forces with American musician/producer Tony Visconti. Rehearse in Visconti's flat. Visconti records Tyrannosaurus Rex at Advision Studios.

20 October
'Go Go Girl', final John's Children single with Marc, released by Track.

John Peel lands residency at underground club Middle Earth (formerly The Electric Garden). Tyrannosaurus Rex make regular appearances. Future *Old Grey Whistle Test* star Bob Harris interviews John Peel at his Fulham home, finds Marc there too. Bob and Marc become close friends.

30 October
Tyrannosaurus Rex make debut recording for BBC Radio 1's *Top Gear* (broadcast 5 November).

Further demo sessions and club gig dates.

1968

Track Records decline to sign Tyrannosaurus Rex. New deal is made with Straight Ahead, allowing them to record on the Regal Zonophone label distributed through EMI.

Napier-Bell amicably relinquishes managerial role.

21 March

Tyrannosaurus Rex support Donovan at charity folk concert, Royal Albert Hall.

19 April

First single 'Debora' released, reaches Number 34 UK chart.

Summer

Tyrannosaurus Rex picked up by Blackhill Enterprises management co. Marc meets Blackhill secretary/future wife June Child (former lover of Pink Floyd's Syd Barrett).

Social and political unrest throughout the world. Many singer-songwriters reflect world events in their music.

3 June

Tyrannosaurus Rex play Royal Festival Hall, supported by various acts including David Bowie, Hyde Park free concert, in support of Pink Floyd, and several other UK dates.

Marc finishes with Terry and June finishes with long-term boyfriend. They camp in June's van on Wimbledon Common. Move into lodgings at 57 Blenheim Crescent, Ladbroke Grove.

5 July

Debut Tyrannosaurus Rex album *My People Were Fair and Had Sky in Their Hair ... But Now They're Content to Wear Stars on Their Brows* released. The track 'Frowning Atahuallpa' features one of the earliest Hare Krishna chants on a UK pop record.

Tyrannosaurus Rex begin sessions at Trident for second album, *Prophets, Seers & Sages*.

Marc commences never-to-be-realised epic, his own 'Lord of the Rings'.

23 August

Single 'One Inch Rock/Salamanda Palaganda' released, makes Number 28 – the band's only Top 30 single.

Play gigs in Belgium and at the first Isle of Wight festival.

Autumn

Make string of UK and European appearances.

1 November

Prophets, Seers & Sages, The Angels of The Ages released, doesn't chart. Despite mainstream failure, begin to build respectable underground following.

Marc and June leave Blackwell Enterprises, strike deal with Bryan Morrison Agency, based at 16 Bruton Place, W1.

December

Record early sessions at Trident for 'Pewter Suitor' and some future *Unicorn* album tracks.

1969

13 January

Band debut their *For the Lion and the Unicorn in the Oak Forests of Faun* show at Queen Elizabeth Hall, Southbank.

17 January

Release single 'Pewter Suitor'. It fails to chart.

Promo dates, Denmark.

February

First Tyrannosaurus Rex fan club launched.

For the Lion and the Unicorn ... UK tour, supported by sitar player Vytas Serelis and David Bowie as mime act.

16 February

The Fairfield Halls, Croydon show is attended by Marc's brother, Harry Feld.

Visconti commences work on the *Unicorn* album.

American singer/*Hair* stage star Marsha Hunt visits studio. Marc and Marsha begin a brief fling.

March

The Warlock of Love, Marc's book of original poetry, published by Morrison's Lupus Publishing Co. Will become highly sought-after collectible after his death.

Marc purchases Fender Stratocaster, experiments with electric sound.

Tyrannosaurus Rex announce first US tour.

16 May
Third album *Unicorn* released.

Steve Peregrin Took's relationship with Marc in decline. Took undertakes American tour drugged and under sufferance.

11 June
Marc reads and discusses poetry from *Warlock of Love* live on John Peel's Radio 1 *Night Ride* show.

2–3 July
Rolling Stones founder member Brian Jones, 27, found drowned in pool at his home, Cotchford Farm, East Sussex.

11 July
Bowie's 'Space Oddity', about launch of fictional astronaut, re-released as single to coincide with moon landing. BBC play it during coverage of Apollo 11 launch and lunar landing on 20 July 1969. At last, Bowie has a hit.

25 July
Fourth Tyrannosaurus Rex single, their breakthrough 'King Of the Rumbling Spires', released, reaches Number 44.

August
First US tour, six weeks, commences. Makes negligible impact.

Woodstock Festival, New York State, featuring Ravi Shankar, Joan Baez, Janis Joplin, The Who, Jefferson Airplane. Shankar unhappy with conditions at festival. Will distance himself from hippie movement during 1970s. Bob Dylan boycotts Woodstock, travels to UK to star at Isle of Wight Festival.

13 September
Band supports The Turtles at a concert in Detroit, Michigan. Marc meets/begins friendship with Turtles singers Howard Kaylan and Mark Volman, aka Frank Zappa's backing singers 'Flo & Eddie'.

Marc meets Gloria Jones. Jones is performing with the US cast of the stage musical *Hair*.

Steve Peregrin(e) Took quits/is sacked.

4 October
Marc advertises for new musical partner in *Melody Maker*.

Meets Mick(e)y Finn, who joins Tyrannosaurus Rex.

21 October
Alcoholic Beat poet/writer Jack Kerouac dies aged 47.

31 October
Work begins on fourth Tyrannosaurus Rex album.

21 November
Embark on short UK tour, commencing Manchester's Free Trade Hall.

Hippie idealism wears thin against backdrop of macho guitar heroes and supergroups. Marc seeks new musical direction. He, June and Mickey decamp to North Wales to take stock.

Bowie pays public tribute to Marc as important personal influence, despite early simmerings of rivalry.

June discovers Marc's fling with Marsha Hunt and confronts them. Marc proposes to June.

Winter
Tyrannosaurus Rex sign to EG Management. Bernard 'Beep' Fallon, former Apple Records' employee, becomes first official publicist.

1970
8 January
Visconti invites Marc to Trident Studios session for new David Bowie single. It is Bowie's 23rd birthday (Elvis Presley's 35th). Marc contributes guitar parts to 'The Prettiest Star' and 'London Bye Ta-Ta'. June behaves disrespectfully towards Bowie. She and Marc walk out, probably in jealous rage over Bowie's slow-burn success with 'Space Oddity'.

16 January
Final Tyrannosaurus Rex single 'By The Light of a Magical Moon' released, fails to chart.

30 January
Marc and June marry at Kensington Register Office.

David Bowie assembles new 'band', Hype, featuring Visconti on bass.

22 February
David Bowie/Hype play the Roundhouse, London, dressed in camp pre-glam outfits. Denim-clad Marc attends.

13 March

Fourth Tyrannosaurus Rex album *A Beard of Stars* released, reaches Number 21.

24 March

Visconti, now living in Bowie's flat in Haddon Hall, Beckenham, Kent, lands free studio time in Wembley, records 'fun' tracks 'Oh Baby' and 'Universal Love', Visconti on bass, Rick Wakeman on keyboards.

April/May

Bowie and Visconti part company for several years. Marc, hitherto quietly credible album artist with cult following, perceives new direction of music scene, begins to crave pop stardom.

May

Singer-songwriter Ray Dorset and pop-blues outfit Mungo Jerry score worldwide hit with 'In The Summertime'. Number One in countless countries and one of bestselling hit singles in pop history, proves a turning point for Marc in making his obscure vibrato vocal style acceptable in the mainstream.

Fleetwood Mac (British-American rock band formed London, 1967) hailed as 'the new Beatles'.

July/August

Bolan and Visconti record sessions for debut T. Rex album.

At Trident, they lay down brand-new song encapsulating everything Marc has been striving towards musically: 'Ride A White Swan'.

Band undertakes promo trips to Austria and West Germany. Tour Scotland briefly in support of Ten Years After. Join summer festival circuit.

Release of Dib Cochran & The Earwigs' single 'Oh Baby' on Bell Records.

September
Marc abbreviates band name to T. Rex, marking change in musical direction.

18 September
Jimi Hendrix, 27, found dead in London apartment hotel.

4 October
Janis Joplin, 27, found dead in Landmark Motor Hotel, Los Angeles.

9 October
'Ride a White Swan' released by Essex Music's new Fly Records.

October/December
T. Rex enjoy strong support from BBC, recording five sessions for Radio 1.

November
'Ride a White Swan' makes Number Two on UK singles chart. T. Rex tour UK extensively, all shows selling out. Bassist Steve Currie hired.

18 December
T. Rex's eponymous debut album released – a 'compromise' of electric and acoustic tracks.

Beatles break up. Ringo, George, John & Paul go on to release solo albums.

Marc raves in interviews about forthcoming sci-fi concept album and book, *The Children of Rarn*. Demos are recorded, but time constraints prevent project from ever being realised.

1971
21 January
Drummer Bill Fifield of band Legend brought in to Advision for 'Hot Love' single session. Marc invites him to join the band.

25 January
T. Rex play turning-point gig at London's Lyceum Ballroom, are hailed as stars.

19 February
'Hot Love' released, soars to Number One, reigns for six weeks. T. Rex suddenly in huge demand for live shows/promotion. Determined to 'crack the States' – where the single reaches Number 72 – they plan an American tour.

March
Sessions at Trident Studios, recording of basic tracks for two songs, 'Mambo Sun' and 'Cosmic Dancer'.

24 March
T. Rex record 'Hot Love' on BBC TV *Top of the Pops* (broadcast several times during March and April).

Publicist Chelita Secunda, friend of June's, does Marc's make-up, applies glitter, the first time he parades the look.

26 March

Fly Records release budget *Best of* compilation of Tyrannosaurus Rex recordings, cashing in on T. Rex's massive success.

6 April

Band fly to New York to begin US tour. Marc adopts phrase for the new T. Rex sound: 'Cosmic Rock'.

T. Rex sign deal with US Warner/Reprise label.

9 April

Play first US gig as new line-up, Detroit, Michigan. New drummer assumes name 'Bill Legend'.

12 April

Play four nights at New York's Fillmore East. Reception is lukewarm.

Concerts throughout the month. Recording sessions in New York, LA.

T. Rex reconvene with Visconti at Media Sound Studios, New York to lay down further tracks for second T. Rex album *Electric Warrior*. 'Jeepster' and 'Monolith' recorded.

18 April

'Get It On' and other tracks are recorded at the Wally Heider Studios, LA, with Flo & Eddie on backing vocals.

19–20 April
Play legendary Whisky A Go-Go, LA, billed as Tyrannosaurus
Rex, joined by Flo & Eddie.

25 April
Support Emerson Lake & Palmer and Procul Harum in
Philadelphia, Pennsylvania.

30 April
Long Island, New York, support Humble Pie.

Marc dallies with Jewish American artist/illustrator Barbara
Nessim, a friend of Visconti's.

May
Marc dismayed to learn that Fly Records have released retrospective Tyrannosaurus Rex compilation to cash in on T. Rex fame.

Chelita styles Marc in new glam lamé and lurex fashions.

Gigs now echo Beatlemania, most T. Rex fans young, female
teenagers. Beep Fallon or *Melody Maker* writer Michael Watts
coins term 'T. Rextasy'.

3 May
Return to UK. 'Hot Love' still Top Ten, almost three months
after release.

2 July
Third single 'Get It On' released, second Number One. John
Peel loathes it. Public declaration of disappointment marks
demise of friendship. Rising star Bob Harris takes his place.

Summer

Following the success of 'Ride A White Swan' and 'Hot Love', Marc and June move from Blenheim Crescent to Little Venice – into a large rented flat at 31 Clarendon Gardens, London W9.

3 July

On second 'official' anniversary of the death of Rolling Stone Brian Jones, The Doors' frontman, lyricist and poet Jim Morrison, 27, is found dead in his bathtub in Paris.

1 August

George Harrison and Ravi Shankar front Concert for Bangladesh, Madison Sq. Garden New York, world's first international benefits concert, to aid refugees following 1970 cyclone and atrocities during Bangladesh Liberation War. Ringo Starr, Bob Dylan and Eric Clapton also perform.

In the light of Marc's huge success, his newly-appointed manager Tony Secunda, former husband of publicist Chelita, attempts to negotiate more favourable contract with Essex Music/Fly Records. Negotiations fail. Platz and Marc never speak again.

24 September

Second T. Rex album *Electric Warrior* released. Features two of T. Rex's best-loved songs, 'Get It On' and 'Jeepster'. Reaches Number 32 on US Billboard 200. Sits at Number One for several weeks on UK album chart. The biggest-selling album of 1971. Later voted Number 160 in *Rolling Stone* magazine's list of the '500 Greatest Albums of All Time'.

October

Play string of German and Dutch dates. Launch *Electric Warriors* British tour. Exceeds all expectations. Amid scenes of hysteria from Portsmouth to Birmingham, and with DJ Bob Harris as MC, the band are hailed as 'the new Beatles'.

Secunda and Bolan launch the T. Rex Wax Co. label; publishing companies Wizard Artists and Warrior Music Projects Ltd and announce new deal with EMI.

Negotiate new contract with Warner/Reprise, US.

Licensing deals in string of territories secured, including Germany's Ariola and CBS France.

T. Rex now managed out of Secunda's prestigious Mayfair offices at 7 Charles Street.

5 November

David Platz releases 'Jeepster' as a single on Fly, controversially (Marc's contract having expired). Reaches Number 2.

9 December

Further UK dates and Trident sessions. Marc and June spend a week in the US for meetings and promo in New York, LA, San Francisco and other cities.

A US tour in support of Alice Cooper is rumoured, but does not happen.

Marc raves about *Children of Rarn* opus as T. Rex's answer to *Sgt Pepper*.

1972

Electric Warrior promo dates.

Marc embraces rock'n'roll lifestyle and new-found superstar status.

15 January

Play one-off gig at Starlight Rooms, Boston, Lincs, for an ATV documentary.

21 January

Single 'Telegram Sam' released, Bolan's first on his own label. Gives T. Rex third Number One, and Top 10 hits around Europe.

'Get It On' enters US chart, re-titled 'Bang A Gong (Get It On)'. Dates in Scandinavia and Germany.

10 February

David Bowie introduces androgynous alter ego Ziggy Stardust and the Spiders From Mars.

14 February

T. Rex fly to LA for two-week US promo tour of *Electric Warrior*. Hailed variously as 'the new Beatles', 'biggest pop sensation in years', and 'the teen idols of the Seventies', but concert reviews generally poor.

5,000 fans attend their Hollywood Palladium show, including Mick Jagger. He advises Bolan to play longer sets.

27 February

T. Rex play debut headline US show, at Carnegie Hall, New York, fulfilling Marc's dream. Paul Simon of Simon & Garfunkel said to have attended. Reviews mixed, show falls short of hype. Secunda and Marc part company.

T. Rex management move to new offices, 16 Doughty Street – famous as the location of the home of Charles Dickens. Chelita Secunda appointed Marc's PA. Fans throng daily on the street outside. They include future singer and Culture Club sensation George O'Dowd, later known as Boy George.

March
Band decamp to Strawberry Studios, Château d'Hérouville near Paris, record LP *The Slider* abroad to avoid tax liabilities. Further work on album takes place later that month at Rosenberg Studios, Copenhagen. Flo & Eddie contribute backing vocals at LA's Elektra Studios in April.

17 March
Ringo Starr releases single 'Back off Boogaloo', produced by George Harrison, citing Marc's supper-time spoutings as inspiration for the lyrics. It is rumoured that Marc contributed to the single. The track reaches Number 9 on the US Hot 100. At Number 2, it is Starr's biggest UK hit.

18 March
Perform two shows at Wembley's Empire Pool. Scenes eclipse Beatlemania. Ringo Starr films the show for proposed documentary for Apple Films. Becomes full-blown feature. Glam rock dominates the music scene. Further scenes are shot at John and Yoko Lennon's Tittenhurst Park, Ascot estate, which Ringo is house-sitting; and at an Apple Studios jam session, featuring Elton John on piano and Starr on drums.

24 March

Still cashing in on T. Rex's fame, Fly Records release further old Bolan recordings, this time an EP featuring 'Debora', 'One Inch Rock', 'The Seal of Seasons' and 'Woodland Bop'. The EP is a Number 7 hit. In April, they release Tyrannosaurus Rex's first two albums as a single unit, and achieve a Number One hit.

14 April

David Bowie releases breakthrough single 'Starman' (recorded at Trident). John Peel calls it 'a classic, a gem' of a record. The milestone hit seals his fate.

5 May

Release single 'Metal Guru' from *The Slider* LP. It is the record which finally turns off Bob Harris. Their friendship suffers. Becomes T. Rex's fourth (final) UK Number One, remaining on the chart for four weeks. Fails to chart in US.

Fly Records release *Bolan Boogie* compilation, another Number One, which will inhibit sales of *The Slider*.

Marc, June, George Harrison and Ringo Starr depart for Cannes, on a sailing holiday.

T. Rex undertake brief promotional UK tour. More mania. Marc dismayed by realisation that safety/security now so compromised, it is becoming virtually impossible to tour. Like his idol Bob Dylan, he is on the verge of becoming a recluse.

June

Bowie releases concept album *The Rise and Fall of Ziggy Stardust and the Spiders From Mars*, a sensation. Promo tour takes US by storm. Marc watches helplessly as Bowie steals his thunder. Bowie is gracious, mentioning T. Rex in his lyrics for 'All The Young Dudes', the song he gifts Mott the Hoople. Bolan bitches. Marc wins injunction against Track Records and distributor Polydor to prevent the release of 20-track Bolan retrospective recording, 'Hard On Love'.

Fans discover their home address. Life at Maida Vale flat becomes intolerable. Marc and June move to 47 Bilton Towers, Great Cumberland Place, London.

Gloria Jones visits London as part of Joe Cocker's roadshow, performs at Crystal Palace Bowl garden party. Bumps into Marc, same night, as he leaves the Speakeasy.

Keith Altham quits music journalism to become a publicist. Replaces B.P. Fallon as Marc's/T. Rex's PR.

28 July
Release *The Slider*, their third studio album. Peaks at Number 4 on UK chart and 17 on Billboard Top LPs & Tapes chart. Reviews excellent.

August
Band return to Château d'Hérouville, record new single 'Children of the Revolution'. Begin work on songs for a new album, *Tanx*. Another single, 'Solid Gold Easy Action', is cut.

New Marc/T. Rex manager Tony Howard appointed.

5 September
T. Rex fly to Montreal, Canada, begin six-week North American

tour – their keenest attempt yet to crack the US market. Reviews are poor.

8 September
Single 'Children of the Revolution' released. Number 2 in the UK, it is a huge hit in several countries including West Germany and Japan.

13 October
T. Rex play Winterland, San Francisco, joined by singers Oma Drake, Stephanie Spruill and Gloria Jones. Gloria now a successful Tamla Motown songwriter and singer, working with the Four Tops, Gladys Knight, Jackson 5, Marvin Gaye, Ike & Tina Turner. Marc visits Gloria's family.

Marc and June purchase large Welsh rectory at Weston-under-Penyard, near Ross-on-Wye, with plans to create their own Château d'Hérouville with recording studio.

T. Rex begin to look over their shoulder at a rising British band intent on stealing their fans: Slade.

2 November
Marc, Keith Moon, Harry Nilsson, and Flo & Eddie jam with Alice Cooper in London. Nothing recorded during the session is released.

10 November
Fly Records re-release two Tyrannosaurus Rex albums, *Unicorn* and *A Beard of Stars*.

From 26 November
Tour of Far East is reduced to Japan-only dates, kicking off at Tokyo's Budokan.

December
Fan club members receive Christmas flexi-single containing Yuletide messages and songs.

1 December
Single 'Solid Gold Easy Action' released, reaches Number 2 in UK chart.

Marc produces himself and T. Rex on rudimentary new track '20th Century Boy'. The track is refined in London by Visconti.

14 December
Ringo Starr's film *Born to Boogie* launched at Oscar 1 Cinema Brewer St, Soho. Box office flop, ignored by US buyers and distributors.

22–23 December
Rexmas Christmas TV specials rumoured to have been recorded. Set includes two new songs, 'Chariot Choogle' and 'Buick Mackane', both of which had had their first airings during the autumn US tour.

1973
T. Rex perform on BBC's *The Cilla Black Show*. Marc duets with Cilla on best-forgotten 'Life's A Gas'.

February
Brief, disappointing tour of West Germany.

2 March

Single '20th Century Boy' released. Brief European promo tour.

23 March

Fourth T. Rex album *Tanx* released.

Single 'The Groover' recorded Rosenberg Studios, Copenhagen. Marc, at only 25, begins to let himself go.

April

Marc records demo at London's AIR Studios for Ringo Starr's album *Ringo*, recorded at Sunset Sound Recorders Studio LA. No evidence that anything Marc recorded in London was used on the album, although confirmed that he contributed guitar on 'Have You Seen My Baby', a cover of a track on Randy Newman's 1970 album *12 Songs* (originally recorded as a 1969 single by Fats Domino).

During Electric Light Orchestra sessions at AIR Studios for their album *On The Third Day*, Marc contributes guitar to three tracks: 'Dreaming Of 4000' (working title 'Mambo' scribbled on the tape box), 'Ma-Ma-Ma-Belle', and 'Everyone's Born To Die' – on which Marc and Jeff Lynne both play solos. Subsequent rumours that Marc also played on ELO's 1973 hit 'Showdown' are unfounded – Lynne borrowed Marc's Gibson Firebird guitar to perform the solo.

10 April

Marc performs with ELO at Watford Town Hall, during their encore – his last UK public performance that year.

'20th Century Boy' peaks at Number Three, UK. On its way down, it passes Bowie's rising hit 'Drive-In Saturday'.

T. Rex operation moves to new premises at 69 New Bond Street, London W1, subletting offices to Pink Floyd's management and to Who and Stones' tour manager Peter Rudge.

Lawyers and accountants set up offshore companies/accounts to handle Marc's financial affairs: 19 July, Wizard (Bahamas); early August 1973, Wizard (Jersey) and Wizard (Delaware); 11 February 1974, Wizard Publishing. Wizard Artists, which had been created in 1972, has share capital transferred to Wizard (Bahamas).

13 April
Bowie releases LP *Aladdin Sane* (recorded at Trident Studios London, and RCA Studios NYC and Nashville, spawning UK Top 5s 'The Jean Genie' and 'Drive-In Saturday'). Bowie hailed by the UK music press as 'most important figure in rock'. Rivalry between Bolan and Bowie at a peak.

1 May
T. Rex film special in Hollywood for ABC TV's *In Concert*. Marc and Gloria Jones meet again.

June
T. Rex decamp to Musicland Studios, Munich, to begin work on new album *Zinc Alloy*, leaving June behind. Marc and June growing apart. Marc's relationship with Visconti unravels. This is their final album together.

'The Groover' released, makes UK Top 5 but denounced as 'too familiar' to thrill a discerning pop audience. T. Rex's appeal beginning to pall. Slade dominate the charts.

July

T. Rex fly to US to support American rock band Three Dog Night. June returns to London after beginning of tour, Milwaukee, Wisconsin. Marc and Gloria Jones begin affair.

3 July

David Bowie retires Ziggy and The Spiders From Mars at Hammersmith Odeon, at the end of their British tour.

10 August

Single 'Blackjack' released by 'Big Carrot' a.k.a T. Rex jamming with Gloria, Sister Pat Hall and Stephanie Spruill. Ridiculed by John Peel, fails to chart.

15 August

June confronts Marc in Seattle, delivers ultimatum, returns to London. The marriage over. Financial complications ensue as assets are moved between Marc's companies to eliminate June's rights. She will sue the estate for compensation after Marc's death.

Single 'Teenage Dream' and other tracks recorded in US during tour.

2 September

J.R.R. Tolkien dies in Bournemouth, England, aged 81.

4 September

Marc returns to London, meets June, with no chance of reconciliation. A week later, he flies to Nassau, Bahamas, on business, and for an illicit rendezvous with Gloria.

19 October

Great Hits LP released to great fanfare, climbs no higher than Number 32. T. Rex now officially in decline.

October–November

Marc draws up his will. His parents, June's parents, Gloria, June, Tony Howard, Mickey Finn, Tony Visconti, Terry Whipman and several charities are beneficiaries. (Although a replacement will was believed to have been made after the birth of Marc's son Rolan in September 1975, including details of a Jersey trust fund for the child, this version is 'lost' – believed destroyed by someone close to Marc. The death of manager Tony Howard in 2002 puts paid to further investigation into the widely-held view that Howard was more responsible for the fate of Marc's fortune than was originally thought.) Most in the fold at that time protest Howard's innocence.

Following overdubs for *Zinc Alloy* at AIR Studios, London, Visconti ends professional relationship with Marc. Accept offer from David Bowie to produce *Diamond Dogs* (April 1974). T. Rex will never sound the same again. According to tapes owned by Caron Willans and Danielz, Visconti continued to work with Marc on *Zinc Alloy* during December.

T. Rex undertake Far East tour – reduced to Japan and Australia – minus Gloria and Pat. During the tour, drummer Bill Legend quits the group.

Gloria arrives in London from LA, lives briefly with Marc at Bilton Towers. They move to a luxurious flat in the Avenue, St John's Wood.

16 November

Single 'Truck On (Tyke)' released, their least successful since Tyrannosaurus Rex.

November 1973–March 1974

Marc writes/oversees material for solo soul album by backing singer Pat Hall. In LA, works with Gloria's brother, singer Richard Jones.

1974

January

T. Rex tour UK, *The Truck Off Tour*, for first time in 18 months, but too early for the LP, unavailable until over a month after the tour finishes. No London dates played.

25 January

Single 'Teenage Dream' released, the only one co-credited to Bolan and T. Rex (all previous singles credited to 'T. Rex'), and to co-producers Bolan and Visconti. Features Lonnie Jordan of War on piano. Spends five weeks on UK Top 40, peaks at Number 13. Operatic and doom-laden, Marc described it as his lyrical pièce de résistance. Gloria Jones names it her favourite Bolan lyric. Later used in the soundtrack for *Scott Pilgrim vs. The World*, 2010.

Marc appears on BBC Radio 1's 'My Top 12', discussing his early influences – particularly Elvis. Talks of creating a rock'n'roll revival show.

1 March

Fifth album *Zinc Alloy (and the Hidden Riders of Tomorrow – A Creamed Cage in August)* released UK only. A 'darker' album reflecting Bolan as a has-been teen idol, losing his grip.

Distracted by his obsession with conquering the US market, Marc had taken his eye off the ball at home. Inclusion of American soul and R&B influences was ahead of its time: eighteen months later, David Bowie's *Young Americans* would be championed as first album by a British glam rock artist to represent the move into soul-based pop/rock.

Spring

T. Rex dropped by their American label Warner Brothers.

Marc leaves UK, divides his year in exile primarily between California and the South of France. He records in Paris, and rumoured to have done so in Munich and Chicago too, desperate to rekindle his magic. Returns occasionally to London for promo. Drinking heavily and has gained substantial weight, inviting comparisons with 'Vegas Elvis'. Eventually, he and Gloria settle in LA. Recordings take place at MRI Studios LA in May and June.

May

Boozed up, coke-fuelled, high on his own hype and having lost perspective, Marc re-activates his *Children of Rarn* project at MRI Studios LA.

21 June

Another 'cash-in album' of demos and early recordings entitled *The Beginning of Doves*, released by Track – the only 'Marc Bolan solo album' released while he was alive. It is *Hard On Love* repackaged – the material set for release on Track Records, aided/abetted by Kit Lambert and Simon Napier-Bell, but which Marc had injuncted successfully in 1972.

Summer

A post-glam fest during which the Bay City Rollers, the Rubettes, Alvin Stardust and Showaddywaddy rule, while big rock guns the likes of Led Zeppelin and Pink Floyd compete for world domination.

5 July

Single 'Light Of Love' released UK, falls two places short of Top 20.

9 August

Watergate, the biggest political scandal in American history, culminates in the fall of President Richard Nixon – the only time a US President has ever resigned. He is succeeded by Gerald Ford.

August–September

Album *Light of Love* released US only. LP comprises three tracks from *Zinc Alloy*, eight songs recorded spring 1974 at MRI Hollywood (which appear on album *Bolan's Zip Gun*). First album without Tony Visconti, and Marc's debut as producer.

T. Rex regroup at Victorine Film Studios in Nice, South of France, to rehearse for two-month US/Canadian tour.

Despite full-on publicity and what turns out to be their final US tour, opening in Upper Darby, Pennsylvania (where T. Rex support Blue Öyster Cult) album fails to chart. This marks the end of Marc's efforts to succeed in the US, and is the last to be released there. Marc resolves to return to UK, and focus on British comeback.

During tour, Marc and Gloria attend Bowie gig at Universal Amphitheatre, Los Angeles, departing after 'All The Young Dudes' (Marc's favourite Bowie composition, thanks to the T. Rex name-check.) Marc cannot handle visual and aural proof that Bowie has moved on while he remains stuck in a groove.

8 November
Single 'Zip Gun Boogie' released while T. Rex in US. Without promotion, it climbs no higher than Number 41 in UK.

1975
January
Marc and Gloria lease Monte Carlo seafront apartment, move to Monaco, but cannot settle. Bored, Marc toys with pursuing a movie career, perhaps inspired by his old rival David Bowie, about to star in *The Man Who Fell to Earth*.

Marc and Gloria return to LA/MRI Studios Hollywood. Mickey Finn has left T. Rex. Only Steve Currie remains.

Move into a Benedict Canyon, Hollywood Hills house , and hang with the Hollywood rock fraternity. Marc sinking deeper into drink-and-drugs abyss. Losing his grip, is violent towards Gloria.

14 February
Album *Bolan's Zip Gun* (content mainly derived from *Light of Love*) released UK. Ahead of its time, largely ridiculed. Appreciated more today than it was at the time.

7 March
David Bowie releases funk/soul-based album *Young Americans*, recorded and produced in Philadelphia and New York by Visconti.

19 March

T. Rex sessions at Strawberry Studios, Château d'Hérouville, recording tracks for 'Billy Super Duper' and 'Depth Charge'.

Spring

As concern for Marc's soaring blood pressure and compromised health mounts, Gloria and Marc decamp to private clinic near Cannes. Gloria is delighted by confirmation that she is pregnant. Marc, inspired to create, returns with T. Rex stragglers to the Château d'Hérouville for recording sessions which go horribly wrong. His ideas to create a 'rock opera' concept album in the vein of *Sgt Pepper* or The Who's *Tommy* prove a fantasy too far.

April

T. Rex reconvene in Musicland Studios, Munich. So bad are the sessions, with Marc drunk most of the time, that studio owner Reinhold Mack bans him in perpetuity.

May

Marc and Gloria return to London, wanting their baby to be born in England. Rent house at 25 Holmead Road, Fulham.

Marc and Bowie attend reception for Gary Glitter in NY but by the time they arrive, Glitter has gone.

20 June

Single 'New York City' released. Reaches Number 15, first Top Twenty chart success for 18 months.

July

T. Rex undertake modest tour of British seaside towns. Marc goes back to his roots, even hanging with his fans in hotel bars.

Loyalty and a sense of security restore his confidence. Stands poised to make triumphant comeback.

September
Veteran TV producer Mike Mansfield launches camp music show *Supersonic*, features Marc countless times during the show's eighteen-month run. Bolan also proves popular on London Weekend Television's children's pop show *Saturday Scene*, where he befriends presenter Sally James.

26 September
Single 'Dreamy Lady' released, peaks at Number 30 in UK.

Baby Rolan Seymour Feld born in The Avenue Clinic, St John's Wood. With his musician parents often travelling, Rolan spends much of his first 24 months with doting paternal grandparents, Phyllis and Sid Feld, at their council flat in Putney.

October
Marc begins to sketch ideas for a *London Opera*; writes furiously. The tracks 'London Boys' and 'Funky London Childhood' are laid down at Scorpio Studios. Both receive their debut on Thames Television's *Today* show.

December
Marc, Gloria and baby Rolan travel to LA for Christmas.

1976
30 January
Sixth studio album *Futuristic Dragon* released.

February

T. Rex embark on British promo tour. Their biggest and most ambitious since 1971, it is not a raging success. Marc raves in interviews about recordings he is still working on with Gloria and her brother Richard; enthuses about *Wilderness of the Mind*, a new book of poetry he is planning to publish. Fantasises about working with Bowie again.

Interviewed on London Weekend Television's *Saturday Scene* by Sally James.

Feeling the pull of nostalgia, he delves into his past. Marc and Gloria return to the studio to finish her album, which they have been working on since 1973.

April

Gloria releases her version of 'Get It On'.

24 April

Marc flies to Finland to join Bowie on Scandinavian dates, attends his shows in Helsinki and Stockholm.

3 May

Bowie returns to London in triumph as The Thin White Duke, bringing his *Station to Station* show to Wembley's Empire Pool – where Marc and T. Rextasy had reigned supreme less than five years earlier. Marc and Gloria attend. Marc drops hints in press interviews that he and Bowie are planning both musical collaborations and a film.

4 June

Single 'I Love To Boogie' released, charts at Number 13 in UK, followed by 'Laser Love', which makes Number 42.

Gloria departs on European tour with Gonzales, supporting Bob Marley & The Wailers.

Marc attends the Hammersmith Odeon, Ninian Park, Cardiff (with Robert Plant) and Belle Vue, Manchester gigs.

June Feld Bolan files for divorce, blaming Marc for adultery with Gloria Jones.

13 July
T. Rex record five-song set for a *Supersonic* TV Special *Rollin' Bolan* at Wimbledon Theatre, to be broadcast on 28 August.

2 August
Marc returns to LA.

10 September
Single 'Laser Love' released, reaches Number 42 in UK.

Marc and Gloria purchase a new house requiring extensive renovation, 142 Upper Richmond Road West, East Sheen, a short drive from his parents' Putney flat.

Single 'Laser Love' is promoted on *Supersonic*, along with a new version of 'Ride a White Swan'. Marc performs inside a huge, moving swan. Children's television is on the rise as the most effective way to promote pop singles. Does not do much for a rock star's cool.

Marc records at AIR and Trident studios, for his next album *Dandy in the Underworld*.

3 December

Gloria's album *Vixen*, produced by Marc, released. Credible soul album featuring original songs by Bolan, plus the only two verified Bolan/Jones co-compositions, 'High' and 'Cry Baby'. There is also an updated take on 'Tainted Love'. But its pre-Christmas release is ill-timed, and the LP makes little impact.

19 December

Marc and T. Rex support Gary Glitter on *Christmas Supersonic*, filmed at the Theatre Royal, Drury Lane as a co-promotion with the *Daily Mirror*'s Pop Club.

23 December

T. Rex leave for Paris to appear live on a Christmas TV special.

The 'new music', punk rock, is on the horizon.

1977

Marc begins comeback.

14 January

Marc and Gloria release cover of The Teddy Bears' 1958 hit 'To Know Him Is To Love Him' (written by Phil Spector). It fails to chart, but is nevertheless viewed as a public admission of their relationship.

February

T. Rex perform short tour of France. Picks up on the new wave, and declares himself 'the Godfather of Punk'.

2 March

A newly-slim, fit-looking Marc (claiming to have ditched drugs and booze) launches seventh studio album *Dandy in the Underworld*. Launch party held at popular punk haunt the Roxy, Neal Street, Covent Garden. Generation X, the Sex Pistols, the Damned, Donovan, Alvin Stardust, Paul & Linda McCartney attend.

T. Rex embark on *Dandy in the Underworld* UK tour, supported by the Damned, receive largely favourable reviews. During tour, Marc keeps fit, eats sensibly, drinks water, focuses on the music.

11 March

Dandy in the Underworld LP released.

Marc's emergence from his drunk, drugged-up years reminds him that his financial affairs require attention. Unsettled, he takes steps to put his affairs in order. Unhappy about various art purchases and business investments. Begins to shed 'advisors' who have been careless with his money . . . but his efforts are all too little, way too late.

20 May

Single 'Dandy in the Underworld' released, fails to chart.

24 May

Last ever T. Rex gig, at the Grona Lund, Sweden.

Summer

Marc is offered regular column on pop magazine *Record Mirror*, which is ghosted by his publicist Keith Altham.

6 June

The Ramones play the Roundhouse, Chalk Farm. Marc attends gig and after-show party, is photographed with the band by his best friend from school, society photographer Richard Young.

26 July

Marc and Steve Harley record together at AIR Studios, resulting in 'Amerika the Brave'.

5 August

Single 'Celebrate Summer' released, flops.

Marc attends performance by Siouxsie and the Banshees at the Music Machine. They cover his '20th Century Boy', to his great delight, and considers producing their next album.

Lunches with producers Muriel Young and Mike Mansfield to discuss his own new TV series, *Marc*, to be recorded at Granada TV's Manchester studios and broadcast during the tea-time post-school slot. He would perform old hits and new, and introduce performances by the pop acts of the day as well as showcase best of the rising new-wave acts, including Generation X, The Boomtown Rats, The Jam. Will be the perfect platform from which to relaunch his own career. Marc takes the show very seriously, looks after himself, avoids partying, goes to bed early, takes up literature again.

For most of the run's filming, beginning 9 August, Gloria is in LA recording next album, *Windstorm*. Rumoured that June and Marc meet up again during Gloria's absence, which June continued to claim after Marc's death, but this is disputed.

16 August

Drug-addled Elvis Presley dies at his home in Memphis, Tennessee. Funeral held two days later, thousands having gathered at Graceland to view his open casket.

7 September

Bowie agrees to appear and perform with his old friend and foe on the final *Marc* show. Bolan and Bowie perform new song which they have written together. Upsets and disputes culminate in Marc falling off the stage. It is too late to re-record.

Gloria returns from LA.

15–16 September

After visiting the Speakeasy, an inebriated Marc, Gloria and her brother Richard gather with friends Eric Hall, Tony Howard etc. at Morton's Club, Berkeley Square. Leaving Morton's at around 4am, Gloria drives Marc home to East Sheen in their purple Mini. Richard follows behind in second car, driven by Morton's pianist and singer Vicky Aram.

Just before 5am on 16 September, Gloria loses control of the car, crashes into a steel-reinforced concrete post and then into a sycamore tree, on Barnes Common. Marc, 29 years old, is killed instantly.

Police logged the accident at 5.58am – but were not first on the scene.

AFTER MARC

His death wipes talk of the death of international opera star Maria Callas from the next day's front pages. Callas, 53, also died on 16 September, following a heart attack in Paris, aged 53.

1977

20 September

Marc's star-studded funeral at Golders Green Crematorium. Gloria, still seriously injured in hospital, is unable to attend.

28 September

The final edition of the *Marc* show, featuring lifelong sparring partners Bowie and Bolan, is broadcast in tribute on the ITV networks.

24 November

Battersea Coroner's Court inquest pronounces Marc's death 'accidental'. Vicky Aram gives evidence as primary witness.

December

Gloria and Rolan return to LA

1980

27 October

Steve Peregrin(e) Took dies.

1981

28 April

Steve Currie killed in a car accident in Portugal.

1991

11 January

Marc's mother Phyllis Feld dies.

19 September

Marc's father Sid Feld dies.

1994

31 August

June Feld Bolan dies. She had begun a new relationship with Paul Varley, of Arrows fame. Their daughter, Ilona, was born in 1978 (Elton John is her godfather), but June's relationship with Paul did not last. June weakened over time. She convinced herself that she had become pregnant by Marc in a dream. She confided in friends about abortions she'd undergone during their marriage, and how she wished that she had those children now. She died of a heart attack while on holiday in Turkey with her close friend, celebrity hairdresser Denni Godber.

1997

PRS Memorial installed at the site of the accident, to commemorate the 20th anniversary of Marc's death. Ceremony attended by Rolan Bolan.

2001

13 April

Gloria's brother Richard Jones dies.

2002

Marc's final manager Tony Howard dies.

Rolan unveils bronze bust of his father at the site, to commemorate 25th anniversary. Plaques since installed for the four most prominent members of T. Rex – Steve Peregrin Took, Steve Currie, Mickey Finn and Dino Dines. Only drummer Bill Legend is still living. Plaque for June Child Feld Bolan added in September 2005, in a small ceremony attended by June's daughter, Ilona Porter.

2003
11 January
Mick(e)y Finn dies.

2012
16 September
35th anniversary of Marc Bolan's death.

30 September
Would have been Marc's 65th birthday.

Marc Bolan's Recordings

There have been endless releases, many by unscrupulous individuals who had no legal rights to the material, of Marc Bolan and T. Rex music in the years since Marc's death. These are too numerous to list here. Please see 'Life and Times' for original release dates and details.

The most comprehensive discography, complete with dates and images, can be found here:

http://rockfiles.co.uk/rockfilesfiles/MarcBolan.html

Of all those who have striven to make sense of the mess that Marc's recordings were left in, no one has been more dedicated to the cause than lifelong T. Rex fan Martin Barden and rock writer/author Mark Paytress.

'Since 1994, Mark Paytress and I have had the privilege to work on many aspects of Marc Bolan's legacy. Marc's death in 1977 created a vacuum; all existing structures seemed to die with him. It is unusual if not unique for an artist of Marc's stature to be seemingly abandoned in the manner that came to pass after the tragedy of 1977. Creative and organisational input into archive releases, documentaries, exhibitions, events and publications has largely fallen to fans, with varying results. Marc has not been here to look after himself and

we, as fans ourselves, have tried as best we can to exert quality control while being creative and respectful. We have tried to promote Marc as a major artist who practised multiple disciplines with a unique creativity. In the absence of any clear strategy by rights holders, we have attempted to restore his good reputation, return him to the public eye and encourage greater respect and understanding of his work.'
Martin Barden

'I first heard Bolan in the aftermath of the Beach Boys' "Good Vibrations" and The Beatles' "Strawberry Fields Forever". First impressions die hard. That's why, throughout his early-70s' glam supremacy era, I never lost sight of him as a figure forged in an earlier, more esoteric pop underworld. The spectacular, sage-like star who sang "Jeepster" or "Metal Guru" on* Top of the Pops *was light years away from Rod, Noddy, Elton, even Bowie, who – initially at least – seemed more closely associated with fellow one-hit-wonders Leapy Lee and Don Partridge.*

'Bolan was and remains important because, like Beefheart and Dylan, Kate Bush and Marc Almond, his personality and exceptional perspective are inseparable from his work. Like many musicians, he raided the past for much of his inspiration. Unlike most, he had the vision and dignity to do something entirely different with it. Cue the creation of a distinctive musical signature.*

'Even detractors from the "Bolan Sells Out" era cannot now deny that his extraordinary run of hits from 1970-73 endures far more convincingly than the progressive rock that was once hailed as music of the future. Bolan was also a pure pop poet, in the sense that his lyrics were a testament to pop's power to illuminate without being unduly troubled by the burden of common sense. He heard words as hooks, as riffs, as through-the-looking-glass illumination. Bolan saw the world as melodrama, rich in textures, aesthetic to the core. And whether alone dreaming up lyrics in his Ladbroke Grove*

atelier, or performing to 10,000 screaming teenagers at Wembley, that's how he lived it, always high on life's great delusions. We gotta thank him for that!'
Mark Paytress

It is widely believed that 'Lady Stardust', a track from David Bowie's recently re-mastered, re-released 1972 concept album *The Rise and Fall of Ziggy Stardust and the Spiders from Mars,* was written about his close friend Marc Bolan.

You decide: www.lyricsfreak.com/d/david+bowie/lady+stardust_20036911.html

Acknowledgements

Every book is a collaborative effort, involving the talents of many. All of these names should be on the cover, in 72pt.

I thank my editor, Lisa Highton, for her great skill and calm encouragement, and for letting me get on with it; Valerie Appleby, for her enthusiasm, and for doing the many invisible things; Camilla Dowse, who is a wonderful picture editor, and who seems to read my mind. She interprets in visuals what I can't always say in words; Alistair Oliver, for designing this beautiful cover; and Rowena Webb, Kerry Hood, Jaime Frost, Jason Bartholomew, Alice Howe, Joanna Kaliszewska, Kate Miles, and everyone else at Hodder & Stoughton . . . what a team. Special thanks and love go to Hannah Black, whose idea this was in the first place.

I can't do much of anything without Ivan Mulcahy, who has long been my agent. I wish I had his cool, as well as that Irish bigger-picture thing he has going on. It really lifts you out of the ditch and over the hurdles. Stephanie Cohen, Jonathan Conway, Laetitia Rutherford and Kate Rizzo at Mulcahy Conway Associates are my friends as well as agents, and deserve special mention for their love and support.

I was stabbing in the dark when I started to research this.

Marc Bolan had been dead for three-and-a-half decades: would there be anybody left? But once word was out, I was inundated. Listening to the experiences and recollections of the many who knew, loved, worked and played with Marc, or who had been involved in his music in some way, and who wanted to share, has been humbling.

I owe them all:

Rolan Bolan, Gloria Jones, Harry Feld, Sandra Feld, Jeff Dexter (Dexter Bedwell), Tony Visconti, Bill Legend, Simon Napier-Bell, Sir Tim Rice, Robert 'Bob' Harris OBE, Trudie Myerscough-Harris, Jeff Dexter, Rachel Garley, David Stark, Mike Hurst, Rick Wakeman, Steve Harley, Joe Boyd, Marc Almond, Brian Patten, Mark Paytress, Martin Barden, Mick O'Halloran, Cliff Wright, Charlie Watkins, Phil Swern, Steve Levine, Dr. Robert, Sally James, Mike Smith, Caron Willans, Danielz of T. Rextasy, Fee Warner, Paul Davies, Keith Altham, Alan Edwards, Andy Ellison, Judy Dyble, Vicky Aram, John Halsall, Richard Young, Gary Osborne, Lee Starkey, Nick Kent, David Hancock, John Blake, Marilyn Roberts, Rod Weinstein, Clair Woodward, Rachel Collier, Dominic Collier, Dan Arthure, James Nisbet, John Logan, Brian Dunham, Nicky Graham, Simon Platz, Ronen Guha, Gill Abraham, Trevor Jones, Debbie Jones, Vicky, Amy & Lily, Kelvin MacKenzie, Jane Wroe, Mitch Winehouse, Brian Justice, Eric Hall, John Burgess, Blue Weaver, David Hamilton, Allan James, Steve Emberton, Mike Batt, Mark Hagen, Bernard Doherty, Colin Joseph, Gerard Shine, Jonathan Morrish, Susu of the Official Marc Bolan Fan Club, David Day, Judie Tzuke, Ellis Rich OBE, Hyacinth 'Hy' Money, Lisa Smith, Lisa Davies, Tony Moore, Ilona Toteva, Sylvester Rivers, Berni Kilmartin, Leo Mcloughlin, James Saez, Neal Preston, Hal Lifson, Nick Elgar, Frank Allen, Natasha Holloway, Michael Watts, Mick Rock, Laura

Jamieson, Richard Hughes, Andrew ByTheWay, Roger Taylor, Lucy Tucker, Anya Wilson, Larry LeBlanc, Rachel & Bill Leigh.

Heartfelt thanks to:
Soho House London, New York and LA, High Road House Chiswick, Babington House, Somerset.

The Bournemouth Daily Echo/Newsquest (Southern) Ltd.

Picture acknowlegements:

© Mark Adams/ TotalBlamBlam@DavidBowie.com: 15 (bottom left). Author collection: 1 (top), 14 (middle left). © Camera Press London: 7 (top right)/ photo Richard Imrie, 12 (top)/ photo Steve Emberton. © Kevin Cummins: 13 (top). © Danielz: 15 (middle left). Courtesy of Electric Boogie, Inc © 2012: 3 (bottom), 4, 5, 6 (top). Courtesy of Alan Edwards collection/ The Outside Organisation Ltd: 9 (bottom right). Courtesy of Andy Ellison: 1 (bottom left & right). Courtesy of Harry and Sandra Feld: 1 (middle left), 7 (middle right)/ photo Tony Visconti, 8 (bottom left), 9 (middle), 11 (bottom right). © Getty Images: 6 (middle)/ photo Jorgen Angel, 6 (bottom left/ photo Estate of Keith Morris, 8 (top)/ photo Anwar Hussein, 9 (top)/ photo John Downing, 10 (bottom)/ photo Redferns/ Gus Stewart, 12 (middle right)/ photo Denis O'Regan, 14 (top)/ photo Maurice Hibberd. © Steve Harley collection/ Comeuppance: 11 (bottom left), 15 (bottom right). © Mirrorpix: 14 (bottom)/ photo Gavin Kent. © Peter Sanders www.petersanders.co.uk: 2 (bottom left & right). © Photoshot: 6 (bottom right), 7 (top left)/ photo Retna/ Michael Putland, 7 (bottom left)/ photo Retna/ Neal Preston, 13 (bottom)/ photo LFI/ Paul Cox. © Ray Stevenson: 2 (top). © Rex Features: 3 (top left)/ photo Harry Goodwin, 10 (top left)/ photo Kip Rano, 11 (top), 12 (bottom)/ photo Richard Young, 13 (middle right)/ photo ITV, 14 (middle right)/ photo Laurence Cottrell, 16/ photo Alan Messer. © Scope Features: 10 (top right)/ photo Allan Ballard. © Caron Willans collection: 3 (top right), 8 (bottom right), 9 (bottom left), 15 (top left).

Every reasonable effort has been made to contact the copyright holders of material reproduced in this book. But if there are any errors or omissions, Hodder & Stoughton will be pleased to insert the appropriate acknowledgement in any subsequent printing of this publication.

Bibliography and References

Associated Newspapers Ltd

Bate & Rasmussen, *William Shakespeare Complete Works*, Macmillan: London, 2007

Boyd, Joe, *White Bicycles: Making Music in the 1960s*, Serpent's Tail: London, 2006

Buxton, John, *Byron & Shelley: The History Of a Friendship*, Harcourt, Brace & World: New York, 1968

Cann, Kevin, *Any Day Now: David Bowie the London Years: 1947–1974*, Adelita Ltd, 2010

Currie, David (ed), *David Bowie: The Starzone Interviews*, Omnibus: London, 1985

Danielz, *T. Rextasy – The Spirit of Marc Bolan*, Wymer Publishing, 2012

Day, David, *Tolkien: The Illustrated Encyclopedia*, Mitchell Beazley: London, 1991

The Guardian/Guardian Media Group/Guardian News & Media

Hall, Eric, *Monster! True Tales from a Showbiz Life*, Boxtree: London, 1998

Honey magazine/Fleetway Publications 1960–86, founded by Audrey Slaughter

Horsley, Sebastian, *Dandy in the Underworld*, Hodder & Stoughton: London, 2007

Hunt, Marsha, *Real Life*, Chatto & Windus: London, 1986

Kent, Nick, *Apathy for the Devil: A 70s' Memoir*, Faber & Faber: London, 2010

Lenig, Stuart, *The Twisted Tale of Glam Rock*, Praeger/ ABC-CLIO, LLC: Santa Barbara, 2010

MacInnes, Colin, *Absolute Beginners*, MacGibbon & Kee: London, 1959

Martin, George, *Making Music: The Guide to Writing, Performing & Recording*, Pan Books Ltd: London, 1983

Martin, George & Hornsby, Jeremy, *All You Need is Ears*, Macmillan Ltd: London, 1979

McLenehan, Cliff, *Marc Bolan 1947–1977: A Chronology*, Helter Skelter: London, 2002

Miles, *David Bowie Black Book*, Omnibus Press: London, 1980

Muldoon, Paul (ed), *Lord Byron (Poems)*, Faber & Faber Ltd: London, 2011

Napier-Bell, Simon, *Black Vinyl, White Powder*, Ebury Press: London, 2001

Napier-Bell, Simon, *You Don't Have To Say You Love Me*, New English Library, London, 1982

Neill, Andy & Kent, Matt, *Anyway, Anyhow, Anywhere: The Complete Chronicles of The Who, 1958–1978*, Virgin Books Ltd: London, 2005

Palmer, Robert, *Dancing In The Street*, BBC Books: London, 1996

Paytress, Mark, *Bolan: The Rise & Fall of a 20th Century Superstar*, Omnibus: London, 2002

Sampson, Fiona (ed), *Percy Bysshe Shelley (Poems)*, Faber & Faber Ltd: London, 2011

Shemel, Sidney & Krasilovsky, M. William, *This Business Of Music*, The Billboard Publishing Company, 1964

Thomas, Dylan & Davies, Walford (ed), *Under Milk Wood*, Penguin Classics: London, 2000

Thomas, Dylan & Davies, Walford & Maud, Ralph (eds) *Collected Poems 1934–1953*, J.M. Dent & Sons Ltd, Everyman's Library: London, 1988

Visconti, Tony, *Bowie, Bolan & the Brooklyn Boy*, HarperCollins: London, 2007

Weird & Gilly, *Mick Ronson: The Spider With The Platinum Hair*, Independent Music Press: Shropshire, 2003

Welch, Chris & Napier-Bell, Simon, *Born To Boogie*, Plexus: London, 1982

White, Charles, *The Life & Times of Little Richard, The Quasar of Rock*, Pan Books Ltd: London, 1985

Young, Richard & Young, Susan, *Shooting Stars*, Metro Books: London, 2004

Richard Young Gallery, 4 Holland Street, Kensington, London W8 4LT: www.richardyounggallery.co.uk

20th Century Boy The Musical: www.bolanicproductions.com

Cliff Wright's band Eat This: www.eatthis.net

Judy Dyble: www.judydyble.com

The Keats-Shelley Memorial House Museum, Rome, Italy, Commemorating the Romantic poets, Piazza di Spagna, 26, 00187 Rome: www.keats-shelley-house.org/

The Official Marc Bolan Fan Club: www.marc-bolan.com/

Brian Patten: www.brianpatten.co.uk

Dr Robert: www.theblowmonkeys.com/

TAG: official, legal guardians of the 'Bolan Tree': www.marc-bolan.org/

Fee Warner: tag@mercurymoon.co.uk

T. Rextasy: www.trextasy.com

Lesley-Ann Jones: www.lesleyannjones.com

http://www.facebook.com/RideAWhiteSwanTheLivesAnd
 DeathOfMarcBolan

Follow me on Twitter: @LAJwriter

The Bolan Sound

US record producer James Saez on the instruments Marc used
 to achieve the distinctive Bolan sound:

'His sound was really based on the Dallas Rangemaster and the
 Vamp Power amps but he used a lot of different gear. Here's
 some good info on that:

http://www.analogman.com/bolan.htm

Gibson made a Mark Bolan Les Paul:

http://www2.gibson.com/Products/Electric-Guitars/Les-Paul/
 Gibson-Custom/Marc-Bolan-Les-Paul.aspx

Marc had an Olympic White Strat that looks a lot like my 63.
 http://www.youtube.com/watch?v=vbuhx0MNeH4

His Les Paul was a modified 59 that went through a few necks
 and wound up with a split diamond custom neck on it by
 August 1972. It had a Bigsby on it at some point early on, and
 was also refinished in Gretsch orange, to match his hero Eddie
 Cochran's.

Tons of great info can be found by paging through here:

https://www.facebook.com/photo.php?fbid=164830060229373
 &set=a.164828760229503.36507.100001071407785&type
 =3&theater

Although most people think of him as a Les Paul guy, I think he
 used the Strat a lot in the studio.

He used many other guitars as well, including Flying Vs, SGs
 and telecasters.

http://www.marcbolanmusic.com/guitars.aspx

Index

An invitation from the publisher

Join us at www.hodder.co.uk or follow us
on Twitter @hodderbooks to be a part of
our community of people who love the very
best in books and reading.

Whether you want to discover more about a book or an
author, watch trailers and interviews, have the chance to
win early limited editions or simply browse our expert
readers' selection of the very best books, including

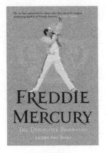  

. . . we think you'll find what you're looking for.

And if you don't, that's the place to tell us what's missing.

We love what we do, and we'd love you to be a part of it.

www.hodder.co.uk

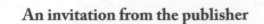 @hodderbooks

HodderBooks

HodderBooks

GIPSY LANE

Nos 8-11

Pomes
Peny-
each